LETTERS HOME

LETTERS HOME

Lessons from the Great Hippie Trail

BRUS L. WESTBY

Waterside Productions

First Printing, 2022

ISBN-13: 978-1-958848-13-5 print edition
ISBN-13: 978-1-958848-14-2 e-book edition

Waterside Productions
2055 Oxford Ave
Cardiff, CA 92007
www.waterside.com

For our children and grandchildren
who continually inspire us.

"If you do follow your bliss you put yourself on a kind of track that has been there all the while, waiting for you, and the life that you ought to be living is the one you are living. Follow your bliss and don't be afraid, and doors will open where you didn't know they were going to be."

—Joseph Campbell

"A journey of a thousand miles begins with a single step."

—Lao Tzu

"A ship is safe in harbor, but that's not what a ship is for."

—John A. Shedd

TABLE OF CONTENTS

INTRODUCTION

I was inspired to write this book about our first overland journey to India after rereading a manuscript I wrote in longhand just a few months after our return. I found it difficult to read my sloppy, careless handwriting—some puzzling entries rivaled hieroglyphics! Still, this supplied me with a fresh and fairly accurate account of the places we traveled and people we met. Without this information, I'd be writing a novel rather than a memoir.

I was also motivated by reading the letters we exchanged with our families. Both our mothers treasured and cached away the letters—aerogrammes, really—that we sent home from different stops on our journey. Perhaps they thought these might come in handy someday, and they have, providing me further information and, more important, conveying the love and support of parents and their children. In that time before social media and cell phones, when India was still a distant and exotic destination, these handwritten letters would arrive every few weeks at home doorsteps and poste restantes in faraway places. They were old news by the time they were read. No matter—the purpose of each letter we sent was not so much to inform our families of details, but to assure them that we were still healthy and safe at the time of writing. The rosy pictures we painted in our letters for our parents' peace of mind was at times quite different from the reality we were experiencing! In reading through these letters, I envisioned our two young travelers as kites, soaring high in ever-changing winds, at times dancing together; at others, battling over a small space in the vastness of the sky, sometimes clearly visible in the bright sunshine, but often lost behind thick clouds. No matter how and where these kites fluttered about, they were never lost for good because they were firmly tethered by their families' heartstrings in the form of these letters. They served as the intimate connection between the young travelers' skies of exploration and discovery and the ground of love and support of their families.

That I'd even consider such a journey was born in college, when I took an elective course titled, "The Journey of the Hero," using as a primary resource the work of Joseph Campbell, *The Hero with a Thousand Faces*. Campbell discusses the progression of the hero's journey, drawing parallels between religious icons, mythical figures, and our human experience. Each hero, whether it be Jesus, Buddha, or Odysseus, embarks on a path of discovery, including: first being called to adventure, encountering allies and enemies along the journey, facing daunting ordeals, discovering the precious elixir, and returning with proof of this discovery. Campbell concludes that the hero is a universal archetype, and as ordinary humans, we can also experience these same stages of a hero's journey. He writes, "We must be willing to let go of the life we planned so as to have the life that is waiting for us." This course opened my eyes to possibilities beyond the expected prospect of continuing through grad school toward some lifetime career. I wanted to take the hero's journey and find the elixir, whatever that might be. A very different world for me was waiting to be discovered.

Yet this was not my journey alone. Our journey began with an initial friendship of two very different people. Traveling together twenty-four hours a day, routinely facing demanding challenges, is a tale of endurance. Our relationship weathered the storms of doubt and distress to eventually blossom into mutual respect and love. Many years later, we're still working together through all that life throws at us. Yes, our relationship has indeed earned the epithet, "enduring love."

Our lives are made of stories. We were inspired by, and learned from, so many travelers we met who shared with us their stories of challenges, victories, losses, of love and heartbreak. So often, we'd develop intense bonds with others, arising from our mutual need for intimacy and security in the face of the unknown. Our stories propelled each other forward in our short time together, only for us to part too soon and go our separate ways, each person, as Joseph Campbell puts it, "following their bliss" toward their own destinies. This story is uniquely ours but is just one of many stories of those who heeded the call of the hero's journey on the "Great Hippie Trail" to India.

CALL TO ADVENTURE

October, 1970
Hi,

 Well, here we are in Amsterdam. We've been here since Thurs. afternoon. Took a boat from Ireland to Liverpool, then hitched across Eng. to Hull and took the boat to Rotterdam, and then hitched up here.

 We will only stay one more day and tomorrow (Sun.) we take the train to Munich. Also "Happy birthday, Mom!" I forgot in the last letter. Sorry. We are very healthy and careful.

Love and Kisses,
Jean

Hello—At present we're in Munich enjoying the gala Octoberfest, while preparing to leave to Istanbul on the Orient Express. Our plans to buy a van in Amsterdam were thwarted by research: the cost of the van, gasoline and an insurance policy proved to be just too expensive, at least from the European side. We intend to keep our eyes open for some deal as we travel east, though ... We'd still love to see Switzerland and go into Italy and Greece but time and money do not allow us at this point. Perhaps on our way back? Quien sabe? Next point to write, of course, is American Express, Istanbul, Turkey. This letter is also for Grandma and Uncle Harry. Will write again soon.

Love, Bruce and Jean

Two reserved tickets in hand, we've just boarded the Orient Express in the München station and are looking for our compartment. The forty-eight-hour journey will take us from Germany through the Eastern European countries of Austria, Hungary, Yugoslavia, and Bulgaria to Turkey. We think we've packed enough provisions for the journey.

"Here it is," exclaims Jean, "26B."

I look at the compartment, crammed with eight large men sitting in a dense cloud of cigarette smoke, passing around beer and bread.

"This can't be it," I say. "Excuse me," I address a man closest to the compartment door, "Is this 26B?"

Instead of answering, the man looks at the others and they all start laughing. They smell like the sweat and stale beer of one of the many Octoberfest tents in the city.

"But this is 26B. Here are our tickets." I display the tickets in the air as they laugh even louder.

I'm thinking that these men don't speak English, when one next to the window of the compartment says in a thick Eastern European accent, "These are our seats now. Go find seats of your own."

Another man leers at Jean and slurs, "But she can stay. Come join us pretty girl. We show you a good time!" More laughter.

"Come on Bruce," Jean mutters, "This is hopeless."

We soon realize as we edge our way down the narrow corridors from one car to the next that there are no available seats on this overcrowded train. It certainly doesn't help that we're both carrying large backpacks. I know now why, when we bought our tickets this morning, the woman in the ticket booth said, "God bless you!" The train starts moving and we begin to panic. No getting off now! In contrast, everyone seems jubilant, constantly chattering, laughing, and passing around bottles of beer and whisky.

I yell to Jean over the noise, "We just have to find a place where we can stand!"

"That's what I'm looking for, dammit!"

We finally reach a car so crowded that there is nothing to do but stop. And this is where we find ourselves, hours into the two-day journey to Istanbul, still with backpacks on, exhausted and joints aching.

Finally, a small man who somehow has managed to squeeze his way up the corridor, puts down a suitcase next to us and says in English, "Please madam, you sit down here."

"Oh no, that's all right. I can stand."

"No, no, better that you sit. You look tired."

Jean sits gratefully and, through tears of relief, says. "Thank you."

More hours pass. We learn from our friend that this train is filled with Yugoslavian laborers who are heading back home after six months of work in different parts of Germany.

"Yes, they end their work with one week at Octoberfest. Now they are all drunk and very happy to be going home to their families."

Great timing for us, I think.

After several more hours, and for a reason beyond us, our train car has become less crowded. Our new friend disappears further down the corridor and returns, saying, "I have found you a fine suite. It is a bathroom that is no longer in use. Come, follow me."

He leads us to a small bathroom with a toilet and sink. The reek coming from the toilet is obviously why it no longer works. Oddly, there is no door to the bathroom. Was there one at one time that broke, or was there never one? Are open bathrooms the custom here?

"Here, you can put your packs under the sink, and even sit down."

Such is our condition that we are grateful for his kindness and quickly occupy the bathroom. We finally have a little space, if not breathing space. We take turns perching on the toilet and looking out from our "suite." I think to myself how malleable the notion of comfort can be as we accustom ourselves to this relatively spacious bathroom. Just this morning, I would have been aghast at such privations!

Several people peer in as they pass by, we just as curious looking at them as they are at us. They seem friendly enough, their comments and laughter seemingly guileless. Our friend sits on his suitcase nearby, sharing stories of his office work in Germany and his wife and two daughters at home in an unpronounceable town in Yugoslavia.

The train stops in Vienna, Austria, where, among others, three travelers board, longhairs like us. They nod as they pass by in their own search for space. Somehow, seeing them is a comfort, a sense that we're not alone on this sea of strangers with their different cultures and languages.

As the train travels through Austria and Hungary through the night, vendors struggle up the corridor selling wrapped meat, vegetables, and fruit. One enterprising man shoulders enough space to set down his small folding table and lays out three shells and a peanut. He continuously chatters away as he places the peanut under a shell and deftly slides the shells around, bills and coins being thrown onto the table by the captive crowd around him. This is the first time I've actually seen the "shell game" and am fascinated by his easy dexterity. I'm glad I haven't thrown down any money because I am wrong about the location of the peanut every time! When enough money and interest is lost, he puts the shells and peanut in his pocket, folds up his little table, and moves on.

We are two young travelers bound to India. If someone is to ask us why, we really have no clear response. We're living in a time fueled by psychedelics, the "Summer of Love," and Woodstock. The Vietnam War is raging, as are the demonstrations against it. Young people are questioning the worldview presented them by the older generation. Dylan is singing "The Times They Are A-Changin'." Many youths are running from the war to Canada, or moving to communes to rediscover a more simple, natural life.

For me, there's a calling to travel to the East. A seed of interest in foreign cultures was planted when, at eight years old, my family moved to Peru. My father's work in New York as a treasurer of a mining corporation demanded that he spend two years at the mining operations themselves, based in the high Andes. Our journey through Cuba and Panama to Peru, our life in an international mining camp, our slow boat back through Ecuador and the Panama Canal, every sensation was so new and exciting! I met new friends from many different countries. Those two years were a grand adventure!

Another influence is an elective course I took in college called "The Journey of the Hero." This was a semester-long study of the works of mythologist Joseph Campbell. He proposed that the journey of the hero is a classic story structure shared by religious stories and myths worldwide. The iconic hero, whether it be Jesus, Mohammed, or the Buddha, must adhere to common stages in their development. These are generally Departure, Initiation, and Return, which can include a range of tests and ordeals to finally attaining the reward of the "precious elixir" of self-discovery. Most inspiring for me was Campbell's teaching that we each are heroes at our core, and we must go on the hero's journey to realize this.

My "planned" future as a history major in college included continuing in academia with a goal of achieving a PhD or law degree. Instead, right after graduation, I opted to travel alone to Spain and Morocco for six months. There, I encountered many travelers en route to and from India. By the time I returned to New York, my mind was made up. I also wanted to take the "hero's journey" to India.

As for Jean, she's on her own hero's journey. As an old friend and new lover, she has decided to come along just for the adventure of it all. Jean has traveled before, living for six months in Cali, Columbia, with an ex-boyfriend. She had just accepted a position as director of a prestigious preschool in New York City, which she has now turned down on the pretext of a family emergency.

Our parents are understandably surprised and concerned by our decision but have somewhat different reactions. My parents have seen my changes from college through Morocco and understand by now that their bearded, long-haired son is seeking a different kind of life. Although Jean's parents have experienced a taste of foreign culture through a short visit to Jean's oldest sister who worked for an international school in Tehran, they have an understandable fear for her safety as a female traveling who knows where with a new boyfriend. Yet, In the end, it's clear to both sets of parents that neither Jean nor I will be deterred from our quest.

We have several thousand dollars between us, no map or compass to guide us, but we have an unerring trust that things will just work out. Knowing from hearsay how long and arduous this trip will be, our only binding pact with each other is that should one of us want or need to leave the trip, the other will see him or her safely aboard a flight back home to New York. We are about as clueless as two kids can be, and therefore perfect candidates for a run on what will become known as the Great Hippie Trail.

In these days long before cell phones and social media, we promise everyone that we will write regularly. This comes mainly in the form of the international aerogramme, just one sheet of paper folded to optimize space for writing and addressing the letter. A typical time frame for sending and receiving each letter is two weeks, sometimes longer depending on access to an American Express office or a poste restante, an office or restaurant with postal service.

Sixteen hours after leaving München, a palpable excitement fills the corridor as we pull into the main station in Belgrade, Yugoslavia. I see a large crowd of people are on the platform and my heart sinks, thinking even more people are about to board. To my surprise, our car empties out in ten minutes! Those people are just there to meet and greet the tired, happy passengers coming home at last.

We wedge ourselves out of the bathroom and wander through the empty train cars, exhausted survivors agog at the availability of empty seats. We see the three long-haired travelers hunched together in an abandoned compartment and ask if we can join them.

The three are German but speak English fluently. Carla looks in her forties, is gregarious, and interested in conversation.

"Oh, I see from the flag pins on your packs that you are Canadian."

"Uh, no," Jean replies. "We're Americans."

"Interesting. But why the pins of Canada?"

"We've been told that Americans are disliked in Europe and Asia because of the war. And I bet there are other reasons as well."

I add, "And it seems nobody has anything bad to say about Canadians."

"I would love to visit America," Carla says. "I have an uncle there, maybe in Birmingham? Is that a city? He says it's nice there, but I don't know. I can't say I like the politics there. If I may ask, are you for or against the Vietnam War?"

"We're very much against it," I reply.

"So, are you running away from the war then?"

"No," I say. "I'm glad I don't have to make that decision yet. They have a lottery system of who will be drafted into military service based on one's birth date. Because I was born on June 3, I have a very high number, so probably won't be called. If I am, I'll have a big decision to make."

Carla states, "America is a big place, and I'm sure there are many beliefs and convictions to go around, no?"

Jean responds, "You've got that right. There are many people in the States who like nothing better than a good war."

Carla sighs, "Not only in the States. Everywhere!"

Hermione, Carla's daughter, is quiet, attractive, with kind eyes. She listens carefully, saying little until she hears when I was born.

"Ah, June 3! You are a Gemini like me. We are twins!" She laughs.

She then leads us into a lively conversation of astrological signs, saying that she is guided by daily astrology readings. She says the signs are good for her to be on this journey with her mother and Rudi.

Carla says, "I want to share the beautiful city of Istanbul with my daughter. I have many memories there."

We're enjoying our conversation, happy to be sharing our thoughts for the first time in days. Rudi, tall, blond, and bearded, is a silent, intense presence. He fidgets constantly, as though he is uncomfortable in his own skin. He says nothing, seeming to listen to our conversation sometimes, but often withdrawing into himself. In just a few hours he has excused himself several times and gone to the bathroom in the hallway.

They are fascinated that we're determined to go to India.

Hermione asks, "But why do you want to go there?"

Jean responds, "We don't know. We really don't. Maybe just because it's an adventure to a land that is so different from our own."

"Hmm, maybe you are looking for spiritual teachings."

Thinking about the book I brought in my backpack, *Autobiography of a Yogi*, I mutter, "Maybe."

Looking over at Rudi, Carla says, "He has tried to reach India several times, but he has only been able to get as far as Kabul. He's an addict you see. He can't be without his drug, which he can easily obtain in Istanbul."

"Oh," is all I can say.

"Yes, heroin," she says. "He is just so afraid he won't be able to find this drug further east."

I peek over at Rudi, scrunched over in a far corner of the compartment. His eyes are closed. Perhaps he's asleep; perhaps he's listening but isn't interested in commenting.

"He can't be alone. He needs me, and I suppose I need him."

We all settle in, sharing more stories and food offerings from our packs. I'm a little embarrassed by our meager offerings of apples and granola bars, compared with their tasty breads, cold cuts, and cheeses. Day turns to night as the train chugs its way through the mountains of eastern Yugoslavia. As the hour grows late, we all agree to try to get some sleep. We each get as comfortable as possible, shutting off the compartment light.

Sleep proves impossible for me, as Rudi's fidgeting increases steadily until he is moaning, his body writhing in pain.

"Is he all right?" I ask Carla.

"No, not now. He is dope sick because his supply has run out."

Now I know why he has gone to the bathroom so often. Rudi's moans grow louder, and now he seems to be pleading in German for Carla to help him. Carla tries to assuage him, giving him aspirin, but we can see that it gives him no relief.

Carla finally says, "We must get off the train at the next station, Sofia. I know the city, and there is a clinic there where we can get help."

Jean says, "Is there anything we can do to help?"

"No, we've been through this before. We'll get through it again."

The train stops at a station in Sofia at the break of day, and the three Germans collect their things quickly. Carla and Hermione give us a warm hug, wishing us well as they leave, half carrying Rudi between them. We're concerned for them, but don't have time to process this, as now four men from that station file into our compartment.

Three of the men are dressed in traditional Turkish dress: long, loose-fitting pants, long-sleeved collarless shirts, colorful vests, and fezzes for headwear. The other is a military man in a pea-green uniform and fatigue hat. They seem surprised to see us at first, stealing glances, making low comments to each other in Turkish, perhaps about our long hair and my beard.

The train, meanwhile, hasn't budged from the station. I wonder if this delay is typical or if there is an engine problem. After a few minutes, one of the men, who has a drooping mustache, says in halting English, "Excuse me. Are you traveling to Istanbul?"

"Yes, we are," I respond. "And you?"

"Oh yes. We live there. I and my brother," he says, indicating a small man with a thin mustache, "and my friends have been visiting our relatives here."

"We are just visitors. This will be our first time there."

"Oh, it is a beautiful city! You must see Hagia Sofia, and the Grand Bazaar, it is very big, very special."

This seems to break the ice. We introduce ourselves and continue talking. Our new friend, Mustafa, seems to be the only English speaker, serving as interpreter for the others' rapid-fire questions. Jean remains quiet, sensing that, in their minds, women are not expected to talk, especially away from the household.

"Where are you from?"

"Uh," I point to the flag pin on my pack, "Canada."

"Ah, Canada," Mustafa says. "I hear it is a very big and beautiful country."

"Yes, it is," I say, hoping he won't ask me anything more about Canada, which I know nothing about.

"And my brother wants to know if you are hippies. He has read about hippies. Do all hippies have long hair and beards like you? Do you like drugs?"

This leads to a lively, enjoyable exchange about similarities and differences between hippie and Turkish lifestyles.

The train still hasn't moved. Suddenly, we hear a knocking on our compartment door and see two officials peering in.

Mustafa says, "Do not worry. This is a Communist country, and they are very serious about checking the identities of all who pass through."

The officials, both large and unsmiling, squeeze into the compartment and announce something I don't understand.

"They want to see our transit papers and your passports," Mustafa tells us.

Jean and I eye each other as Jean produces our American passports for the officials and all to see. The man I assume to be the head official looks through each passport thoroughly, comparing the photos with our faces. I glance at Mustafa and see a look of confusion on his face. He then exchanges looks and quiet words with his compatriots. The head official says something official, not expecting or receiving a response, and hands us back our passports before leaving.

The train slowly pulls out of the station. Now, instead of the previous animated exchange with the Turks, there is silence. I feel terrible. We've told them we were Canadians yet produced American passports. We are caught in a lie. I try to explain but Mustafa turns his back on me. For the rest of the day's journey through Bulgaria and eastern Turkey to Istanbul, we no longer talk. Time together in the compartment becomes endless as I stew in guilt, gazing unseeing out the compartment window at passing hills, valleys, and forests. It is obvious that, from the point of view of Mustafa and his friends, we can no longer be trusted and nothing more should be said to us.

When the Orient Express finally arrives at the station in Istanbul, the men wordlessly gather their belongings and leave. Jean and I feel bad but relieved, a great weight lifted.

I realize sometime later that I've learned two important lessons from this painful experience. First, living with a lie, even a small one, often invites bad consequences. In this case, these curious, interested men came away with distrust and contempt for us and for Americans. I certainly can't say that I won't lie again, particularly to protect ourselves, yet I know that any lie I tell has a way of coming back to haunt me. Then I'll have a choice. I can either come clean, admit my lie, or lie again to cover up the original lie, promoting an endless cycle of lying. I see this often in some of our political leaders in the past and today. Lying has become a way of life, so one lives the lie, becomes the lie. There is no trust, no confidence in those who propagate lies.

The second lesson is, by lying that I am not an American, I'm denying my birthright as a citizen of my own country with its freedoms of speech and press that allow me to participate fully in elections, a stark contrast to the countries we've just passed through. Better to tell the truth, no matter how difficult that might be.

We find lodgings at the Hotel Gongor in the Sultan-Ahmet district in central Istanbul. Our room is small and windowless, but clean. The first thing we do upon entering, even before throwing ourselves on the bed in utter exhaustion, is remove the Canadian flag pins from our packs.

November 1970

... Istanbul is a lovely port city, where the waters of the Bosporus and Marmara converge—the site of the legendary swim of the Greek hero What's His Name and, in heading east, where Europe ends and Asia begins. We stay at a small hotel in the Sultan-Ahmet district, close to the famous indoor bazaar filled with thousands

of items from meerschaums to puzzle rings and Afghani coats. Everyone here bargains as just part of business. Makes no difference whether the item for sale is expensive or cheap—which is all we can afford—they love to bargain. We made some Turkish "friends" here who continually ply us with tea as we kibbutz over prices.

That's all for now folks. We'll be traveling by bus from here into Eastern Turkey and then Iran.

Love, Bruce and Jean

We stay in Istanbul for only three days. This gives us enough time to check mail and procure the necessary visas to enter Iran, the next country east. We also tour the remarkable Blue Mosque on the first day and visit the massive Hagia Sofia and Topkapi museums on the second. We're close enough to the Grand Bazaar to regularly peruse that enormous, cavernous maze of glittering shops, displaying, among myriad other things, gold and silver jewelry, meerschaum pipes, and alabaster figurines. After some haggling over price, I buy a meerschaum pipe, its bowl the head of a bearded man, for my father, a lifelong pipe smoker. I shove it down to the bottom of my pack, where it will stay until I mail it home months later.

We recognize that we aren't paying due respect to all the sights this remarkable ancient city can offer, but we're impatient to push on into Asia. And besides, we tell ourselves, when we come through again on our way back home, we'll spend more time here.

The Hotel Gongor's guests are mainly travelers from Europe. Most are young, like us—some on their way to India, others returning. Manuel, the manager of the hotel, is a tall, handsome Latino, maybe forty. He seems kind and well-respected, regularly checking with travelers in the hotel's spacious sitting room to make sure they are comfortable and content. In seeing our two fresh, inexperienced faces, he is somewhat concerned about our intentions to travel further to India.

"The journey from here is long and can be difficult. Many have turned around and come back after just a few weeks. Are you sure that this is what you want to do?"

"Yes, we're sure," I reply.

Manuel asks, "Do you have maps?"

"Uh, no."

"How do you expect to travel then?"

Jean starts, "We've heard …"

"Please don't rely on hearsay! There are just as many wrong notions as there are right. Please at least buy a proper map. Do you have the necessary visas?"

"Well," I respond, "we've been to the visa office this morning and they say they will be ready tomorrow."

"That is good, but please, you must be absolutely sure you want to make this journey. Instead, you could spend more time here in Istanbul. It is a remarkable city, and there is much to explore and enjoy. Afterward, you can just take the train all the way back to Paris."

"Thank you for your advice, Manuel. You've given us much to think about."

This conversation with Manuel is eye-opening and a little disturbing. A seed of doubt has been planted. Are we capable of such a journey? Are we putting ourselves in danger? This is the first time Jean and I have really had a heartfelt conversation about our intentions and their ramifications. In the end, we agree that we have not come this far to turn back.

Resigned to our determination, Manuel directs us to a travel shop, where we buy an atlas of maps and information of the countries we'll travel through. He also writes all that he knows of upcoming transportation, lodging, and border crossings.

Our taxi comes in the morning to take us to the station, where we'll train to Erzurum, a city in eastern Turkey close to the Iranian border. We bid goodbye and thank you to Manuel, who replies, "God bless you." I think to myself, this is the second time in a few days that someone has given us this benediction.

PUSHING EAST

The train ride to Erzurum is another long one: forty hours. This time, though, we're seated in an open train car across the aisle from two other Americans, Mitchell and Barbara. We met them at the Hotel Gongor the day before, discovered we all had tickets on the same train, and decided to travel together for a time. They're from Buffalo, New York. Mitchell is short, with hair even longer than mine, while Barbara has short brown hair and is inches taller than Mitchell. As our train chugs through the gray hills and plains of western and central Turkey, they are both good company: lively, engaging, and, like us, enthusiastic about the journey and working on their young relationship.

Mitchell is reading a book by British theologian, Allen Watts, *The Way of Zen.*

"Man, he's really turned me on to Zen. It's a Buddhist meditation they do in Japan, and now there are some Zen centers in the States. Barbara and I tried to visit a center in Buffalo, but it was a bummer because it was closed to outsiders on that one day. But I really want to learn to meditate."

"Me too," I reply without thinking; but now bringing this idea to consciousness, I add, "I think this is the reason we're going to India."

Every train stop brings more Turkish nationals into our car: men with vests and caps, the women wearing head scarves, loose blouses, and pajama pants. Some women are in *burkas*, covering themselves from head to foot. By the time we reach Ankara, the country's capital, our car is completely packed. Every person upon entering is agog at us four travelers, not able to take their eyes off our every move. The men are the worst, riveting gazes at Jean and Barbara, and looking away quickly when they stare back at them. Jean coins the term, "Lurking Turks'" to describe their behavior. At first disconcerting, we inure ourselves to their stares as the hours roll along.

Fitful sleeps and many conversations later, the train starts climbing into mountainous terrain. We finally arrive during a driving, late-afternoon rain at the station in Erzurum. We've learned from Manuel in Istanbul that there is a small hotel and adjacent bus station within walking distance from the station, so we slog through the rain to the hotel. Soaked to the skin, we all stop first at the bus station and buy tickets for the next morning on a "luxury bus" coming from Ankara to the border, a smart move we think, as the ticket counter is about to close for the day. Then, renting two rooms at the hotel, we share our packed food of cheese, bread, and fruit with Mitchell and Barbara before saying goodnight. Our room is on the second floor overlooking the bus station. It is tiny and musty, with just a double bed and small table with a dim lamp. It matters little to us. We're so exhausted, we're asleep moments after our heads hit the pillows.

I awaken sometime in the middle of the night with red, itchy splotches all over my body! Jean is scratching in her sleep too. I wake her and we throw the covers and sheets off the bed to reveal dozens of crawling insects.

"Oh God!" Jean screams. "What are those?"

"Bedbugs," I say, even though I'm not sure what they are.

"We can't stay here! We have to get another room."

I dress and go downstairs to the lobby. I pound the desk and yell, but there's nobody around.

Returning to the room, I say, "It'll be light in a couple of hours. Let's try sleeping on the floor."

We shake out two blankets as best as we can, making sure they're bug-free, and wrap ourselves up on the floor. I do fall asleep, but I don't know for how long. Jean is asleep when I wake up. We pack our things and go down to the lobby. Our friends are already there and scratching! It probably wouldn't have helped getting another room after all. Fortunately, Barbara has a small travel bottle of calamine lotion to pass around, relieving the itching somewhat.

The bus station has a small restaurant, offering cheeses, sweetbreads, meat kebabs, and strong black coffee. We chow down as we wait for our bus—our first real meal in a couple of days. Finally, our "luxury bus" arrives, chock full of people! There's absolutely no room for even one of us!

We locate the man we bought tickets from the evening before. Mitchell takes the lead, waving our tickets at him. "These are our tickets for this bus. You have to let us on!"

The ticket man responds in broken English, "Not possible. Bus full."

"But we have tickets, see? How are we going to get to the border?"

"Next bus. Luxury. Tomorrow, yes?"

"No, we must get to the border today!"

Ticket Man thinks. "You wait. I come back."

He disappears around a corner, is gone for several minutes, and returns with a driver and old minibus.

"This man drive you to border. Not much money."

I yell, "But we already paid for this bus!"

"Not much money," Ticket Man repeats.

Mitchell jumps in. "We want our money back for the bus!"

"Not possible."

We're irate, but see that further arguments will get us nowhere, and we might not even get the minibus ride. After conferring with each other, we agree to pay the jeep driver. Several Turkish people who've also been waiting for the full bus have been listening to our negotiations and now offer money to the jeep driver as well. By the time we leave, we are eight passengers and the driver in an old minibus, headed for the border.

The trip takes just three hours, as the jeep steadily climbs through mountain passes. Our driver is young but handles the precipitous curves with the ease of a veteran. As for us, we're turning a

16

little green from motion sickness. The driver points out the snow-capped volcano of Agri Dagi on our left, which we later learn is the same Mount Ararat where, according to Judeo-Christian belief, Noah landed his animal-laden ark at the end of the great flood.

We arrive at the border to join a large crowd of people lined up at a small cement building, waiting to pass through immigration and customs. I'm surprised that there are quite a few Western travelers like us. I feel nervous. Although we have nothing to hide, we've heard tales of how strict these border patrol guards can be if a person is caught with illegal arms, drugs, or black market cash. Our fears are confirmed when guards start yelling and beating a Turkish or Irani man traveling with whom I assume is his wife and two young children. He is hauled to the back of the building, out of sight. We don't know what his offense is, or what his punishment will be, but his distraught wife and children move out of line and squat under a nearby tree, awaiting word of his fate.

All the Western travelers pass through easily with the officials' cursory glances at visas and quick stamping of passports. We enter the Iran side to a lively bazaar of street vendors, restaurants, and clothing and jewelry shops. Several people are selling tickets for different buses, but one claims to have the cheapest tickets on a "nonstop, luxury express" to Tehran, the capital city.

"Leaving right away," the vendor declares.

Most of us Westerners choose this option and soon load ourselves onto a brightly painted bus with red window curtains until every seat is full. And there we wait. A half hour becomes an hour. We yell to the vendor to find the driver or give us back our money, but he seems to have forgotten all of his English. Finally, two passengers start pounding on the seat backs, and soon we're all following suit. Within minutes, a fat, surly man appears, leers at us in disgust, hops in the driver's seat and we're on our way.

Forty-five minutes later, we stop in a small dusty town. The driver announces that here we'll stop for the night and then travel to Tehran in the morning.

"There is a nice, clean hotel right here," he offers.

From all the Western travelers, our response is immediate.

"No, you cannot stop! We have paid for an express bus direct to Tehran! You must drive us there right now!"

The driver simply leers at us, then snorts a derisive laugh as he climbs down from the bus and disappears around a corner. We are captives! The Irani travelers quietly collect their belongings and exit the bus to seek lodgings for the night. We Western travelers sit in shock, not knowing what to do. I'm thinking that the driver must get a regular commission from the hotel owner for bringing him all this business.

Finally, a heavyset young woman with unruly red hair and flowing yellow skirt states, "I'm not leaving this bus!"

"Yeah," an older man with his wife adds. "If we leave, there's no guarantee this bus will be here for us in the morning."

We see the logic in this and agree that, to the person, we'll stay on the bus until it leaves. Someone in the front shuts the bus door so no one can get in. The driver comes back after some time, sees that we're not leaving, and mutters some local expletives as he leaves. Our group decision has an uplifting effect. We strike up conversations and share what food we've packed away. One longhair produces a joint of tobacco and hashish he has foolishly but gratefully smuggled through the border and passes it around the bus. A blonde woman plays Joan Baez songs on her guitar, accompanied by her partner's harmonica. Soon, we've all transformed a difficult situation into a celebration of comradery and relaxation.

We share questions and answers of what to expect on the road ahead with some of the older travelers with enough sense to have researched the entire route to India.

Karen, the redheaded woman, reminding me of Janis Joplin, is vocal in her impatience. She now asks an older guy named Andy, who has been on this "Hippie Trail" before, "What's the fastest route to India?"

"This is it, unless you're flying."

"But, I mean, how long does it take from here?"

"Depends on how fast you want to go. Some people might take a couple more weeks, others a couple of months. Sometimes you just get stuck in a place for a while."

"Yeah, like on this bus!" People around break out in laughter.

Many of us now crowd around Andy, thirsting for more information of what lies ahead. Our questions pour out of us like water.

"How about Afghanistan? Is it worth staying there awhile?"

"Is Pakistan safe to travel through?"

"Tell us a little about India. Is it as cool as people say? Any good places there you recommend?"

Andy answers our questions diplomatically, saying more than once that our journey is personal. His opinions of places and people are his own, and we may have an entirely different experience. Still, I find his information valuable.

We're still in high country, so it gets colder as the night wears on. Conversations dwindle to whispers as we all bundle up and settle in as best as we can. Needless to say, no one gets much sleep. We're all awakened at first light by an explosive bus horn.

Karen is in the driver's seat leaning on the horn, screaming, "It's fucking morning and you fucking drivers better get your fucking asses out here right now!"

Yes, I think, Janis is definitely her role model.

The driver and his ticket-taker sidekick run up, yelling curses, pounding on the bus door. When we open the door, the driver pushes Karen out of his seat and gives us all a look to kill. We respond by chanting, "Drive the bus, drive the bus, drive the bus ..." and we don't stop until the local passengers who have left the bus for the night clamber back on and we're on the move.

We stop for a short while in a light rain for a bathroom break and gas in the city of Tabriz, a large industrial center renowned for its woven fabrics, carpets, and jewelry, but few of us travelers know this at the time. Jean has taken a long time in the bathroom and confides with me that she is having an attack of diarrhea, combined with the start of her menstrual period. She looks ashen, and there are still hours to go before we reach Tehran!

The rest of the trip brings us down from the highlands through plains and farms, now bathed in sunshine. The bus is quiet as everyone tries to catch up on lost sleep. Jean leans up against the window, eyes closed, her stomach occasionally rumbling. I keep asking her if she's okay until she finally shoots me a look to shut up.

We enter the outskirts of Tehran at dusk. Andy announces to our bus troupe—for that's what we have become by now—that we'll arrive at the general bus station, which is in the "tire district," a poorer section of the city. He knows a hotel nearby, the Amir Kabir, which is clean and welcomes foreign tourists. The best way to proceed is to stay close together and walk quickly, as many locals see us as infidels and, in particular, the women without head coverings as whores. When we unload and follow Andy the three blocks to the Amir Kabir, his words prove accurate as people yell at us, some throwing small stones, and some men actually grabbing at the women. Many locals are laughing, enjoying the sport of harassing the infidels.

We're all emotionally and physically exhausted when we arrive at the Amir Kabir. Serving as an oasis in this poor section of the city, the rooms of the three-floor hotel look onto an open courtyard with a central fountain. It's owned and run by a friendly old Jewish man. Andy tells us he welcomes foreigners because, in the eyes of Iranians, he is an infidel himself. The hotel also has a good restaurant—a relief to us all, as we won't have to leave the hotel during our short stay.

Jean is in the bathroom as soon as we check into a room on the second floor. I'm amazed at her strength of will, being able to hold it all in for hours on end. When she emerges, she declares that she absolutely has to have a shower, our bathroom just being a stool and sink. I contact the owner who informs me that the showers are in the basement, and that he'll send a boy up to take us there. A sixteen-year-old Iranian boy arrives a short time later and shows Jean to the shower while I flop on the bed. Within minutes, Jean storms back into the room! "That little bastard tried to jump me in the shower!"

"Oh my God, what did you do?"

"I screamed and clawed at his face until he ran out crying. What do you think I did?"

"I mean, are you all right?"

"No, I'm not all right, Bruce. I'm a mess!"

Tears streaming down her face, she sits on the bed, and I put my arms around her.

I say, "I know this is hard, but that boy just misunderstood. Remember what Andy told us, a woman without a veil here is a whore."

"So, you expect me to wear a veil when I take a shower?"

"No, I'm not saying that. I'm just saying that we need to put in some effort to understand and appreciate their different customs."

Jean looks at me agog, as if I just flew in from Mars. "Oh boy, oh boy, what can I say?"

"Say you'll try to understand their customs."

This is the last straw for Jean. "Understand … understand their customs? I just got attacked in a shower, you, YOU ASSHOLE!"

I really don't fathom the severity of Jean's trauma; a terrible time holding herself together through the day, only to a be attacked at the end. And I, so clueless, asking her to understand! This marks a low point in our young relationship. For the rest of the day, we barely talk.

Sat. Oct 17ᵗʰ—Night
Hi Again,

Here we are in Tehran. We've been here since Thurs. night, and we leave here tomorrow evening—6:00—for an overnight train to Mashed, Iran, for a very short time there only long enough to get our Afghanistan visas, then by bus to Herat, Afghanistan (no American Express there). And then on to Kabul for a while. The trip to here from Istanbul was long & boring—we took a train for 40 hours to Erzurum, Turkey, spent the nite there and took a mini-bus to the Iran border—went thru customs (one hour) and then took another bus to Tehran, but spent the nite in a small city near the border. The bus was supposed to go straight thru, but they lied and we had to stop—there were about 15 of us (Hippies) on the bus and we refused to get off and go to their hotel, so we all slept on the bus. It was quite a night for us.

I don't know how Carole lived here for 3 yrs. It is worse than any city I've ever been in. The men are <u>disgusting!</u> We walk down the street and they try to grab us and touch our rear ends, to avoid them you must move like a football player. I'm never alone, Bruce tries to scare them off—I'm even wearing a scarf on my head to turn them away, to no avail, they are the most frustrated up-tight people—no wonder their women wrap themselves up like mummies. Today, we went to the bazaar, and it's horrible there, just surplus Sears Roebuck clothing, rubber shoes, tires. The only thing is their rugs and tablecloths and a few jewelry stores, nothing like the bazaar in Istanbul! I have seen <u>Nothing</u> here, except mosques, worth buying or seeing—and the men make it so hard to enjoy the city—Please tell me what you did or where you went so if we must return here on our way back, I can see it differently!!

I've had a slight case of diareaha (there is that word to spell again) but went to the drug store and bought two more bottles of entro-vioform and toilet paper today. And I feel better. Please write Carole and tell her, maybe she can explain this city?

HAPPY ANNIVERSARY to you both!! What did you do to celebrate? Did you get my letter from Istanbul? Write to: me, Poste-Restante, Kabul, Afghanistan—I'll be there in about 1-1 ½ weeks from now—we are well and miss and love you, Jean and Bruce.

The next morning, we discover that there were even more Western travelers staying at the hotel. Many are young longhairs like us, confirming the epithet Great Hippie Trail. Much of each day is spent at the hotel restaurant or talking with new friends in the spacious lobby, in part because we're feeling uncomfortable with each other after the shower incident. Besides Mitchell and Barbara, our closest friendships develop with Quenton and Ginger, and Roslyn and Candice. Quenton and Ginger are Californians.

Tall, with long, flowing blond hair, Quenton looks the quintessential surfer, which he is. Aside from Ginger, his constant companion is his guitar, which he plays at any given opportunity. Nobody objects as he's quite good. Ginger is short, standing no higher than his shoulders, and older, maybe by ten years. At times, she seems more like Quenton's mother than his girlfriend, and it's soon evident who makes the decisions in their relationship. They bought a motorcycle in Amsterdam to drive to India but were attacked with stones by locals in the mountains of Yugoslavia. The battered motorcycle is now in storage in Istanbul.

Roslyn and Candice are a lesbian couple from New York City. In contrast to ours and most other travelers' dull clothing of jeans and tee shirts, they display a delightful array of multicolored flowing robes, nose rings, and sparkly necklace bangles. They've been at the Amir Kabir for several weeks, resting up from a year on the road through the African side of the Mediterranean—two Jewish girls on their way to visit Israel, braving the heart of the Islamic nations: Morocco, Algeria, Tunisia, Egypt, and Iraq. In Iraq, they purchased *chadors* and secretly visited a sacred mosque. If they were discovered, they would have been stoned to death! They are so relaxed and full of humor that they really do embody the newly adopted expression we often hear on the road: "go with the flow."

They convince us one day to venture out of the Amir Kabir to a nearby bazaar, so we brave the locals' stares and men occasionally grabbing as we wander through the streets. Roslyn and Candice seem unperturbed by the all the attention, laughing their way from one stall to another in the bazaar. The bazaar itself is a disappointment, offering more of the same cheap trinkets in each stall, nothing like the exciting wares of the Great Bazaar in Istanbul.

As our focus is to pass through Iran as quickly as possible, it never occurs to us to visit the Tehran Community School, an international school where Jean's sister, Carole, and her husband worked and lived for three years. The school is located in a somewhat more upscale section of the city than where we are, but still poorer than the "European Zone," marked by wide boulevards, expensive housing, and modern malls with their boutique shops. The leader of the country, Mohammad Reza Shah Pahlavi, was educated in Switzerland and has built a modern countrywide infrastructure with the financial support of European, Russian, and American investors. Tehran under the Shah is really a city of two peoples: the wealthy and urbane, and the poor, often fanatically religious masses.

We book tickets, along with Mitchell and Barbara, and Roslyn and Candice, for an overnight train to Mashhad, Iran's second largest city in northeastern Iran. I find space to lay out under a long bench and have a surprisingly good night's sleep, awakening just as our train pulls into the station in Mashhad. We immediately set out to find the Afghan embassy for visas. Again, our friend Andy has previously given us unerring directions to the embassy, where we obtain free visas within minutes. Unlike in Tehran, the people we pass hardly give us any notice. We're baffled, and relieved, by this. We find out later that Mashhad is a more multicultural center than Tehran, populated by Persians, Turkmen, Uzbeks, Tajik, and Kurds among others. In the center of the city sits the Ali al-Rida Mosque, an impressive memorial to a ninth century martyr. We find a small hotel near the mosque and bargain with the hotel owner for a room large enough to fit the six of us. We tour the city center later in the day, stopping at stalls to buy food. Again, the locals are busy shopping, selling, and conversing with neighbors, with no one giving us a second glance. What freedom!

Our sleep is fitful at best, but the next morning we board a bus to take us to the border. A part of me wanted to see more of Mashhad as it's obvious that this city, with its tolerant citizens and rich cultural history, has much to offer; but, then again, Afghanistan awaits!

AFGHANISTAN

Oct. 28—Thurs.
Hi Y'all,
*   This is a very large Aerogramme to fill up—so it will take a few days—Also it is supposed to cost 8 afghanis and he charged me 12, so I must get my monies worth. The last time I wrote was in Tehran and we are now in Kandahar, Afghanistan. After spending one week in Herat, Afghanistan, all I can say is it's a pleasure to be out of Iran and in this country. The people here are much more relaxed and friendly—the men stare at you but <u>don't touch</u>! The children all scream "hello" & "goodbye" to you & most of the women cover themselves like mummies. On Sat. we will leave toward Kabul where we will try for our Indian visas & get our mail—not to stay there long as it is very cold now—then on to Pakistan.*
*   The streets here are filled with bazaars and donkeys, horses & camels—they sell surplus American clothing and beautiful embroidered shirts & the <u>BEST</u> pomegranates in the world—they're the size of grapefruits and taste fantastic!*
*   I'm going to leave the rest of this until I get to Kabul where I'm sure to find a letter from you with many questions to answer, so until Kabul …*

Love and Kisses,
Jean and Bruce

We're excited to arrive at the Afghan border, both of us hoping to leave the ongoing tension between us behind in Iran. We've heard many stories of this country of mountains and desert, sun, delicious fruit, and plenty of hashish! Our bus will take us directly from Mashhad to Herat, so we only need to disembark for quick passport and visa checks before hopping back on the bus. We pull away from the border slowly as sellers run beside the bus selling fruit and hash to the windows of outthrust hands. We've heard that hashish is illegal in Afghanistan, but authorities look the other way as long as a person is not caught buying or selling it. Indeed, marijuana, hashish, along with opium, are among the biggest economies in Afghanistan, with a thriving worldwide black market export business. Mitchell buys a large chunk of hash for 100 afghanis, or $1.25, and loads pipe after pipe, passing it around the bus. Soon, one can't see in or out through the fragrant fog of smoke!

It's Candice who first says, "Man, this stuff is crap!"

"Yeah," I reply, "I don't feel high at all!"

Mitchell laments, "Damn, I'm not in this country for a half hour, and I've already been ripped off!"

This brings gales of laughter. Bad weed or not, nothing is going to dampen our relief in being out of Iran and in this new, exciting country.

We arrive in Herat after just a few hours and, as the sun is low on the horizon, we disembark in search of New Behzad, the hotel Andy told us about in Iran. Soon Jean and I are in a room on the second floor of the small hotel, with a small balcony overlooking the main street. Roslyn and Candice are across from us, while Mitchell and Barbara are at the end of the hall. We have a shared bathroom in the middle of the hallway. Meanwhile, Quenton and Ginger have decided to get a room in another hotel down the street.

Our room is oddly shaped. Nothing seems perpendicular. Each wall is painted a different bright pastel color. Its effect makes us feel claustrophobic. We assess how we can rearrange the room for maximum comfort. First to go is the large creaky bedframe. We convince the hotel manager to remove it with my help to an empty room. He doesn't seem put out, probably happy that the hotel finally has some guests. Next, we place the mattress on the floor, covered in blankets and surrounded by straw mats. The new low decor now makes the room seem more spacious. When our friends see the change, they all insist that they have their bedframes removed. We compliment each other on the new look of our "hippie pads."

Although Herat is the third largest city of Afghanistan, sitting in the low mountains of northwest, we are struck by how quiet it is compared with the cities we've come through. Just a few cars, a taxi, and a horse-drawn carriage, with its distinctive ringing of jingle bells, pass by beneath our window. A call to worship from a nearby *minaret,* or tower, mingles with birds singing and dogs barking. Scents of garden incenses mixed with roasting meat waft through our open window, reminding us that we're hungry.

Both sides of the hotel's street are lined with vegetable and fruit stands, as well as food stalls; we settle on a stall with a small table and chairs. The owner, a short, heavyset man with graying beard, speaks some English.

"Are you from America?" he asks.

"Why, yes," I reply, remembering instantly the painful hours on the Orient Express when I tried to pass us off as Canadians.

"I like Americans. I have many friends from America."

"Oh?" I say. "Where in America?"

Misunderstanding my question, he says, "Right here. They come to my shop. They like my food. It is the best in all of Herat!"

He introduces himself. "I am Hamid. I was born here and hope to die here also."

I introduce us, as Jean is reluctant as usual say anything for fear that a woman speaking in public will offend this man.

I ask, "Well, Hamid, what do you suggest we eat?"

This opens the floodgates; a wide smile creases his face as he takes us through a culinary menu of his wares. I try the lamb *koftas* (meatballs) and *kaddu burani* (sweet pumpkin) while Jean settles for a *palaw,* a rice dish of lamb mixed with vegetables, dried fruit, and nuts. All is washed down with glasses of *doogh,* a sweetened mixture of yogurt, water, and mint.

At the end of the meal, I compliment Hamid on his excellent food.

"I hope you come to my shop again. I don't only serve food, you know. I know the best people to see to change money and for hashish!"

We and our friends soon become regulars at Hamid's stall.

Short of afghanis, we enter a bank the next day to change American traveler's checks. The line to the cashier is long and has just moved a foot in a half hour. I approach a traveler several people in front of us and ask, "Excuse me, but have you been waiting long?"

He replies, "At least an hour. Do you have bank business or are you just wanting cash?"

"Just cash," I answer.

"In that case, I recommend you get cash on the black market. Here, you'll have another hour or so on the line, and then have a lot of paperwork to fill out. The exchange rate on the black market is a little lower, but hassle free. I'm stuck here because I have to transfer funds from my account in London. No choice for me."

We thank the man, leave, and find Hamid. He directs us just around the corner to a woman in an open doorway, who takes our checks and gives us a handful of afghanis, a five-minute transaction!

Jean and I are determined to slow down and try to heal our relationship, strained since the shower incident at the Amir Kabir. We walk and take the "jingle bell carriages" throughout the many neighborhoods, gardens, and bazaars, amazed at how extensive the city is. Men with long beards and turbans openly regard us, but with none of the malice we experienced in Iran. Passing women peek at us from under *chadors*. At a clothing stall, I buy *pyjamas*, loose-fitting pants, a *kurta*, or shirt and a vest, while Jean finds colorful tops and skirts. Jeans and shirts are stuffed in the bottom of our packs. We are sloughing off our Western apparel completely!

While having breakfast one day at a small restaurant attached to the New Behzad, we strike up a conversation with an American and two Afghans. All are middle-aged; two are wearing Western-style shirts and pants, while the third is in an Afghan Army uniform. They tell us that they are part of an international geological team. For the past year, their job has been to create the first accurate geophysical map of Afghanistan by using coordinates from its three largest cities—Kabul, Kandahar, and Herat—to bounce back beams from American satellites. The job has been grueling, demanding long treks into the mountainous terrain, and always having to deal with Afghan bureaucracy. They have just completed the final stage of their task here in Herat.

For their part, they're interested in who we are and why we are traveling such a long way by bus and train. Colonel Shribe, in his army uniform, is the project leader as this work is under the auspices of the Afghan military. He's particularly interested in our hippie lifestyle and in Jean's upbringing as a "liberated" Western woman.

"I am stationed in Kabul, but I was born here in Herat. My family lives here still and are happy I am back for a while after being away all year. I am busy finishing all this work today but, if you'd like, I can show you some of the beautiful sights of our city tomorrow."

We agree to meet him at the restaurant the next morning.

Later that afternoon, we go to Quenton and Ginger's room in the nearby hotel. The room is on the ground floor, larger than ours, with its own bathroom—only a toilet and sink, but what convenience! After Quenton entertains us with a few guitar solos, his voice not up to his skillful guitar riffs, Ginger suggests we all go to a nearby *hammam*, or bathhouse, a good idea as none of us have showered since Tehran. At the hammam, we must first pay the price of a shower before entering separate changing rooms, where we're given towels. The rooms are hot and steamy, naked people darting through steam clouds to the shower rooms. After days of washing our bodies with hand cloths, the showers are such a luxury! After this, we enter a large room with two separate hot pools for women and men. I'm the first in and the first out in a half hour, overwhelmed by heat and steam. We all emerge squeaky clean and grateful for fresh, cool air. "Our hammam" becomes an essential daily destination.

We return to our hotel where we catch up on the day's activities with Mitchell and Barbara, and Roslyn and Candice. Like us, Mitchell and Barbara are sporting Afghan-style clothing they bought at a bazaar: *pyjamas* and kurta for Mitchell, and a long, flowing skirt decorated with beads for Barbara. We all laugh at our apparel change in just a few days in Afghanistan! Roslyn and Candice, meanwhile, have run into a *dutar* player named Amir who was playing his long-necked, two-stringed instrument in the streets. He has invited them to come this evening to a local *chaikhana*, or *chai* house, to hear him play. So, after we all have dinner at Hamid's, we go off to the chaikhana.

This chaikhana has six carpeted platforms, each with beaded pillows and space enough for four. At the foot of each platform is a large *samovar*, or urn with spout. We remove our shoes at the entrance and clamber up on the platforms. The room is lit with candles and hazy with the smoke of tobacco and hashish. Amir sits at one end in the center of several musicians with drums and recorders, already deep into a repetitive, mesmerizing melody. He has a *chillum* in his lap. This is a conical pipe, often held aloft and smoked through a cloth wrapped around the smaller end. The song over, he deeply inhales from the chillum and blows out a cloud of hashish smoke, coughing and roaring with laughter. He packs the chillum again and passes it around, laughing as we try our hands at smoking from it. We're all stoned in no time, drinking chai and thoroughly enjoying the music and Amir's and his friends' company. Quenton has brought his guitar along, of course, and tries to accompany the dutar. He gives up after a few minutes, saying that the dutar's scales are too different for a guitar. Perhaps so, or perhaps he's simply unable to follow the magical notes of Amir's talented instrument. Finally, in the wee hours of the morning, we thank Amir and his band for the wonderful evening and stumble back to our rooms.

The next morning, bleary eyed from hashish and lack of sleep, we meet Colonel Shribe at the hotel restaurant. He has changed his uniform for casual Western-style short sleeve shirt and slacks.

"Today, we are going to visit some very famous sites for Afghans," he declares.

His driver opens jeep doors for us, and he drives just a short way to what appears to be a fortress.

"This is the Herat Citadel," Colonel Shribe proudly states, "famous throughout the world!"

"Why is that?" I ask.

"This was built in 330 BC by Alexander the Great when his armies invaded this area. His Greek army occupied this area for centuries before the Persians drove them out. The citadel has since been occupied by different occupying armies and has been destroyed and rebuilt many times."

We seem to be the only people in the whole complex. With its dark echoey chambers and two-foot-thick walls, it isn't hard to imagine the citadel as a pivotal outpost of defense from centuries of invaders.

Colonel Shribe then takes us to a large garden area enclosed by two *minarets*. Very different from our notion of a garden, there are plants, low shrubs, but no flowers to be seen in this high, dry climate during this time of year. A number of old bearded men are sitting along the garden path that brings us to a large tomb in the middle.

Colonel Shribe says, "This is the tomb of Sultan Husayn Bayqara, the Persian king who ruled Herat from 1469 to 1506. His reign is considered the golden age of Herat when Herat was the center of the Persian Empire. He is considered a saint, so this garden serves as a sanctuary for holy beggars. All who come here to visit this shrine are responsible to give them alms."

Of course, we live up to our responsibility, receiving in turn toothless smiles from the beggars.

We travel next to a large, impressive mosque.

Colonel Shribe informs us, "This is The Great Jami Masjid, also known as the Friday Mosque. It is also very old, but I don't know exactly how many years. If you would like, we can go into the courtyard."

As non-Muslims, this is as far as we can go. A few steps in, the colonel asks us to return to the entry and leave our sandals outside. We're a little embarrassed not to remember this simple yet important custom, not only for mosques but all households as well. We're immediately struck by the beauty of the courtyard. The surrounding walls and fountains are intricately adorned with inlaid tile, mainly of blue hues.

Colonel Shribe explains, "The central fountain here, and the ones in each corner of the courtyard are for performing ablutions before entering to pray. The several passageways leading from this courtyard go to different areas for prayer."

There is something about the aura of this courtyard in the center of this mosque that produces in me a calmness that is new, yet somehow recalled, like rediscovering a hidden part of myself. I feel like I would be satisfied if my journey to the East would just end here. We eventually, and reluctantly, leave this wonderful courtyard.

Finally, we accompany Colonel Shribe to his camp outside the city, where we have tea outside his large tent. The two Americans we met the day before say hello on their way to their own tents. We're filled with questions from the day, and for the colonel's part, his curiosity about our upbringing and lifestyle has not waned one bit.

As we prepare to leave, Colonel Shribe says, "This evening, my family is having a party to celebrate my return. I would be honored if you two could join me as my guests."

We enthusiastically accept, thanking the colonel for a wonderful tour as the jeep driver takes us back to our hotel to rest.

Two hours later the driver returns and brings us to a large, two-story house just blocks from the hotel. Colonel Shribe is there to greet us, leading us into a living room with Western-style chairs and a sofa. The house seems surprisingly empty, and we silently wonder what this "party" is all about. The colonel puts on some Indian music on an old 78 record player.

"I'm afraid this is as modern as I get. This is the latest music from Bombay. It is very popular in Kabul."

A young man enters the room, looking like a younger, thinner version of the colonel. "This is my son, Abdul. He is in his last year in school here."

Abdul adds, in only slightly accented English, "Yes, I am facing a decision to go to university in Kabul or join the military."

Colonel Shribe laughs, "You may think that I am pushing him toward the military, but I would really like him to continue his formal education."

A man comes to the entrance and nods to the colonel, who says, "I am told that the preparations for the party are completed. Please follow me."

He leads us across the dark street to an even larger house. After taking off our shoes, we're escorted into a long room. Seated on cushions against the walls are perhaps fifteen turbaned and bearded men. Everyone stands as the colonel happily greets the men in Dari (a local language with its roots in Persian), introducing us as his guests. All are family: uncles, nephews, and cousins. We're shown seats on cushions across from him. There are no women other than Jean to be seen. We understand that, because this unveiled woman is from a country with different customs, Jean's presence is acceptable to the men in this room.

Colonel Shribe explains to us in English that where one sits in this room indicates his place in the family hierarchy. Though he is being honored tonight, his is not in the first place. That is reserved for his father, the elder and family head, a wizened man with a long gray beard, a large *hookah*, or water pipe, at his feet. His father now regards us candidly, silently assessing who we might be. Looking around, we see that he is not alone. The men sit in silence, all eyes on us, as I suspect Colonel Shribe is telling them how we met, and perhaps some of our reactions on the day's tour. For the first time, I see several women in the doorway, peeking through their veils, their children behind their skirts openly staring with unabashed curiosity. I've no doubt we're the first Westerners these men and women have seen closely enough to fully scrutinize.

Now these women come in with cups and pitchers to serve chai, a tasty concoction of sweetened green tea, cardamom, and ginger. When all are served, the elder fills the hookah with tobacco and lights it, drawing a long pull and exhaling a great plume of smoke. Then he offers the hookah to me; I suppose he hasn't offered it to Jean because it's generally understood that a woman never smokes. I take a much smaller draw of the pipe than he did, and yet am convulsed by a massive coughing fit, setting off peals of laughter by the men. This is the icebreaker, opening the way for all to relax in laughter and conversation. Some men feel comfortable enough to ask us questions, with Colonel Shribe translating: "Are you from America?" "Where in America?" "Where are you going now?" "Why?" "Are you hippies?" "What is a hippie?" "Do you smoke hashish?" I answer these familiar questions as best as I can for both of us, as Jean is reluctant to say more than yes and thank you.

Tea consumed, the elder turns his cup over and stands, a signal for the rest of us to do the same. Then we all file out behind him to a small antechamber where women are waiting with pitchers of water for us to wash our hands. Next, we follow the elder to a much larger room where we take our seats in the same order as before.

In the center, on a large, beautiful Persian carpet is a feast: such an array of lamb, beef, and chicken kebabs, rice, vegetables, fruit, nuts, curries, curds, and chutneys! The women place plates in front of us, Colonel Shribe instructing them to place forks for Jean and me. The elder, placing kebabs on his plate, signals the feast to begin as we all reach to the center for food. As is custom, all eat with their right hands, the left reserved for cleaning the body. Jean and I avoid the forks and dive in with our right hands. We're not very agile at this, our messiness a source of amusement for the men, but we certainly manage to consume our share of delicious food. Colonel Shribe continuously encourages us to eat more until we are completely stuffed!

"Here, try the lamb kebab. More rice and curry?"

The feast ends with plates filled with strawberries, kiwis, and pomegranates. At this point, Colonel Shribe asks Jean if she would like to visit the women's quarters. Of course, she does! A small woman is summoned, whom the colonel says is one of his wives. After she ushers Jean out, the elder and the rest of us stand and return to the original long room, taking our usual places. More tea is served, the hookah relit and passed—this time I don't cough as much—as we all engage in easy conversation. Sometime later, Jean returns, her face beaming. I want to know about her experience, but she shoots me a look that says, "later." Some of the men notice and smile themselves, perhaps appreciating this special opportunity given this Western woman to personally engage with their own women.

Now well past midnight, we take our leave, thanking the elder for hosting us. Colonel Shribe escorts us out to the waiting jeep. We can't thank him enough for his kindness in opening his world to us. He tells us he must leave for Kabul in the morning to "wrap things up" for a few days. We can only express our hope to see him again. We ourselves are leaving for Kandahar soon, so we all understand that this will likely not happen.

In our hotel room, Jean tells me of her adventure in the women's quarters. "There were more women there than those who served at the feast. There must have been ten or so, and about the same number of children. And first of all, they had no veils on there, and they are beautiful, every one of them! Three of them introduced themselves as wives of Colonel Shribe!"

"Wow," I exclaim. "He told me that the woman who escorted you there was one of his wives."

"Yes, she was the oldest of the three, and I think the boss. She directed the others to bring me a seat and some chai."

"Maybe she was his first wife. They seem the same age."

"Maybe. But you remember my Turkish puzzle ring, the one I bought in Istanbul?"

"Yeah, but I haven't seen it since then."

"It's always been in my purse. Anyway, all of the women were eating and laughing together, a real difference from their quiet, veiled public personas. None of us spoke each other's language, so

I was a little self-conscious. Then I remembered my puzzle ring. I showed them the whole ring first, and then let it fall to pieces. They were dismayed because they thought I had broken the ring. Then, as they watched, I slowly put it back together. There was a lot of laughter, as others then let the ring fall to pieces and tried to put it back together. Not one of them could do it. I'm happy I practiced with it so much in Turkey, and that it only had twelve pieces, not like some of those with sixteen. Otherwise, I would certainly have confirmed their fears that I broke my ring."

The story told to us by the merchant who sold Jean the ring was that the men of Turkey had little trust in their wives' fidelity, fearing that they would take lovers if they went away on business. One man devised a clever method of making a wedding ring that would fall apart if the wife removed it from her finger to take a lover. As it was generally thought by men that women were not smart enough to be able to put the ring together again, they would know upon their return if their wife was still faithful or not.

Jean continues, "I was really sorry to leave them, but the oldest wife told me that the men were preparing to leave."

"At least you got to see who the women really are behind the veil."

"Yeah, I won't soon forget that!"

We have a last breakfast the next morning with Roslyn and Candice, and Mitchell and Barbara, who have tickets on the morning bus to Kandahar. We've made arrangements to meet them there the next night, unaware that we won't get to see the three of them again, only running into Roslyn eight months later in Delhi. The rest of our day is spent at a bazaar, enjoying a last bath at the hammam and packing for the next day's bus ride with Quenton and Ginger to Kandahar.

Arriving at their hotel with our packs in the morning, however, we find Quenton in bed with a fever and unable to travel. They've managed to get their bus money back, though not an easy feat. They're now considering taking an airplane from the local airport to Kabul, where they'll meet us in a few days.

Just before we leave them, Ginger says, "I know you guys have been going through a hard time. I want to loan you something that might help."

She pulls out of her pack a book, *Gestalt Therapy Verbatim* by Fritz Perls. This is the first time we've heard of the book.

"It's incredible," Ginger exclaims. "This book is all about how we can heal our problems through dreamwork. Perls is a psychiatrist at Esalen Institute in Big Sur, and the book covers the sessions he holds with small audiences at Esalen. You guys need to read it."

Jean and I look at each other. We thought our difficulties were private but, when you travel in such close proximity with others, it seems there are no secrets. Everyone knows each other's problems.

Ginger continues, "It's been such a help in our relationship, I think it may also help yours."

We thank her for the book, Ginger adding, "But please give it back when we get together in Kabul. This is our bible and I don't want to go on to India without it."

We promise, wishing Quenton a speedy recovery as we leave to catch the bus.

10/29/70

Howdy,

Now I'm not going to write a large thing as I'm sure I'll be receiving a letter from you in Kabul; so, I'll respond in a bit more detail then. We are in Kandahar, Afghanistan, an oasis city located on the Russian-American highway between Herat on the western border and Kabul in the northeast. The city itself is a grand bazaar, with each shop vending anything from Care Package clothing and food to beautiful carpets from all over the East. Noises as I write include a minimum of car honking, the distinct clanging of bells from the million odd horse carriages, Afghan music—slightly repetitious—and popular Indian music from next door, also repetitious. Days are broiling while nights can become three blanket temperature. Our room in the "Tourist Hotel," costs 20 afghanis—money not the people, comparable to 25 cents, and is cave like: very small, triangular with blue, orange and white walls, always dark, has a small wood burner, and no beds. Really, it resembles a theater setting, but is not without its charm. I'm going to end this letter by telling you that Kandahar is the pomegranate capital of the world and wishing you a Happy Halloween, and by saying hello to everybody else, particularly Randy and Merle who I'll write to shortly, and finally reminding you to buy a lottery ticket!

Love, Bruce and Jean

We are the only Westerners on this bus. Several Afghans are playing popular music on their boom boxes, a cacophony of competing noises seemingly acceptable to the ears of the local travelers. The ride on our multicolored, curtained bus out of Herat is lined with tall cypresses for several miles before we begin our slow descent to the southeast desert city of Kandahar. The sun blazes down from an azure sky with a few high cirrus clouds. We ride through a land of brown hues with occasional riverbanks and dwarfed trees of faded green. It has been a long hot day by the time we reach the bus station in the center of Kandahar.

As usual, our first goal is to collect our bags, which have been secured on the top on the bus, and search for a suitable hotel. Within a block of the station, we enter the Tourist Hotel. The hotel is on the second floor above a restaurant and behind its balcony. Ascending narrow, winding steps, we come to a small registration desk. A tall, older man with a long, stringy beard greets us, introducing himself as Hayatullah, the owner of the hotel and restaurant.

I ask, "May we see a room?" He nods, leading us through a hallway behind his desk onto a large, rooftop garden.

"I am very proud of my garden." he declares. "This is an oasis of beauty and rest."

Small potted trees, plants, shrubs, and benches line narrow gravel paths, leading to a dozen rooms surrounding the garden. Most benches have hippies lounging on them. Local men squat against the room walls, drinking chai and smoking chillums. We see that most, if not all, of these garden denizens are stoned. In one corner of the garden is a large cage containing many pigeons.

Hayatullah explains, "These homing pigeons are my pets. Caring for them is my duty and pleasure."

"Do they always stay in the cage?" I ask.

"Oh no. I let them out every evening at sunset. They like to fly over that mountain," he indicates distant, low-lying hills to the east, "but they always come back to this cage, their home."

Hayatullah then shows us to one of the rooms off the garden. It is small and dark. Its walls are different colors and curve into a triangular shape. A double bed, small table with lamp, and a central wood furnace are its only furniture, covering a worn Afghan carpet. It seems acceptable.

"How much for the room?" I ask.

"Only 20 afghanis, a good price," he responds. "Wood for the furnace and shower are a little extra." I calculate that this amounts to slightly more than a US quarter a day!

"May we remove the bedframe?"

"Of course. Many hippies like to do the same."

A short time later, we've settled into our cave-like room. With only the mattress on the floor, it does seem a little larger. As it's growing dark and we're tired, we decide not to explore this new city until the next day, opting to have some rice and kebabs on the balcony of the restaurant. The evening has grown colder, so we now understand the need for our room furnace. While eating, Jean comments as she waves with her free hand, "There seem to be a lot of flies about. I hope they don't crap in my food."

"Yeah," I respond. "Probably be gone in the morning."

We're just finishing our meal when Jean exclaims, "Look over there. Isn't that Roslyn and Candice?"

I look to a window of another hotel across the street. "That's them all right. Let's go and say hi."

After a pause, we decide that we just want to get some sleep. Now that we know where they are, we tell ourselves we'll see them in the morning. After paying only 8 afghanis for two meals, we return to our room, light the furnace, and settle in for a surprisingly comfortable night's sleep.

The next morning, we have an omelet and chai breakfast on the balcony, noting that the flies not only haven't gone away but seem to have multiplied! Other diners, mainly locals, seem undisturbed by them, nonchalantly waving their left hands over their plates as they eat. We soon adopt this gesture ourselves at each meal, dubbing it the "Kandahar Wave." Afterward, we cross the street to the other hotel. We ask for Roslyn's room but are told that the two women checked out for the morning bus to Kabul. We ask if another man and woman were with them but were told no. We're surprised that they left Kandahar so soon after arriving, and disappointed that we didn't see them when we had the chance. And where are Mitchell and Barbara?

Hoping that these friends are still in Kandahar, we spend the morning looking for them throughout the bazaar. Kandahar is certainly hotter and dustier than Herat, and seemingly poorer as well, as there are beggars everywhere, many with missing limbs. Other than ubiquitous hash sellers, there is nothing really different in this bazaar. We've already seen the same clothing, jewelry, and dishware in Herat, but we do buy some giant pomegranates, grapes, and a melon at one stall along a narrow bazaar lane. Walking further down a lane we see a large black object hanging from the roof of a stall.

Jean asks, "What is that thing?"

"I don't know," I reply. "Looks like a bag of something."

As we come closer to the stall, the shopkeeper appears with a broom and starts pounding on the object. Suddenly, a thousand black flies explode out into the air, exposing a large bloody slab of meat!

"Oh my God!" Jean exclaims.

I add, "Tonight's dinner."

This spectacle marks our change to becoming vegetarians, mainly. Certainly, we'll eat no more meat in Kandahar!

By the time we return to the Tourist Hotel, we're convinced that Mitchell and Barbara must have left with the two women. We share a pomegranate and some melon—delicious! Neither of us have tasted fruit this good!

"Who needs meat," I pronounce. "We'll just live on fruit."

At sundown, we wander out to the garden and join the hippie crowd just as Hayatullah opens the cage for his pigeons to fly en masse into the sky. He then steps up to a giant hookah, which has been filled with hash and tobacco by one of the locals. The hookah is so tall he actually climbs a step to reach its mouthpiece. Lighting the big bowl with a long match, he sucks in the smoke for long seconds, his eyes bulging and cheeks hollowing into caves, before he explodes in great coughs of smoke and flames flaring from the bowl. I can see there is great appreciation by the garden crowd for his massive expulsion. As we watch, both men and women step up to the hookah for their turn.

"All right if I give it a try?" I ask Jean.

She responds, "Better you than me."

I'm not much of a hash smoker, but I step up and take the longest pull of smoke that I can. However, instead of coughing, I hold in the smoke as I sit back down.

"You're supposed to cough the smoke back out," Jean cautions.

All I can say is, "Oh," as I now become consumed by coughing spasms.

I start to feel nauseous and faint after a few minutes. "I think I'll lie down for a few minutes," I tell Jean as I head back to our room.

No sooner do I lie down on my sleeping bag then I pass out. The next thing I know is that I have a terrible headache and it's morning of the next day. I've been asleep for thirteen hours!

I don't feel like moving from my bed, so Jean suggests we start looking through the book that Ginger loaned us in Herat, *Gestalt Therapy Verbatim*. I'm reluctant at first, but soon we're immersed in the book to such a degree that we don't leave the room for the rest of the day, eating only our fruit. The basic premise of the work is that understanding one's dream images can expose and release any trauma or emotional difficulties one experiences in the waking world. Psychiatrist Fritz Perls believes, as did Sigmund Freud and Carl Jung before him, that all dream images are actually latent parts of a person. His method of bringing these images to light involves his inviting a person in the small Esalen Institute audience to come up on stage, where in front of Perls are two chairs facing each other. After the participant sits on one of the chairs, Perls asks if they have a dream that has been troubling them, or at least a dream they remember. In recounting the dream, the participant will mention different images. For instance, "I'm walking through a jungle with a friend, chopping vines to clear the way. It's a very hot day and I'm sweating. Suddenly a tiger appears and stares at me. I should be afraid, but I'm not. Our eyes meet, and then the tiger moves on."

Perls will then place one of the dream images, the tiger, the friend, even the jungle, with its heat and vines, in the empty chair opposite the person. Perls will then facilitate a conversation between the participant and the dream image. Questions and responses between the two invariably bring insights to light, which Perls describes as "mini-Satoris." The participant will begin to recognize some of the fears or prejudices they have suppressed, clearing the way for them to make positive changes in their life.

With the book as guide, Jean and I work to uncover the difficulties we've been experiencing. We each take turns as facilitator while the other converses with dream images. Much comes to light about our own views and how we communicate, and particularly issues with each other we've suppressed on our journey. One day turns to two, and then extends into the third day, as we pause only long enough to sleep and buy food to bring back to our room. By the end of the third day we're exhausted but inspired by the further understanding of ourselves and each other. I'm seeing myself more clearly and appreciating Jean as she is, devoid of my expectations of how I want her to be. I know she's experiencing the same of me. The dark cloud over us since Tehran has lifted. We now recognize that, with all our differences, we truly love each other, an understanding allowing for a relaxed and passionate release of lovemaking. We've moved a light year beyond our initial pact as friends agreeing only to see the one having difficulty on a one-way airline ticket home.

A loud knock wakes us the next morning. I open the door to Quenton, uncharacteristically without Ginger.

He exclaims, "There you are! We've been looking for you all over town for the last two days!" He seems angry.

"Hi there," I respond. "I see you're much better."

Jean calls from bed, "Hi Quenton. Where's Ginger?"

"She's back at the hotel, packing. We leave in an hour for Kabul."

I say, "I thought you were going to fly directly there from Herat."

He replies, "I wanted to, but Ginger was afraid we might not see you again. So, we came to get the book back. She can't live without it. At least that's what she keeps saying."

Handing him back the book, I say, "Thank you both so much. This book has been a lifesaver for us."

When Quenton doesn't respond, I add, "Well, we leave here in a few days. Leave a message for us at the poste restante in Kabul, so we know where you're staying."

"Yeah, sure," he mutters as he leaves.

When he's gone, Jean says, "Are they angry at us?"

"I don't know," I reply. "Maybe Quenton is just frustrated that he's had to search for us for two days."

"Yeah, maybe." (But when we check the message board at the poste restante in Kabul days later, there is no message from Quenton or Ginger. We're not to see them again.)

While we were holed up in our "cave," Ramadan had begun. This is a forty-day period of fasting to emulate the forty-day fast of the prophet Mohammed in the wilderness. Whereas Mohammed did not eat or drink the entire time, fasting now is only observed during the daylight hours. During the days, everything comes to a crawl: no food or drink, besides water, available. And no hashish smoking! People are grumpy. The hippies still smoke and lay like lizards on the benches of the garden, much as they always do, while the locals squatting against the walls look sullen as they continuously knead marijuana in their hands to make hashish. With

no food to feast on, even the ubiquitous flies are lying low. But, as
the sun sinks lower in the sky, conversations pick up, the solemn
mood lightening among the citizenry of Kandahar until, at sunset,
life returns to the city: restaurants open, music plays, and laughter
abounds as the happy locals in the garden load the hookah with
tobacco and hashish. After releasing his homing pigeons to the sky
and mountain, Hayatullah, as always, is offered the first draw of the
pipe, with the garden denizens lining up to take their turns. After
that first experience with the hookah, I pass. Then most of us head
to the restaurant balcony or downstairs for dinners of kebabs, rice,
and vegetables and plenty of chai. Some of the wealthier Afghans,
like Hayatullah, have wine. We return to our room after a few hours
but can hear the feasting and music going on all night! In the morning, all of Kandahar is once again as silent as a tomb.

November 3
Hi Again,

*Well, I just got letter #2 and sat down right away to write to
you & to tell you that we are both __very__ well, no diarrhea anymore.
I took one Entro-Viaform and felt fine. We are very careful about
water—I have not had any since Germany, only hot tea. We eat
__no meat at all__, just rice and cooked vegetables & only fruit that
can be peeled—or melon with thick skins. We take our vitamins
every day and stay in hotels where we have clean bathrooms and
showers. I know how you worry—I'm a chip off the old block!—but
we are careful. I don't want to be sick and Bruce watches me and I
watch him. You must not think that we are here alone—there are
100's traveling this route—all give info to each other about the cities, etc.—even many middle-agers are here in Kabul—it's a very
western city. We met a man who was driving his jeep from Europe
to India at 60 yrs. old. Also, some are going by bicycle which is the
hardest way. The buses are very good here, no problem w/ them and
the roads are fine—the Russians and Americans built them, nothing compared to the S.A.—we just go from city to city (about 8 hrs.
on a bus) stay a few days and go on. We got our Indian visas today*

& our mail (only one letter so far (#2)—I'll check again tomorrow.
Maybe I'll buy a few things tomorrow (tues) …

We leave for Kabul the next morning, the only Westerners on a hot, crowded bus. Recently repaved by the Russians, this ancient trade road is now a straight eight-hour shot, with just three short stops along the way. The passing scenery outside is bland: a cloudless blue sky and the browns of desert broken only by low shrubs along dry creek beds. In our haste to leave in the morning, we've brought no food with us and are feeling hungry by early afternoon. As it is Ramadan, nobody is eating or drinking on the bus. We've resigned ourselves to our circumstance when an old woman in front of us turns around and offers us a pomegranate. Her young seatmate then hands us chunks of bread and cheese. They speak no English, but their generosity in offering us food speaks volumes. They've realized that we're hungry, and as non-Muslims, we can't be held to their religious observance of Ramadan. Their generosity brings Jean to tears. Later, we reflect on how different these Afghan women are to those Iranians who offered up only verbal and physical abuse.

It has grown colder by late afternoon when we arrive in Kabul. Although the road seemed mostly flat to us, we have climbed to an altitude of 5,873 feet. Kabul, the capital of Afghanistan, is larger and more modern than either Herat or Kandahar, with tall office buildings, impressive mosques and museums, wide boulevards, and large parks and shopping plazas. Searching for a hotel, we notice that, although it's Ramadan, quite a few restaurants and shops are open for business during the day. Even more striking is the dress of many citizens: men in suits and casual Western wear, and women in stylish dresses, many without *chadors* or veils.

We settle into a large, sparsely furnished room in the Olfat Hotel, recommended by one of the hippies on the rooftop in Kandahar. The room's best asset is its large windows overlooking the city's central park. Also, the hotel is within easy walking distance to many restaurants, the post office, and Indian consulate. We've agreed to stay in Kabul only long enough to accomplish our business, as we're anxious to move on quickly through Pakistan to India. Our ratio-nale, as it was in Istanbul and Mashhad, is that we'll spend more time in this city when we return from India, whenever that may be.

After an unremarkable meal of soup and omelets in the small hotel, we settle in to a fitful night's sleep. The next morning, we go to the Indian consulate to obtain our visas. We are the first in line, so the process takes just half an hour and is free of charge. Next, we wander to the post office, are handed two letters, one from each family, but are disappointed to find no messages from any of our friends on the notice board.

We wander about the city, enjoying the sights. It's early November, and the air is cold and crisp. Trees in parks and lining the streets are shedding their golden leaves. The jackets we've retrieved from the bottom of our packs are barely warm enough! We buy a bag of pine nuts at a street stall, a specialty of the north. We've heard that the Afghans have pine nut eating contests, the winner eating the most pine nuts and leaving the cleanest shells in a certain amount of time. As we walk along, Jean easily bests me in our own contest. The few nuts I've managed to eat before Jean finishes off the bag are delicious!

Looking for lunch off the central plaza, we come across the Khyber Restaurant. We've heard about this place before, a haven for travelers. There are only a few available tables, as the rest are taken by travelers, mainly hippies, who can order a breakfast and then occupy their tables for the whole day. A large board filled with messages hangs on an entrance wall. I check it out, but there are still no messages from any of our friends who may have passed through. We eat a tasty vegetarian lunch, but don't return. We're just not interested in "staking our claim" to a table and "vegging out" for days on end at the crowded Khyber Restaurant.

The next day is spent touring the older, medieval section of the city where we've heard there is a thriving black market to exchange US dollars for Indian rupees. There are several on the very first block, all touting the same exchange rate. We change $100 in traveler's checks for 1,300 rupees. As the bank rate in India is only 7 rupees to the dol-lar, we've almost doubled the value of our money! Aware that this is an illegal transaction, we'll have to smuggle the money through the Indian border. The very least we can expect as punishment if we are caught is to have the rupees taken away—hopefully not jail! Fewer shops and restaurants are open than in the more cosmopolitan section, but we do find a pine nut stall. Jean is already halfway through the bag while I struggle with the few in my hand. We poke into the few open shops, admiring the fur-lined coats, hats, and boots for sale. Our packs are already full, so we buy nothing, promising ourselves that we'll really shop when we return from India.

During our last evening in Kabul, as we're having a meal at the hotel restaurant, we notice a man continuously glancing over from his table. Jean is uncomfortable, but I sense he wants to talk.

Finally, he comes over and says, "Excuse me, but may I say hello. My name is Habib. I am a pharmacist from Karachi."

"Oh, we are traveling from America."

"I do not have the chance to meet Americans. I would like to know more about your country. Would you please to join me in my room for a glass of wine?"

I look to Jean, who nods her assent. "I suppose we could," I reply.

Habib's room is a carbon copy of ours, only with a dismal view to another building. He pours three glasses of red wine, unusual for a Muslim and the first alcohol we've had since Octoberfest in Munich. The wine is syrupy sweet.

Taking advantage of his opportunity, Habib peppers us with questions. "Where in America do you live?" "Do you work in America?" "I have heard of hippies who have long hair and smoke hashish. Are you hippies? Do you smoke hashish?" We give our standard answers to such questions.

Then he asks, "Where are you going on your travels?"

I reply, as Jean as usual is reluctant to speak with a Muslim man, "We're going to India."

"Oh no," he admonishes. "India is not a good place! It is very dirty, and many people are poor and sick. Better that you stay in Pakistan. It is much cleaner and so beautiful."

47

I respond that we will be leaving to Pakistan in the morning and will be happy to see his lovely country. He then launches into a long spiel of how Pakistanis are so brave and how they defeated the cowardly Indians in the war of 1947, despite India's superiority in weapons and troop numbers.

As he talks, something about his noticeable interest in Jean makes us both uncomfortable.

Then he asks, "Excuse me, but are you two married?"

"Yes," I immediately lie.

"Oh." He seems disappointed, perhaps because he's hoping I'd offer Jean up, or maybe we could all enjoy a threesome. "Yes, that is good," he replies. "I myself have three wives."

Just like Colonel Shribe, I think. He further explains, "It is necessary for a Muslim man to keep himself happy with the pleasure of many wives."

I can feel Jean coming to a slow boil!

"Yes, a woman must have a menstrual period for ten days each month. During that time, they are no good for a man. Therefore, more wives than just one will keep a man satisfied."

Jean can no longer hold herself in. "Ten days? You must have some strange women in Pakistan who have periods for ten days."

"Yes, ten days," he replies. "I know this, you see, because I am a doctor."

"And I know this is not true," Jean counters, "because, *you* see, I am a woman!"

This seems to take to wind out of his sails. We go to leave when Habib says, "Please, before you go, please accept this small gift from me. I have in my possession the very latest antibiotic. It is called tetracycline."

Handing Jean a packet, he adds, "It is far more powerful than penicillin. This will protect you from all the diseases in India."

We thank him, unaware yet of what a timely gift this is.

FURTHER

... We'll leave here Weds. morning for Peshawar, Pakistan (8 hrs. from here)—we'll be there for one or two nights and then by bus to Lahore (10 hrs.) for one or two days and then by bus to New Delhi for our first stop in India.

It is hard to explain why we want to go to these countries—I can only say for the Adventure. Europe was nice, only nothing was new, life was similar to N.Y. and it was expensive—yes I (we) will go to Greece when we come that way again, but now the most foreign and strange is what we want to see. The people here are kind and good—we have made many friends. It is nothing like Iran—I'm sorry I write so strongly about them but they were madding (sp?) These countries are not as poor and helpless as those in S.A. and we need to travel and learn from them, esp. in India we will learn how to meditate and find peace within ourselves and how to live a good human life. Yes, we know you can learn this at home, but this is part of our dream. Please try to understand and worry as little as possible—I know you worry out of love but you must try to accept also my needs and dreams—we are both happy and healthy and try-ing to be wise—Enshala—which is Arabic for God Willing. Please write next to American Express in New Delhi, India. We should be there in about 1-2 weeks.

Love and Kisses,
Jean and Bruce

The next morning we're off on another bus loaded with Afghans and Pakistanis, everyone's luggage packed into an impressive mound atop the bus, to Peshawar, Pakistan. This journey takes us through the famous Khyber Pass of the Safed Koh mountains, part of the Hindu Kush range. Important for centuries as a trade route, this pass served as a strategic military route for Alexander the Great's armies in his conquest of India and, centuries later, a stronghold when a small British platoon known as the "Khyber Rifles" defended India from an attack from the Barbarian hordes of Mongolia and Afghanistan. The pass itself descends a barren, narrow valley between high mountain walls, just a one-hour ride by bus.

The border crossing is easy, just an obligatory stamping of our visas and passports. By nightfall, we pull into the bus station of Peshawar. Our objective is to pass through Pakistan as quickly as possible, so we buy bus tickets for the next day to Rawalpindi before searching for a hotel. We agree on a nearby hotel and settle in a rooftop room, which is expensive compared to the prices in Afghanistan. We're the only Westerners during a hotel meal of soup, rice, and curried vegetables. We go to bed early, both feeling lonely and adrift without our traveling companions.

An old bus with tiny windows awaits us in the morning and is already filled with people and luggage. We don't see how any more can fit, but when we show our tickets to the driver, he yells some orders for people to shove over on the wooden seats so we can squeeze in. Throughout the trip, we are both fighting nausea. The heat and crowd, combined with curves and hairpin turns on a bus with no shock absorbers, are a jolting horror! I think that there must be a better way to travel than this. (Later, we discover that there is indeed: an excellent train, built years before by the British Raj, traveling down through the Khyber Pass to the cities of Pakistan. We just don't know it at the time.) As we descend, we see water buffalo grazing along the roadside for the first time. These powerful yet gentle long-horned beasts have served farmers in Pakistan and India for centuries.

Several people get off at a midway stop, allowing two men to board and sit in front of us. One is obviously caring for the other, who is wrapped in a white sheet and moaning. Every so often, the sheet flies open, and a wild-eyed man stands and starts screaming in Pakistan's language, Urdu. It takes all of his caretaker's strength to pull him back down to the seat and wrap the sheet around him again. On one such wild outburst, the demented man sees us behind him and lunges for me before he's dragged back by the caretaker. My adrenaline is racing! For the rest of the trip, I have to be on my guard for attacks. I don't know it yet but, aside from the nausea, I'm getting sicker.

One has never seen two people so relieved to reach their destination. Our nausea has abated, but I'm still feeling weak and feverish. The city surrounding the bus station is crowded and noisy, with exhaust from a steady stream of traffic irritating eyes and clogging breathing. We've been told by an English-speaking man at the bus station to take the train—"Yes, very much faster than the bus, you see."—to our next destination, the city of Lahore. We're not interested in staying in Rawalpindi, much less sightseeing, and just want to leave as soon as possible. We locate a nearby taxi and slowly make our way through a maze of narrow, crowded streets to the train station miles away.

> ... *After the breathtaking Khyber Pass, we found ourselves in Peshawar, Pakistan, where Coca Cola is more plentiful than water, and the curry dishes precipitate Atahualpa's revenge! After one night there we took a rickety government bus 100 miles and 6 hours to Rawalpindi, the capital, a whole city slightly below the level of Broadway and 42nd Street. It was there where I contracted some diarrhea and fever. Jean's care brought me around though* ...

At the station, we're disappointed to discover that the train for Lahore has already left and that the next one won't leave until nine o'clock the next morning. By regulation or custom, we won't be allowed to buy tickets until one hour before departure. The taxi has already left, so our only option is to walk the street parallel to the train tracks to look for accommodations for the night. As we walk along with our backpacks, people we pass openly stare at us, some laughing and pointing. We feel as though we're back in Tehran again! We finally find a run-down, two-story building with a faded hotel sign and are shown a downstairs room off a courtyard serving as a car mechanics garage, littered with dozens of worn tires.

The room is dark and long with high, echoing ceilings. On one end are two small single beds; on the other, a toilet and sink behind a threadbare standing screen. In the center of the room is a massive empty desk, but no chair. The bare walls are a sickly green color, the floor a gray tile. At any other time, we'd walk, if not run, away from this hotel immediately but, by now, my legs are wobbly from the weight of my pack. I'm nauseous again and running a high fever. Jean keeps eyeing me anxiously. We pay the owner a price we know is too high, and I collapse on the bed.

In the two days following, I am chilled and delirious with fever. Jean acquires blankets from the owner and wraps me to keep me warm. She helps me across the room to the toilet several times each hour so I can vomit and crap out fluids. I have an unquenchable thirst but, as it is still Ramadan, no food or drink is available on the streets during the day. There is water from the sink tap that we know isn't safe to drink, most likely carrying parasites. Jean asks the hotel owner if we can have tea, but he refuses to give it during the day, telling us we are able to have as much tea as we want after sundown. However, Jean has discovered an old Coca-Cola machine in the mechanic's shop. The shop is empty, probably for Ramadan, so Jean is able to keep me hydrated with Coke during the days. She has also remembered the tetracycline the pharmacist Habib gave us in Kabul and, thinking she must do something more, doses me every few hours. I've eaten nothing. Jean won't leave the hotel, so survives only on the bread, cheese, nuts, and fruit we've remembered to stock for Ramadan. By the end of the second day, my fever and nausea have abated. I'm weak but know I'll be okay.

(Later, in Delhi, Jean receives a letter from her mother. Enclosed is a New York Times article about a cholera epidemic sweeping across Asia. The port of Istanbul was closed a month before, only days after we left there. The article states that cholera is a disease that strikes suddenly and is often fatal. Its symptoms include high fever, delirium, vomiting, diarrhea, and an unquenchable thirst. The only effective treatments are regular hydration and antibiotics. We have always believed that I did have cholera, and that Jean's care, Coca-Cola, and the pharmacist Habib's tetracycline saved my life!)

We leave for the station early the next morning and buy second class tickets to Lahore, giving us two of eight seats in a compartment. Jean helps me climb up to the luggage rack above the seats, where I recline for the entire trip.

Only one man, perhaps a farmer, is in the compartment with us to begin with. He simply stares open-mouthed at Jean, as he has obviously never seen a Western woman before. Fortunately, he disembarks at the first stop. Other passengers come and go, each amazed to encounter a woman sitting alone on a bench with a man lying on the luggage rack above.

A military man enters, surveys the compartment, and sits opposite Jean. He speaks some English and obviously wants to practice his skills.

"Madam, I see you are not alone. But why is your man lying above you?"

"He has been sick. He's better now but must rest."

"But he is in the luggage area. That is only used for sleeping at night."

"But the only luggage are our packs, which are on the rack above you."

"Yes, but these racks are only for sleeping at night." This is something that he must think about deeply. I'm silent above, unwilling to explain or defend such a "brash violation" of the norm.

The military man learns that we are passing through Pakistan quickly on our way to India.

"Oh, but you have not experienced this wonderful country properly. My home city, Quetta, is in the south. It is more beautiful than any city you will find in India."

I know Jean and I are of the same thought. All we want to do is get through this country as fast as we can. At the same time, I realize

I'm prejudiced. I'm sure there is much more to see and appreciate in this country than our subjective experience of two cities. Yet, we didn't travel all this way to explore Pakistan.

Before we disembark at the modern Lahore station, the military man recommends the Continental Hotel as an excellent choice for international travelers. We leave the station to a throng of drivers of taxis, bicycle rickshaws, and horse-drawn carriages. We opt to take a carriage and direct the driver to take us to the Continental Hotel.

"Oh no," he exclaims, "you do not want to go to that hotel! It is much too expensive! Why don't I take you to a nice hotel where other hippies go?"

"No, please take us to the Continental Hotel," I command.

Grumbling, he drives us several miles along a wide, tree-lined boulevard to a large luxury resort. "The Continental," the driver announces.

We're a little intimidated by the sheer size of the place and fear that it might be too expensive. We pay the driver and climb the wide steps to the registration desk in a stately lobby with a large central fountain. The desk clerk runs down the prices of rooms, the smallest being much too expensive for our limited budget. Disappointed, we leave the hotel, only to find the carriage driver waiting for us.

"Okay," I tell him. "Please take us to the hippie hotel."

He laughs, "That is what I told you to begin with!"

Minutes later, he pulls up to what can only be described as a slum dwelling, the sign displaying "OTEL," the H missing. We pay him again, receiving his big toothless smile in return.

The building is in ruins, with holes in the walls and doors falling off their hinges. The odor of hashish permeates everything. The proprietor leads us up a creaky stairway with no railing to a small shack on the roof. When he opens the door, we all gag at the smell emanating from the room. "What died in here?" I think. Inside, the only furniture are two hemp beds. We can see the hemp crawling with bugs.

"Oh, I will send a woman up to clean the room," the proprietor says hopefully. "And I will give you a good discount."

It takes just one look from Jean for me to say, "I'm sorry, but we can't stay here."

We thank the proprietor for his attention and make our way as quickly as possible down the street. Just around the corner, and a world away, we come upon the New Chowhan Hotel. A one-story structure surrounding a well-manicured courtyard, the room we're shown is well furnished and clean. In the three days we are in Lahore, these accommodations prove comfortable and the staff friendly.

As it's almost dusk, the day's fasting soon over, we decide to look for a restaurant or food stall in our neighborhood. To our surprise, both the train station and Continental Hotel are only blocks away from our hotel! It seems our carriage driver has ripped us off, not only once, but twice! This gives us a good laugh.

Among the many shops, there are caged government stores legally selling opium. We've heard that you can also buy hashish there, which is illegal, so I approach the shop owner and indicate I'd like to buy some hash. He disappears into his shop and soon returns with a block of dark hash the size of a fist. First looking up and down the street, he slips me the hash for what I am sure are too many Pakistani rupees. We intend to smuggle the hash through the Indian border, as we've been told, and we hope that, if caught, the hash is just confiscated. Our rationale is that we're already smuggling the Indian rupees we obtained in Kabul, so why not take some hashish along as well?

We want to leave Lahore as quickly as possible, but we must first obtain a "road permit" from the Indian consulate, located in the modern section of the city. We've already obtained our Indian visas in Kabul, but we've been told the road permit is necessary as well to be able to enter that country.

A rickshaw ride takes us just a few blocks to the Indian consulate. Although the modern and old sections of the city abut, the contrast between the two is extreme: the wide boulevards, tall buildings, and international stores of the new, and the narrow streets and crumbling structures of the old, where we are staying.

We learn at the consulate that we must apply and pay a healthy fee, allowing a day for them to process the applications and give us the permit. Just out of interest, I ask if they also give Indian visas there, but am told no.

So apparently, two necessary papers to enter India must be obtained in two different cities. Efficient they aren't!

With a full day to wait, we decide to visit the famed Shalimar Gardens the next day. Built by Shah Jahan in 1641, the same Mughal ruler who built the Taj Mahal, these impressive gardens are laid out in three terraces of flowering bushes and cypress and poplar trees. Unfortunately, as it's November, all the flowers have died, their stems bowing low, lending the gardens a sense of melancholy. Statuary throughout reflects Persian, Mughal, and Hindu influences over the centuries. As we walk through the gardens, a small man and boy approach us.

"Excuse me," the boy says in surprisingly good English, "but my father says that he would like to show you the gardens properly."

We agree, knowing this will cost us some rupees, but also that there is no one else in the gardens for them to solicit. He introduces himself as Faisal, which is also his father's name.

Faisal explains, "My father knows more about these gardens than anyone living. He cannot speak or hear, and so he speaks to me in sign language. I am his interpreter."

We spend the next two hours wandering through the gardens with the pair, stopping at statues, monuments, and fountains. Faisal Sr. enthusiastically gestures with his hands at lightning speed while Faisal Jr. flawlessly interprets the meanings of various inscriptions carved into centuries of stone to us and our questions back to him. We're both charmed by the knowledge, enthusiasm, and humor of the man and his son. We laugh a lot just because we're happy to be enjoying these wonderful gardens together. We give them more rupees than they ask for in the end. As Faisal Jr. has been carrying an old camera, he asks if he can take a picture of us with Faisal Sr. We bid both Faisals goodbye and leave the gardens feeling lighter than we have since entering Pakistan, our faith restored that, below surface differences with others in language and culture, we do share a deep, abiding human bond. I sometimes wonder where that photo of Faisal Sr. and us is today.

We complete the business of procuring our road visas late the next morning. We're told at the consulate that the Indian border closes at 5:00 p.m. each day, so we take a taxi back to our hotel and ask the driver to wait as we pack. But what to do with our smuggled goods? We decide that the Indian rupees will be rolled up in my sleeping bag at the bottom of my pack, and Jean will hide the hash in her panties, which we cut into thin slices and seal in plastic. We then take the taxi directly to the border, just thirty or so miles away. There are only a few people there when we arrive at the Pakistan side of the border. Over the hour we have to wait and fill out paperwork, more people, including several Westerners, arrive by bus. Finally cleared, we then walk a short distance to the Indian side of the border, both nervous that we'll be busted, and sure that we look it!

After presenting our visas and road permits to a turbaned military officer (the first Sikh we've seen) and filling out still more paperwork, we're directed to a nearby bench, where several Westerners are sitting. More join us in the next half hour, a number of them longhairs like us. We've been singled out, and I can see that others are as nervous as we are!

Soon, a stocky woman in military uniform walks over to us from the office. After traveling through four Muslim countries, where a woman is barely recognizable behind covering garments, here is a woman of authority!

Jean whispers to me, "I think that's her!"

"Are you sure?" I reply.

"No, but it must be."

We've heard stories on the Hippie Trail of a military woman at the Indian border who is "psychic" in her ability to find even the most concealed contraband and drugs on travelers. Now, she faces our group, assessing each of us slowly. I can feel myself sweating.

Then she addresses us. "It is now four thirty. Why do you people insist on coming here at this hour when you know the border closes at five o'clock sharp?"

When we say nothing, she continues, "Well, I suppose I have to deal with you." Looking stern, she says, "Please answer these questions truthfully." Eyeing each one of us again, she repeats, "Truthfully! Do any of you have tape recorders?"

We all shake our heads. "Please answer the question!" she commands.

"No," we respond.

"Thank you. Now that wasn't so difficult, was it?"

"No," we respond.

"Any guns?"

"No."

"Any Indian rupees?"

"No."

"Any hashish?"

"No."

"Hah," she laughs. "You're all a bunch of damned liars!" Then after a long pause, she says dismissively, "But it is late and I can't be bothered. You're free to go on ahead."

Relieved is an understatement as we hustle across the border into India. After two months of travel, we've reached our destination!

MOTHER INDIA

... Finally went from Lahore to Delhi, both of us noting an inexplicable but pleasant change in walking over the border to the Indian side. We are presently staying at a guest house in New Delhi, and are enjoying the many luxuries (such as English speaking movies!) that this new city offers.

That's it, geographically to here. There are countless incidents and people we meet every day—stories which will keep until we see you again. We go next to Benares so please write us c/o Poste Restante there. Peace and Love, Bruce and Jean

Birds sing, the soft light of the setting sun caresses the tips of tall reeds dancing in a gentle breeze, casting long shadows on our path as we stroll a short way to waiting taxis and carriages. An unveiled woman with her bundle sits beneath an ancient Banyan tree. A man and his water buffalo plow a field nearby. We feel light and free, joyful to be finally treading the earth of this ancient country that many refer to as "Mother India."

Our immediate destination is the nearby town of Firozpur, where an overnight train is leaving to Delhi at 9:00 p.m. As we have plenty of time, we opt for a horse carriage. The short, skinny driver, happy for our business, is friendly and talkative, anxious to use his English.

"Greetings *sahib* and *memsahib* [sir and madam]. My name is Arjun. Where are you from?"

Jean surprises me by replying, "Oh, you speak English. We are from America." She would never talk publicly in Muslim countries unless she had to.

"Oh yes," he replies with an odd waggle of his head, a mannerism we're to see throughout India. "It is very important to speak English if one wants to get ahead in life, you see."

I say, "I suppose the British taught many people English when they were here in India."

"Oh yes, they taught us many things. I, for one, was sad to see them leave."

After three centuries of British rule, India and Pakistan achieved their independence in 1947. Whereas the Indians' struggle for independence had begun many years before, it was Mahatma Ghandi, Jawaharial Nehru, and others who, along with thousands of followers, successfully resisted the powerful rule of the British through the practice of *ahimsa*, or passive resistance. Railways and businesses would come to a stop when workers peacefully refused to work, often despite beatings by the British guard. This, combined with Great Britain experiencing a waning influence in the rest of the world, produced an agreement to split their empire into two countries: a primarily Hindu India and Muslim Pakistan. There were, of course, many growing pains in this newly acquired self-governance, but the legacies of the bureaucracy and railway system still function much as it did during the British Raj. There are a still a good many Indian "anglophiles" who, like our driver, Arjun, miss the stability of British rule.

Unlike the numerous gawking people in the Muslim countries, those we pass on our way to Firozpur pay little attention to us. Arjun pulls to a stop at a small chai shop on the outskirts of the town, where several men are playing a game of dice.

"We can have some chai here," he says.

I reply, "Arjun, I think we should just go to the station. I'm afraid we may miss our train."

"No worries. There is still plenty of time."

This is obviously his regular stop, for he's warmly greeted by all the men. As we sit down, the proprietor brings a pot of chai, three cups, and a plate of biscuits.

I ask Arjun, "What is that game these men are playing?"

"This is a game of dice called *passa*. It is very popular in all of India."

"Do you bet in this game?"

"Oh yes! I am very good at this game. I often win."

We watch as each man rolls two dice. One rolls two fours, and the group erupts in clamor, as rupees exchange hands.

"How did that man win?" I ask.

"He has rolled a *hare*, which was his bet," Arjun explains. "A *hare* is either two fours or two sixes. The ones who lost bet on a *jeetae*, or rolls of two ones or two threes."

I'm about to ask Arjun more about the game when I notice another man leading our horse carriage with all our belongings away! I leap up from the table and start to chase the cart, Arjun running behind me yelling "Sahib, sahib, please stop!"

"Stop that man, Arjun," I yell. "He's stealing our belongings!"

Arjun reaches me, saying, "No, sahib, he is just taking the horse for some water and food. The horse needs to eat as well. He will return very soon, I promise."

Slightly embarrassed but still leery, I return to the chai shop. The men have stopped play but resume when I've settled down. The man leads the horse and carriage back to us a half hour later. Arjun tells us that as his guests, we don't need to pay for our chai and biscuits. We arrive at the station in plenty of time for the train. I pay Arjun ten rupees for our ride. I know it's too much, but where else would I learn the popular game of passa?

We buy tickets for second class compartment, a process involving time to fill out forms in triplicate. We're to discover that all offices in India demand patience to fill out forms in triplicate, a holdover from the British Raj who demanded thoroughness over efficiency from their Indian employees. One form is for the clerk's records, one for the filer, and one added to a mountain of decaying boxes in a back office, never to be seen again. Having bought our tickets, we're then told that we must then pay another fee for reservations! We haven't been in India for longer than a few hours before we feel assaulted by bureaucracy! We greet several other travelers on the station platform who we recognize from the officer's grilling at the border. We board the surprisingly empty overnight train to Delhi and occupy a compartment with other travelers. We don't realize that, as far as comfort goes, we've all made the same mistake. Thinking that second class must be better than third class, we discover our seats on wooden benches won't allow for us to lie down for the night. We later find out that, unless one pays a good deal more for first class, the best ticket is for a third class reserved berth. This allows the rider to have a padded berth each night for an entire journey, and journeys can be days long on the vast subcontinent of India. As it is, we have a long night ahead of us and fill the time with conversation.

One man, Jack, powerfully built with "all-American boy looks," is particularly talkative, more than willing to share his life story.

"Yeah, I've been married and divorced twice."

"Really?" I say. "You must have gotten married quite young."

"Or maybe each marriage was really short," Jean adds.

"With the first one, you're right," Jack responds. "But I was married to the other for ten years." After a pause, he asks us, "How old do you think I am?"

I guess, "Maybe twenty-five." Actually, Jack looks and acts more like he just graduated from an Ivy League college.

"I'm forty-two." Seeing the looks on our faces, he adds, "Yeah, I know I look young, but I certainly feel my age. I've been all over the world and seen a lot. This is my third trip to India."

"Wow! So, what brings you to India this time?" I ask.

"I'm looking for a woman … and her son."

Jack goes on to explain that he fell in love in Kabul with a woman traveling with a young son.

"She told me she was Mickey Spillane's daughter. She's a hard-headed woman, believes it's every person for herself in this world. She's an opium junkie, hardly able to care for her son, who's dressed in rags and always sniffling and coughing."

"That sounds like child abuse," Jean says.

"It is," Jack concedes, "but I love her. Anyway, I got tired of buying her drugs and feeding her son. I split to Lahore, but she followed and found me there. She told me she loved me and that she'd kick her habit. We lived in an apartment near Lahore Fort for a couple of months. She was behaving, more or less, and her kid was starting to look healthier. Then one day, she and the kid just up and left."

"My God," Jean exclaims. "Do you have any idea where they've gone?"

"No, but they told me at the bus station that a blonde woman and her son had left that afternoon to the Indian border."

"So, you're on her trail."

"Hopefully but, you know, I feel that I'm damned if I do find her, and damned if I don't!"

After this, we all try to get some rest on the hard, wooden benches. I think to myself, what a heartbreaking story! And, what a difference between us: me, young, enthusiastic, opening to my first experience of India, and Jack, who has been everywhere before, yet still trapped in a cycle of emotional turbulence.

We arrive at Old Delhi Station, reputed as one of the most crowded stations in India, but sparsely populated on this early morning. Our arrival in Delhi marks the branching out of the Great Hippie Trail into many smaller paths as travelers now choose their own destinies into the Himalayas, or onto the plains and beaches of India.

We follow Jack's lead, as he's been to Delhi before. We locate a nearby taxi. Jack first checks the driver's meter, whispering to us that many say their meters aren't working and then charging exorbitant rates, and directs the driver to a guesthouse on Janpath Road in New Delhi. Our route from Old to New Delhi takes us through the Chandni Chowk marketplace, renowned for its silver, perfume, and spice shops, as well as fabrics, especially for wedding gowns. As with the train station, the market is not crowded at this time of day, and soon we're driving from the narrow streets of Old Delhi through wide modern boulevards to Connaught Circus, the grand central roundabout of New Delhi. Just a few streets away, we drive onto a quiet Janpath Lane to Colacco's Guest House.

It's still early morning, so only a *chowkidar*, or caretaker, is there to greet us. Yes, he says, they do have available beds, but they won't be ready for a couple of hours. The chowkidar suggests we leave our packs with him and find breakfast in nearby Connaught Circus. The Georgian-style buildings around the plaza are impressive, quite a contrast to the old, decaying structures of Old Delhi! Many restaurants and stores are still closed, but Jack leads us to a small place he likes that serves us eggs and *lassis*, a delicious, sweet yogurt drink that we'll order many times in the future. Jack is as happy as a kid at Christmas to be back in Delhi.

"This is the most modern shopping area in all of India. You can find many of the stores here in Europe and the States."

Jean replies, "The British certainly had their act together!"

"Yeah. Well, it's named after Lord Connaught, the son of Queen Victoria and Prince Albert. The whole layout of this place is two concentric circles of big buildings, with seven streets radiating out to all parts of Delhi."

"Hmm, like the rings of a circus, maybe?" I posit. Sounds to me like as good a theory as any why they call it Connaught Circus. Jack shrugs while Jean looks at me as though I've told a bad joke.

I press on, "I've heard some refer to this as Connaught Place. Is it Circus or Place?"

"Dunno," Jack replies. "Same place anyway, no?"

Back at the guesthouse, beds are ready at 7 rupees a night. The policy is that one sleeps wherever a bed is available. We're lucky that a two-bed room is empty, so we occupy that while Jack sets up his own South American hammock on a back patio.

Colacco's Guest House is a quiet refuge, with comfortable seating in its central courtyard where one can peruse available magazines and books or play cards and chess. Of course, there is a fair amount of hash smoking, now called *charas*, and marijuana, or *ganja*. As in Afghanistan and Pakistan, these are illegal in India, but small amounts are tolerated as long as one is not caught buying or selling these in large quantities. The beds are full each day as travelers arrive by train, bus, or plane, staying a few days before departing to different destinations. The dominant conversation in the courtyard, filled with questions and opinions, is "Where should we go?" The two most popular directions among the younger travelers are north to Kathmandu, Nepal, and south to the beaches of Goa, a Catholic state on the west coast, below the city of Bombay.

Jack, meanwhile, seems antsy, coming and going every few hours. We're puzzled by this but figure he's probably catching up with acquaintances from previous visits to Delhi. After only a day, he tells us that he just got a Nepali visa. He remembers his girlfriend mentioned she wanted to go to Kathmandu back in Kabul and has an intuition that this is where she is, waiting for him. We tell him that we'll probably go there as well, but just need more time to rest in Delhi before we travel anywhere. Jack leaves the next night on a bus to the Nepali border, promising to leave us a note at the American Express office in Kathmandu when he knows where he's staying. As it happens, we won't connect with Jack again.

After a few days' rest and deliberation, we decide to go to Kathmandu as well and taxi to the Nepali embassy for visas. However, the clerk in the office tells me that I will have to cut my hair to receive a visa! Short of that, I can get permission from the American embassy to waive this requirement. We had heard that President Nixon and Secretary of State Rodgers are using the financial clout of the United States to curtail the flow of drugs in and out of Nepal. Although the drugs they're concerned about are primarily heroin and opium, and in amounts that could only be handled by large cartels, the long-haired hippies have provided the US administration an excellent scapegoat to convince an electorate that they are tough on drugs.

I am incensed and inconsolable. To have a whole country reject me is a big blow to my ego.

Leaving the Nepali embassy, Jean says, "Well, you could just cut your hair."

I spit out, "I'm not cutting my hair to satisfy those assholes!"

"Well then, we could try to get permission from the American embassy."

"That's the last place on earth I want to go to!" I add, "Maybe we're just not meant to go to Nepal."

"Good," she smiles, now maybe we go somewhere else."

Jean has already had in mind the "somewhere else": Darjeeling, a British hill station in northwest India. She has periodically mentioned her desire to visit Darjeeling ever since we visited a tea and scone shop in Beverly, England. The black tea we were served was different, a richer flavor than the store-bought teas of the States. The server told us that it was Darjeeling tea from India. Jean even bought a bag to carry with her, never opening it, just as a reminder, or portent, of her desired destination in India. She agreed to go to Nepal because of my enthusiasm to go, but now that door has closed, opening another one to Darjeeling.

That afternoon finds us in the Foreign Registration Office, just off Connaught Place. We obtain visas to Darjeeling for just one week, as that area is close to the Chinese border and therefore heavily guarded from potential attack.

We also visit the American Express office nearby, as we're anxious to hear from our parents. Jean particularly wants to hear from her mother. They've always been close and the time between correspondence, as much as three weeks, is hard for her. A letter received is a new aerogramme sent out the very same day.

Nov.14—Sat.

Hello Everybody!!

We finally got to India on the 10th, crossed over the border into Firozpur and took an overnight train to Delhi. It's a beautiful city w/ many fountains and parks and yesterday we went to the zoo—the best I've ever seen—white tigers, elephants with ivory tusks, all kinds of animals and plants. It's a little expensive here, but the food is good, all vegetarian. We will stay until Mon. or Tues. And then take a train to Benares and stay there until around the 28ᵗʰ, when we'll go into Darjeeling for a week. That's all the time they allow you there and you need a special permit to go. We were going to go to Nepal but when we went to get our visas here, they would not let Bruce go without getting his haircut & maybe shave off his beard—an American request of the Nepal gov't—no more Hippies in Nepal! So, disgusted, we went to get our Darjeeling permit—and now I'm happy. There shouldn't be too many tourists there and by comparison to Darjeeling, Switzerland looks dull! We go there from Dec.1–Dec.7, and then we head south—I hope all the way to Ceylon. We're even thinking of going further to Bali & the islands. There are cyclones in East Pakistan, with 100,000 people dead. I don't know if that made the news back there. There are supposed to be 5000 Hippies in Goa for Christmas—I don't think I want to go there either! All is well and good here—I hope the same where you are—my love to you all, Jean and Bruce

Back at Colacco's, we meet Eric. At seventeen years old, he's young to be in India and seems quite vulnerable, apparent in his need to be liked and accepted. His life so far is an interesting story. He was born in France, has a French passport, but grew up in California. His father has been studying with a Hindu master in South India, and he was determined that Eric and his brother, just a year younger, attend a private boarding school in India, in the hill station of Dehradun.

"The school was terrible!" he tells us. "We didn't understand the lessons, and the teachers didn't help us. We were the only foreigners there, and our Indian classmates made fun of us. After months of this, we escaped. We had enough money from my father and caught a bus to Delhi. We were told that we could get a cheap room here at Colacco's. So now I've been here one month."

"Wow," I reply. "Is your father looking for you?"

"We called him and told him where we were. He sent us some more money but told us we were now on our own."

"Was he angry with you for running away?" Jean asks.

"No ... well, a little, I guess. He said he was happy that we were safe, but I think he's ashamed of us."

"So, where is your mother?"

"I don't know, maybe in France. My parents were divorced just after my little brother was born. We never saw her again."

I ask, "So is your brother here, Eric?'

"No. After we received money from our father, my brother took his half and went to Goa with some friends he met here."

"And where are you going to go?"

"I don't know."

Eric is nearly broke but hopes for more money soon from his father. So we become his benefactors, taking on the roles of big brother and sister. He actually proves a resourceful, engaging companion, as he accompanies us to the markets and restaurants of both Old and New Delhi. He just seems to have an easy ability to gather information from the people we meet. He leads us through the markets of Chandni Chowk, where he bargains with a shop owner for a small primus stove we tell him we want so we can cook our own meals. On another day, visiting the Red Fort, he becomes our guide, having been on a tour before. The Red Fort was reconstructed in 1638 by Shah Jahan when he moved the capital of India from Agra to Delhi, and the subsequent residence of many Mughal emperors. Still another day, he takes us through the sprawling National Zoological Park to enjoy the wild animals, particularly the rare white tigers.

Eric introduces us to his favorite restaurant, Raisika. Much like the Khyber Restaurant in Kabul, it's inexpensive and regularly inhabited by travelers. We eat *samosas*, a fried wanton filled with vegetables, and *masala dosas*, rolled pancakes, also filled with vegetables. Our favorite dish, though, is the restaurant's "Russian Roll," a fried vegetable patty that Eric says is found only at Raisika.

As we prepare to leave to Benares, the first leg of our journey to Darjeeling, Eric asks if he can come with us. He promises us that he only wants to go as far as Benares, as he's heard so much about it, and that he'll have to return to Delhi to reconnect with his brother and get more money from his father. I'm reluctant as this means we'll have to pay for Eric's ticket and boarding in Benares, but Jean is adamant.

"C'mon, Bruce. He's just a kid," Jean says.

"So are we," I respond. "We're not his parents."

"No, but as close to family now that he has."

"So, I have a choice here?"

A look from Jean answers my question.

Eric and I spend a good part of a morning buying first class tickets for the next day's train to Benares. When we mention where we're going to some guests back at the hostel, we're surprised at their reaction.

"Why would you go there?"

"I've heard that place is filthy!"

"Me too. Not only that, they throw dead babies and cows in their river."

I think to myself, I don't know if that's true, and they don't know either. But it'll be interesting to find out.

We board the overnight train the next night to Benares, about fifteen hours to the east. The station is crowded as usual, but as we're traveling first class, it's a simple matter to find our compartment. Unlike our horrific experience in Munich when our compartment was full of unmoving Yugoslavians, the Indian Railway Service prides itself on accountability; the ticket one has is the seat one gets.

Eric is excited to be on the train to Benares with us. As our compartment seats four, we're curious to see who will join us. Shortly, several Hindu monks, dressed in traditional ocher robes, crowd into the compartment. They're surprised to see three Westerners; one monk, seeing our own surprised expressions, explains in English that his friends are just seeing him off. His fellow monks leave just as the train is pulling out.

The monk introduces himself as Ramakrishna. "I am named after two of our gods. Are you familiar with them?"

I pull the book from my pack that I've been carrying since New York, *Autobiography of a Yogi*, saying, "No, but I hope to learn more in this book."

Ramakrishna looks through the book and concludes, "I have heard of this man and his teachers. He is very holy. I, myself, am a follower of Lord Vishnu. Other Hindus worship Brahma and Shiva."

Eric says, "We heard that Benares is a holy city for Hindus."

"Oh yes," replies Ramakrishna, Varanasi is very holy."

"Varanasi?"

"Yes, this is the ancient and true name for Benares. It is our belief that every good Hindu who seeks merit in this life must make at least one pilgrimage to Varanasi in this lifetime, there to purify himself by bathing in the River Ganga [Ganges] and perform *puja* [Hindu prayer service] in the famous Golden Temple."

Ramakrishna continues to enthusiastically explain various aspects of Hindu beliefs and customs, interspersing this with compliments to Jean for being such a liberated woman. Jean says nothing but is visibly uncomfortable with his continually ogling her as he speaks, probably bringing up for her all she had to endure in Tehran and Pakistan. And here is another lascivious man, dressed in monk's robes. She finally stares at me for help. I interrupt his lecture by saying I'm tired and want to prepare my bunk. Jean follows suit. Soon all four of us have bunked down and turned out the main compartment light. Still, I have a hard time falling asleep, imagining our monk's eyes still staring at Jean in the dark. Jean tells me the next day that she didn't sleep a wink!

We pull into the station in Benares late the next morning. Another group of monks are there to collect Ramakrishna. It occurs to me that he must be an important figure in his society. He bids us goodbye, shaking our hands, and Jean's hand a little too long.

Leaving the crowded station, we choose two bicycle rickshaws: one for us and one for Eric. Eric, always resourceful, heard in Delhi that a clean, inexpensive place for us to stay in Benares is a nearby government tourist bungalow. The rickshaw drivers know where it is and take us directly there. We're to learn that many cities and towns have government tourist bungalows, a holdover from the days when British families would stop for a night or two en route to distant destinations. This bungalow is large, with two central gardens and a restaurant. The cost of a bed is just two rupees a night, and a room with two beds, 2 rupees 50 paisas (100 paisas to the rupee). Eric settles for a bed in a small dormitory, while Jean and I take a room off a central garden. Our room is well furnished, and the beds surprisingly comfortable. We join a number of people just outside our door in the garden, both Westerners and Indians, relaxing in conversations, reading, and playing chess and cards. Jean says she'd just like to spend the afternoon in this quiet, idyllic setting, but Eric and I convince her to join us in exploring the city for a few hours.

The bungalow office has supplied us with a general map of Benares, which indicates we're not far from the Ganges. Walking toward the river along wide streets leading to narrow lanes, we're astounded at the sheer volume of people: women in *saris* pulling children; men in pajama pants and long, loose shirts called *kurtas*; others wearing *dhotis*, cloth folded to make baggy pants; shopkeepers squatting in open doorways; street sellers and beggars. Some beggars are simply destitute, while others are holy men seeking alms. Of the latter, some seem to be giving blessings to those who provide coin or food, while others sit in a circle, sharing a chillum of charas, hashish. We learn later that these are *sadhus*, holy men who follow the god Shiva. For them, charas is a sacred substance, enabling them to come nearer to the divine. The streets and lanes are splattered with the red dye of *pan*, betelnut and sweet paste wrapped in leaves and chewed mainly by men. This stimulant is the Indian "nicotine," turning the mouth red and rotting the teeth, with the chewed remains spit onto the streets of villages and cities throughout India.

On the narrow streets, small shrines are marked with ash, red powdered dye called *vibhuti*, and burning incense. At entrances to the alleyways leading to the river are stone, tube-like *lingams* resembling male penises and ranging from a foot to five feet in height. These are symbols of the regenerative power of Shiva. Some lingams rise up from a lipped, disk-like structure of the goddess Shakti's *yoni*, or vagina, representing the spiritual union of male and female, two abiding principles of life.

Looking up, I see families of monkeys peering down on people from rooftops. Interspersed with the crowd are roving cows and pigs. They are generally regarded as garbage cleaners, their noses constantly sweeping the ground before them. Cows are considered sacred in India, a symbol of Shiva, a belief that allows them to roam wherever they want. Even in modern New Delhi, painfully skinny cows move docilely and unconcernedly through meandering traffic in their constant search for food. Many of these have eaten so much street garbage that their rectums have been blown out, leaving gaping black holes beneath their tails. Pigs in Benares, on the other hand, are ugly, hairy beasts that are tolerated even though they can sometimes be dangerous to children, particularly those who are squatting in the street to defecate.

The sensory experience of walking through the streets and lanes of Benares is an overwhelming assault of color and sound mingled with odors of incense, charas, feces, and urine.

An alley takes us to the main *ghat*, basically a large, flat cement platform with steps leading down and into the Ganges. A *Brahmin* approaches us, saying, "*Namaste*, Welcome! Would you like to know more about this famous place?" His hands go up in prayer, and then he extends his palm to receive the few rupees we give him.

He continues, "This is the Dashashwamedh Ghat, the most famous and perhaps the largest of the eighty-eight ghats in Varanasi. Oh yes, it is here that pilgrims come from all over the world to bathe in the holy waters of the River Ganga and to purify themselves for this life and the next."

"So," Eric asks, "do all the pilgrims believe in reincarnation?"

"Oh yes! This is without question!"

I say, "We have heard of the 'burning ghats.' Do they cremate bodies here?"

"Oh no. Never here. Over there," the Brahman points down the river to rising clouds of gray smoke. "I will show you."

We pay him more rupees and return with him to the main lane, working our way through crowds and down a narrow alley to another ghat. The smoke and smell here almost overwhelms us! We descend the ghat and sit on a step, as a corpse, covered in a white sheet, is brought to a pyre, followed by several mourners whom I assume are family and friends. Several other corpses are already burning on the pyre.

The Brahmin says, "This ghat is called 'Manikarnika.' It is one of the two burning ghats in Varanasi. Pilgrims who have died are brought here every day. Many thousands are burned each year. It is very good karma to be cremated here."

"Quite the job," I say, "burning corpses."

"Oh yes! The ones who build the fires and carry the corpses are *Dalit*, or Untouchables. But the pujas, special ceremonies for the dead, can only be performed by a Brahmin, like that priest who is now performing puja for the dead one. I, myself, am of the Brahmin caste. Whether Brahmin or Untouchable, it is very good karma for those who assist the dead to cross over, you see."

We watch for a while as a line of corpses are brought to the funeral pyre—men in white shrouds, women in red, the Brahmin tells us—before we ascend the steps again. The Brahmin offers to take us to a special temple for the dead, but we decline. He looks crestfallen as we say goodbye, so I slip him some more rupees, which instantly eases his sorrow.

I'm to learn later more about the caste system. There are more than one thousand castes in India, arising in ancient times to connote lineage or kinship groups. The primary religious group, the Hindus, break down the caste system to four main groups: the highest group, the Brahmins, are priests and scholars; the next down are the *Kshatriyas*, warriors and kings; then come the *Vaishyas*, who are merchants, tradesmen, and farmers; the lowest caste are the *Shudras*, laborers. There is a fifth order, below the caste system entirely. These are called *Dalit*, meaning "broken, scattered." Also called Untouchables, these are the masses of poor, often tribal peoples. The British Raj did much to strengthen this distinction of castes, primarily to assign workers specific jobs in their massive bureaucracy.

We stop at a small bazaar on the way back to the tourist bungalow to buy rice, vegetables, and an unleavened bread called *roti* at one shop, and a pot, pan, plates, and cooking and eating utensils at another. We settle in that evening to a "home-cooked" meal made on the small stove we bought in Old Delhi.

Over the next days, Jean and I develop a habit of walking through the markets and streets near the Ganges in the mornings, returning to a tasty lunch of vegetable samosas and banana lassis at the bungalow restaurant, and enjoying the quiet and beauty of the bungalow gardens in the afternoons. Much like our days in Hayatullah's rooftop room in Kandahar, we both feel relaxed and happy, at ease with our surroundings and each other. A constant source of interest is the "murder" of large black crows, a dozen or more, sitting in the trees and on the rooftops, cawing their conversations as they look down on the bungalow guests eating meals in the garden below. A meal finished brings a riot of activity as the crows swoop down to contend for leftovers.

During these idyllic afternoons in the garden, I finally get around to reading *Autobiography of a Yogi* by Paramahansa Yogananda. It is a simply told story of a young man, Yogananda, who meets his *guru*, or spiritual teacher, Sri Yukteswar, who introduces him to a discipline called *Kriya Yoga*. The role of the guru in Hindu belief is of tantamount importance, as only the guru is able to help the disciple, or *chela*, to end the suffering of many lifetimes to finally see the "face of God." As the chela must be developed enough spiritually to properly receive these teachings, a well-known saying is, "When the chela is ready, the guru will come."

Through his guru's guidance and years of devotion and discipline, Yogananda achieves a level of enlightenment. He is then given the task in 1920 of bringing the discipline of Kriya Yoga under the auspices of his organization, "Self-Realization Fellowship" to the United States, there to found numerous *ashrams*, or spiritual centers. Paramahansa Yogananda died in Los Angeles in 1952. However, the Self-Realization Fellowship continues to thrive and expand, with centers teaching Kriya Yoga throughout the world.

Yogananda's simple, humble words as he writes of his guru and his training further cements my inspiration to develop myself through the practices of yoga and meditation. One of the teachings he gives in his book is to develop concentration through a simple breathing technique. So periodically, I stop reading the book, sit up straight, and practice the breathing exercise. As she is by now very familiar with my chronic enthusiasm to jump into new situations, Jean looks on with not a little humor at this guy sitting ramrod straight, breathing heavily with his eyes closed. I'm her "guinea pig." If this meditation technique seems to work for me, she may try it herself.

Not one to sit still for long, Eric pops in and out of the bungalow regularly and, upon his return, shares some discovery or another before disappearing on another adventure.

I ask him, "What have you been getting yourself into this time, Eric?"

"Oh, this and that. Talked to a lot of people. Most are so friendly!"

"Like talking about what?" Jean asks.

"Just things, like where they grew up, how they like Benares, what are some places they'd recommend for me to see."

"And what do they recommend?"

"Oh, a bunch of different temples. I'm not into seeing those too much, but I've spent a lot of time at the burning ghats. You know, that first one we visited, and then a second one, not so big but still regularly firing up the bodies. Got to talking with a bunch of Brahmins, and some of those Untouchables too. They call themselves *Doms*. I don't know why."

"Hah," I laugh, "maybe you'll end up being a Brahmin yourself!"

"Don't think so," Eric replies. "They all got mad at me when I took off my clothes and jumped in the water."

"What?"

"Yeah, I saw so many people bathing in the river at other ghats, and people telling me how holy it was to do that, I thought it was okay to just jump in and swim around a bit at the burning ghat."

"Apparently not," I reply.

"No. But now I feel purified."

This, in a nutshell, is Eric: young, enthusiastic, engaging all whom he meets, resourceful and rambunctious at the same time.

A day later, Eric tells us that he has really enjoyed Benares but has to get back to find his brother and hopefully receive some money from his father. We see him to the train, wishing him well and that we hope to cross paths again. Like so many we've already met on the road, we doubt we'll see Eric again. (But several years later, while in San Francisco in December, we run into him as he's flipping crepes at the Heidelberg Hut at the Charles Dickens Christmas Fair. He's overjoyed to see us, telling us that his father flew into Delhi and took his sons to meet his guru in South India. His father's guru became his guru. He stayed at that ashram for a year before returning to the States. He is now bigger and stronger, exuding a calm sense of confidence. We laugh together about his upsetting the Brahmins by jumping in the Ganges, and he assures us that he is now staying out of trouble.)

Monday, Nov. 23, 4:00 P.M.
Hi All,

We are now in Benares for almost 1 wk. The weather is very warm and beautiful every day. We are staying in the Government Tourist Bungalow and have a nice room which opens onto a lovely garden where I sit now (while Bruce plays chess.) About two doors down is the restaurant and so we have been doing very little these days, resting and sunning. This city is known as the holy city for Indian Hindus for it is situated right on the Ganges river. Every morning, the religious go there to bathe and pray—it's quite a spectacle. We got up at 5:00 A.M. the other day to go and see this—hundreds of men and women were in the rivers—it is indescribably filthy water. And that's where they put all their wastes, including their dead animals. And yet the whole scene is so peaceful and beautiful at that hour. We also took a tour to Sarnath about 8 miles away, where the enlightened Buddha gave his first lesson to his disciples—another holy aura surrounding these ruins …

A brochure in the tourist bungalow office is advertising two tours: an afternoon visit to Sarnath, the site of the Buddha's first teachings, and a sunrise boat tour of the Ganges. Jean and I decide to purchase tickets for both.

We board a small bus that afternoon for Sarnath, just a few kilometers away. There are just six of us tourists, all Westerners, and the driver, who is also our tour guide.

The driver introduces himself as Ashok, saying, "We are going to a very sacred place. You will see with your own eyes just how special Sarnath is for Buddhists and those of other religions."

In less than a half hour, we arrive at a wide field of temples and ruins. We walk through the ruins with Ashok as he explains, "This whole area, also known as Deer Park, is an archaeological dig, a World Heritage Site, as this is the site where Lord Buddha taught his first disciples after he had attained enlightenment. Over here is the great *stupa*, built to commemorate those first teachings."

We look over at a towering, round gray structure.

"A stupa is usually a solid structure like this one, and it is built in the shape of the sitting Buddha. This is one of the world's first, built three hundred years after the Buddha's *Parinirvana* by Emperor Ashoka, after whom I am named," he proudly adds.

"Parinirvana?" I ask.

"Yes, this is a term for death used only for teachers who have realized enlightenment. Unlike common people like us, who must continue to struggle lifetime after lifetime, sometimes as humans, sometimes as animals, the enlightened teacher has reached the highest state of realization: the state of non-returning."

The group is silent for several moments as we continue to walk, trying to take in this information.

"And over here," Ashok says, pointing to his right, "is a beautiful Jain temple. Like the Buddhists, the Jains also believe in the path of enlightenment. Their main practice is *ahimsa*, or nonviolence."

Now, pointing left, Ashok continues, "This large temple is of the Hindu religion. The Lord Buddha himself was born of the Kshatriya, or warrior, caste of the Hindu religion. As the story goes, he was first named Siddhartha. His father, a king, was told by an oracle that his son would either become a Buddha or a world emperor. Choosing the latter for his son, he supplied him with all the pleasures of this world: food, drink, and yes, women. His only restriction was that he was never to leave the palace grounds. He was even married to a beautiful woman named Maya, and they had a son named Rahula."

"Then one day, prince Siddhartha wandered off the palace grounds. There he saw an old man. At that moment he realized that no matter how comfortable his life was, he was going to get old. On another occasion when he left the palace grounds, he saw a sick man and realized he himself would become sick. On the third occasion, when he saw a corpse on the back of a cart, he knew for certain that he would die. With this, he realized that no amount of pleasure or protection could prevent sickness, old age, and death, known as the "three marks of existence." So, he left behind his family to go into the forest and seek the path to end his suffering."

"You mean he just left his family behind?" a short, bespectacled woman in our group asks.

"Yes," Ashok replies, "for he had a higher calling. The calling of Buddhahood."

She presses, "What kind of man abandons his family?"

"Ah," Ashok counters. "After he achieved enlightenment, he returned to his family and taught them the path to liberation."

The woman doesn't seem appeased by his response but says nothing. As we continue the tour, I hear her grumbling under her breath to her husband who grunts in response. I imagine he has perfected the art of feigning interest while not listening.

Monks in different colored robes are involved in a variety of activities throughout the grounds: some cleaning shrines and replacing candles, others cooking food in large pots, still others sweeping the pathways clean. Vendors trail behind us, respectfully offering paintings, statuettes, even children's toys. Here, it seems, proponents of different faiths abide and work together peacefully. An aura of calm among these ruins and temples is pervasive, and I know for certain that, whatever I need to learn, this is a life path that I yearn for.

The tour over, we're driven back to Benares, giving Ashok a generous *baksheesh,* or tip, for his expertise in guiding us through that remarkable place.

We board a boat early next morning at Dashashwened ghat for the River Ganges tour. Several of the same tourists as yesterday are also there, but not the complaining woman and her husband. The sun has risen just several minutes before we set out upstream, and there are already hundreds of bathers along the many ghats. Some of these are performing offering rituals, while others are simply enjoying their morning baths. Our guide on this tour is reluctant to say much, as I can see that he's both shy and struggling with his English. For the most part, he lets the river speak for itself, as we enjoy the colorful ablution rituals and the beautiful, ancient temples and buildings lining the shore.

We come upon a small boat where two men, probably Untouchables, are using long poles to push a dead cow further from the shore.

Our guide says, "These men are paid to push dead animals to the main current of the river. There, the current takes them to the sea."

"Just animals?" I ask.

"Sometimes dead babies too, those who died being born. But do not worry, nobody gets sick from the waters of the Mother Ganga. She protects all who bathe in and drink her waters."

I don't follow up with another question because I can see he's reluctant to say more. (I'm to read later that this claim has been substantiated, at least in part, by teams of Western scientists who have determined that the Ganges's high mineral content does act as a preventive to infections.)

Further upstream, the guide points out a painted black line high up on the wall of a building.

"This line marks the highest recorded floodwater maybe twenty years ago. Mother Ganga floods almost every year."

Then he directed our attention to a sandy bank, oddly devoid of buildings, on the opposite shore. "There is a saying in Varanasi: 'He who prays on the far shore is a fool.' Some think this is because then one would pray with the sun to his back, but the real reason is that he would then be living there, and would soon lose his house to the seasonal floods."

Upon disembarking from the boat, I amble down the ghat steps to the river's edge. To Jean's amusement, I wash my hands and splash water in my face, as a final blessing from Mother Ganga. The rest of the day is a long, hot affair of buying third class tickets with berth reservations for the next day to Darjeeling through Siliguri, a northeast city at the base of the Himalayas.

We pack our bags the next morning and take a bicycle rickshaw to the train station. Not for the last time, I admire the strength of the skinny rickshaw *walla* pedaling the distance with two large Westerners and all their belongings.

The two-day train ride is hot and dusty, even in November, as we wend our way through the Indian states of Uttar Pradesh and Bihar, with regular stops and a long stretch in Patna, the capital city of Bihar. Our third class compartment seems a revolving door of transients traveling a few stops, many with bundles so large I think they should have an extra ticket! Some passengers are openly curious, others ignore us, but all seem friendly enough. A mother and daughter, who have boarded with us in Benares, stay through-out the entire trip to Siliguri. Both are thin, dark-skinned, wear-ing bright *saris*, earrings, and nose rings. They're both very shy, but periodically flash beautiful smiles our way. We bond over long hours together, even though we don't speak each other's language. Soon, we're sharing food, fruit, rice, and *chapatis* (unleavened bread) from their basket, and potato samosas we've brought from Benares, laughing together as we try speaking each other's words: *khaana*, "food"; *bahut accha!*, "very good." At several stops, I purchase tea for us all from the *chai wallas*, tea sellers, hawking their product: "Chaiiiii ... Chaiiii *garam* [hot]!" For a few *paisas* they pour a sweetened, milky black tea into small, baked clay mugs. The tea must be drunk in a timely way, or the taste will become muddy. Drinks done, the clay mugs are thrown out the train windows onto the tracks, where they soon transform back to earth.

Though we have sleeping berths at night, the wooden benches are uncomfortable during the long days. Our backs and butts are greatly relieved to finally arrive at our station. Our two new friends indicate that they are staying on the train, as they still have a day's ride to their home in Dacca, the capital of East Bengal. Hugging goodbye, I realize once more that the human heart bonds us so much deeper than differences in language and culture.

DARJEELING

... Anyway, two days on a train brought us to Darjeeling. The last 30 miles took seven hours on a choo-choo train, best described by one traveler like "a toy train set of the son of a nineteenth century merchant." This novelty, and the remarkable scenery made the time pass quickly. I hope you're all well and have had a fine Thanksgiving. You know that I think of you often. The cold of the mountains will probably drive us south by the 7th of Dec., so why don't you write me c/o American Express, Calcutta, India. Love, Bruce and Jean

Siliguri serves as a supply city to the many villages and hill stations of the Eastern Himalayas. We present our seven-day permits to Darjeeling in a small office in the train station, where we also confirm that our tickets are good to Darjeeling. However, as the Darjeeling train won't leave until the following morning, we can stay overnight in a room on the second floor of the station itself.

"What is the charge for the room?" I ask the office clerk.

He replies, "Oh, there is no charge. This is a service of our great Indian railway system, to give lodging to those travelers in transit. May I ask, what is the class of ticket you are holding?"

"Third class, sleeping berth."

"Well, normally you would be given a room corresponding to this class of your ticket. But, as you and the memsahib have already had a long journey, I can arrange a first-class room for you."

His offer confirms for me the hold the British Raj still have on India years after independence. White sahibs and memsahibs are still venerated in the Indian bureaucracy, considered above the caste system they promulgated.

The clerk shows us to a spacious room furnished with comfortable chairs and two single beds, with a window overlooking the train tracks. He lingers at the doorway until I remember to give him a baksheesh for his service. It is already dark, so we eat a quick meal at the station restaurant and, exhausted from the days on the train, settle in for a surprisingly sound night's sleep.

In the morning, we're astonished to see the Darjeeling train pull into the station: a wood-burning engine leading brightly colored cars and a red caboose at the rear; a life-sized replica of a toy train! Although we have third class tickets, all the seats in the third class cars are full. We decide to hop aboard the one first-class car available, thinking that, if questioned, we can pay more money or stand in a third class car. As it turns out, there is no conductor on the train, just the engineer and an assistant to stoke wood. Initially, there's just one Indian couple in our car, which has large panoramic windows for us to enjoy viewing the journey's changing scenery.

I expect the train will pick up speed as it pulls out of the station, but it never does, taking seven hours to our destination fifty-six kilometers away! We're moving so slowly in fact that children in villages we pass run beside the train, hopping onto the car steps and jumping off at their village boundaries. There are several stops along the way, with more people joining us in first class, but the car remains far from full.

As our train smokes and "choo-choos" its way into the mountains, the air grows colder, necessitating us to pull our jackets from our packs. Lush foliage of the low foothills changes to alpine forests. People change as well: Indians seem darker, more gnome-like, their colorful clothes a stark contrast to the predominant whites of the plains. We get our first glimpse of other Asian peoples: Chinese, Nepalese, Bhutanese, and Tibetan refugees who have fled their homeland from the Chinese invasion of their country.

At last, we round a mountain bend to view our destination: Darjeeling. This town is situated on several hills overlooking a deep, green valley. At 7,200 feet high, most of the town is wrapped in clouds, even in the afternoon. Disembarking the train, we spend the next hour exploring the town. This is a change from our usual routine of immediately seeking a hotel upon arriving in a new place, just because everything we see is so fascinating! Much of the town's architecture of stately wooden, Victorian-style structures were built for elegance and comfort by wealthy British tea plantation owners, and by those seeking a summer refuge, or "hill station," from the heat of the plains. These are now inhabited by a melting pot of people from the Asian nations—India, Nepal, Sikkim, Bhutan, Tibet, and China—each with their own language, customs, clothing and, most important for us, food.

We stop at a Tibetan restaurant and enjoy a bowl of noodles the Tibetan server calls *thukpa*. Fortified, we climb a steep street to the top of a hill, where we were told at the restaurant there are guesthouses. It's growing darker and colder, so we settle on a guesthouse with a small grass yard in front and a sign that reads, "Sham Rock." The Nepali owners, who introduce themselves as Mr. and Mrs. Ungle, seem happy for our business, showing us a room with a fireplace and large window overlooking the valley for six rupees a day. Importantly, the room is dominated by a large, comfortable queen-size bed, piled with blankets and quilts. We don't know it yet, but we're to spend a month here, the bed serving as our "living room," particularly on cold and cloudy days.

White and gray cloud covering has held sway over the town during our first two days, with only a pale, cold sun popping through to reveal patches of green hillside. On the third morning, I awake early and walk out the front door of the Sham Rock to see a magnificent sight! Clouds have given way to blue skies and bright sunshine, and there, looming over the valley is snowcapped Kanchenjunga, the third-highest mountain in the world! I'm so excited, I run back into our room just as Jean is waking up.

"What are you so excited about?"

"Just sit up and take a look!"

Her sleepy expression changes to awe when she looks out our picture window.

"Oh my God!" she exclaims.

"Yep," I reply with exaggerated pride, "I built it myself."

"Shut up. I can't believe it's been hiding in clouds this whole time."

"Amazing! So, it turns out we have a room with the best view on the planet!"

For the rest of our time in Darjeeling, Kanchenjunga is fully or partly visible, always an awe-inspiring presence.

Dear Family,

We're living in Darjeeling, a town in northeast India, 7000 feet in the Himalayas. From our window, we're able to see clearly Kanchenjunga, the world's third highest mountain. From a pt. several miles away, Everest can be seen, and several miles beyond that has to be the fabled "Lost Horizon!" This town becomes quite cold at night and when cloudy. Although at times we're genuinely freezing despite polar bear clothing, there are enough compensations to make ours an enjoyable existence. For one, Darjeeling is made up of Tibetan refugees and Nepalese, people known for their fantastic physical appearance and kind deportment. There's also a nightly changeover of movies, many of them American; we just saw In the Heat of the Night (so who cares if I've seen it before;) finally, for those who don't want to go to the movies, Tibetan beer or "thumbas"(pronounced toombas) can be drunk to ward off the cold—these are drinks made by pouring hot water over millet to create alcohol, and sipped through a straw—a sort of poor man's hot rum toddy. The market, filled with many Tibetan and Nepalese products, is fantastic! We travel next through Calcutta to the beaches of Puri. Please write to me: c/o Poste Restante, Puri, Orissa, India. Love, Bruce and Jean

Our first week in Darjeeling is a delightful exploration of restaurants, shops, and markets. We're in easy walking distance down the hillside to an Asian culinary delight: Indian *pakoras,* Tibetan dumplings called *momos,* and Chinese egg rolls are daily dishes. When we tire of restaurants, we buy rice and vegetables in the marketplace and take them back to our room to cook them over our primus stove. I'd bought a small English-Hindi dictionary in Delhi and now put it to full use communicating with merchants through a combination of Hindi, English, and hand gestures. We buy colorful Bhutanese and Nepali cloth with little concern over how we're going to manage to shove more stuff in our burgeoning packs.

We discover two large halls in town that show older English-speaking movies projected on old pull-down screens at certain hours of alternating days. A movie buff can then see a movie at one theater on one day, another on the second day, and return to a new movie at the first theater on the third day. Before each movie begins, the audience, sometimes as few as a dozen people, stands for the Indian national anthem crackling on old speakers. Jean and I enjoy movies occasionally yet, in our time in Darjeeling, we only see *The Heat of the Night* and *Bonnie and Clyde.* The projectionists probably speak no English because both movies are projected second reel first. Good thing we've seen those movies before or we'd really be confused!

Toward the end of our week-long visas, we locate the government office and extend our visas for another week. The process is quick and simple, costing just a few rupees. We'll visit this office on two more occasions, each time extending another week.

December 9th
Darjeeling, India
Hi,

I think and hope you're here—I sent a postcard to Tempe, but I doubt you're there—I haven't heard since Nov. 5 before you left N.Y. I'm sure I missed one in Delhi and maybe one in Benares, & as yet none in Darjeeling. We were only going to stay until Dec 7th but loved it so much we extended our permit until Dec. 14. There will be a small package arriving at Carole's to be shared and enjoyed by all—while enjoying you must think of Darjeeling and the Himalayan mts.—make sure everybody drinks some. I know Norma will love it. Think of us as we'll be thinking of you.

The weather here is true blue Christmas weather. It runs from 40 degrees in early morning and after sunset, but right now we sit on a rooftop, Bruce is shirtless and I wish I could be too—it sure is hot! But as I look to my left there are the magnificent snow-capped Himalayas—almost look like clouds. This city is like a ski resort— pastries, ice cream & milk shakes. Movies for only 15 cents! It's hard to leave here. Love and Kisses XXOO Jean and Bruce

We visit the Darjeeling Zoological Gardens one day, an ambitious title for a sad excuse for a zoo. Most of the animals look malnourished, sadly pacing in cages and small outdoor enclosures. We fall in love with two Koalas, feeding them some caramel candy we've brought, and watching them chew away; probably not good for them, but at least they have something to occupy themselves for a short while. The only animals with decent outdoor space are two Siberian tigers, a plaque stating that they are a gift from Russia to India. But even they look underfed, skin sagging off their bodies.

As I watch through the bars, one of the tigers slowly approaches me, starts to urinate, and then quickly whips his hindquarters around, spraying me with smelly urine!

"Arghhh," I yell. "That beast just pissed on me."

"Oh yes," a small Indian man close by pipes up. "This is a favorite trick of the tigers. They've been doing this to tourists for years."

"Well, why didn't you warn me?" I demand.

"What, sahib," he chuckles, "and spoil their only fun?"

Fortunately, the zoo has a fountain where I can at least clean up a little.

Another day, we visit the Himalaya Mountaineering Institute. This is far more interesting than the zoo, boasting a school of mountaineering founded by Tenzin Norgay, the famous Nepali Sherpa guide who accompanied Sir Edmund Hillary in becoming the first humans to scale Mount Everest. As a result, he has been giving lectures throughout the world and dedicating himself to the education and welfare of young Nepalis. That he is held in high esteem in India, due in part to Hillary's support, is a milestone in raising the status of all Nepalese in India, who, like Tibetan refugees, are considered Untouchables and ordinarily can find only menial labor.

One part of the institute is the school for young Sherpas that provides a basic education and trains them to be successful mountaineering guides, a growing industry throughout the Himalayas. The other part of the institute is a museum dedicated to those who have succeeded or attempted to climb Everest and other peaks. Here we learn that Darjeeling is a supply city for Everest expeditions. Display cases show us some of the early axes, pitons, and ropes used by climbers through the years. In one case, we see the stubby boots of a climber who had previously lost all his toes to frostbite, only to have these special "toeless" boots made for yet another assault on Mount Everest. We read of another climber, the English aviator Maurice Wilson who, in 1934, attempted to fly his biplane halfway up Everest and then climb to the top with no oxygen, proving that the mind could transcend all bodily restrictions. His plane was confiscated by the Indian government in Siliguri but, determined to push on, he sneaked across the border to Nepal and onto Mount Everest. Years later, his body was found, frozen to death in a tent at twenty-three thousand feet. No one knows whether he died on the way up to the peak or on the way back down. The cases display many other stories and photos of those who succeeded or failed to conquer Mount Everest. As Tenzin Norgay lives in Darjeeling, I am hoping we might run into him, but the museum guide tells us that he is away giving a lecture in Australia.

One evening while drinking *thumbas* in a popular restaurant, we get into a conversation with James and Scott. Both have been traveling for a long time and have many road tales to share. James, a Californian, arrived in India through the East Asian countries and has spent a long time in Bali.

"In fact," he tells us, "I left Bali to come to India once before, but only got as far as Bangkok before I ran right back to that island."

"Really?" Jean asks.

"Yeah. It's so beautiful there, and the people are incredibly friendly. And the surfing is world class!"

James and Scott met each other recently in Calcutta. An older Englishman, Scott is quiet and shy, letting James do most of the talking. However, I sense that his life has already been filled with many adventures and lessons learned. In the coming days, we all quickly become good friends, as travelers on the road often do. Both men decide to move into our hostel, the Sham Rock, as they're blown away by our view of Kanchenjunga.

Scott appears at our door one evening and, with an enigmatic smile, says, "Follow me. I have a surprise for yeh."

"Where are we going?" I ask.

"If I told yeh, it wouldn't be a surprise, would it?" He laughs.

Jean says she's too tired to negotiate the hillside again, so Scott and I meander down through the streets until we come to a large building with a red door.

Scott says, "This place used to be a British gentlemen's club. Now it's owned by a Nepali family who'll let us in for a few rupees."

"Let us in to see what?" I query.

"As I said before, young man, follow me."

I follow Scott up a steep stairway lined with old photos of British men, some in uniform. A door at the top leads us into a high-ceilinged room lined with dark wood paneling. In the middle is the largest pool table I've ever seen, its felt surface appearing to be in immaculate condition.

"What is this?" I ask.

Showing surprise, tinged with a trace of disappointment, Scotts replies, "Why, this is a snooker table, my boy. And it has been maintained in fine condition."

"What's snooker?" I ask.

"Oh dear," he replies, "yeh really are a son of the colonies, aren't yeh? Well, now I'll enlighten yeh as to the venerable game of snooker."

Scott proceeds to teach me the game, played on a table larger than a standard pool table with slightly smaller corner and side pockets. A white cue ball must hit, or "pot," one of the fifteen red balls, each worth a point, into a pocket before attempting to pot different colored balls of greater point value. As we're playing, the smiling Nepalese owner enters, asking us if we would like a beer.

"Of course!" Scott replies. "What is snooker without a beer!"

The owner produces two Kingfisher beers, and we thoroughly enjoy our evening of snooker.

In the days following, Jean and James join us, each taking a turn at the two-person game, which Scott invariably wins. Nobody but us and the Nepali owner are ever there, and so we come to refer to the place as "our club."

One day, James returns to the Sham Rock towing a little black dog with white paws.

"I found her in the marketplace. She looked so lost and lonely."

"What are you going to do with her," Jean asks.

"I don't know, but look how skinny she is! The least we can do is beef her up a little."

It isn't long before the puppy makes herself at home in the Sham Rock, sharing her time between James's and our room. We laugh at her antics, spinning like a top as she chases her tail, getting a surprising bath by overturning the cleaning woman's bucket of soapy water, attacking laundry hanging out to dry, and pouncing from one lap to the other and licking our faces clean.

After a couple of days, James says, "I think I'll call her Bagus [Bahgoose]."

"Bagus?" I ask, "What does that mean?"

"It means "good" in Balinese."

I laugh, "But she's not good. She's a mischievous little imp!"

"Sometimes a name is given," James wisely posits, "as a goal to shoot for."

"Well," I respond, "she's a long shot, for sure!"

90

Two days later, James tells us, "I'm leaving in a week for Nepal."

"Oh, we were hoping you might stay on until Christmas," I reply.

"I'd like to, but two of my friends from Bali will be in Kathmandu then, and we've talked about starting up an export business there."

After a pause, he says, "Uh, you guys really like Bagus, don't you?"

Jean replies, "She's a sweet little mischief maker."

"Yeah, well, it's like this, you see. I don't really want to travel into Nepal with a dog, and I was wondering if you two would take her."

"Take her where?" I smirk, "Back to the marketplace?"

"No, no, I don't mean that, I …"

"I know what you mean, James."

I peer at Jean, who is holding the puppy on her lap.

"Look, James," I say. "We're leaving soon too. I don't know if we want to travel with a dog either."

"Oh, I don't think she'll be any trouble," Jean says quietly, as our eyes meet in understanding. An apartment dweller all her young life, this is her opportunity to have her first pet other than a goldfish. I realize that further objection on my part is futile. This decision final, our future travel plans now include a dog.

Later, back in our room, Jean says to me, "One thing, though, I really don't like the name James gave her."

"Really?" I respond. "What do you want to call her instead?"

"I don't know, but Bagus?"

"It does sound a little like 'bogus.' Well," I propose, "how about Pouncer? She loves to pounce on our laps."

"No, I don't think so. Doesn't seem right for some reason."

We try out a lot of names—Shammy, for Sham Rock, Kanchi, for Kanchenjunga, even Snooker—but nothing seems to fit.

Jean ends this discussion by stating, "Let's not tie ourselves in knots here. Her name will come to us eventually."

James has been visiting the room of a man named "Ganesh Baba." He tells us that Baba is a hash-smoking *sadhu*, or holy man, who, as a young man, walked throughout India and was known as "the man who smokes one hundred chillums a day." James says that Baba teaches Kriya Yoga, the same discipline propagated by Paramahansa Yogananda.

"But Yogananda didn't smoke hash, at least according to his book." I point out.

"No?" James replies, "But this man does. You two have to come and meet him!"

As is typical for us, I'm enthusiastic to go, but Jean is uncertain, only coming when I tell her that, as we're going down the hill anyway, we'll probably find something to eat after. We follow James, with Jean carrying the puppy, down the hillside to a hut below the Darjeeling train tracks next to a small, colorful Tibetan temple.

The old man who answers our knock seems surprised but delighted to see us. He has the same matted hair, beard, and ocher robes of those hash smokers in Benares who were followers of Shiva.

"Oh ho, I see you've brought some friends, James. And a little dog as well."

He shows us into a small, dark room with two beds and several chairs. He then sits cross-legged in *lotus* posture on one of the beds while we occupy the chairs and other bed. Then he takes three deep breaths, exhaling loudly through his mouth. Behind him on the wall are pictures of Yogananda and his teacher, Sri Yukteswar. He's seems delighted that I've recently read *Autobiography of a Yogi*. He then launches into a lecture on Kriya Yoga, how it is a specific science of how to properly balance our "body/mind machine." This is done through the yoga practice of assuming certain postures, and practicing *prana*, or breathing techniques. Only when one has this mastery of a balanced mind and body can one begin to see clearly the nature of the universe, which is exactly the same as the nature of one's own mind. As he speaks, his gaze moves, eyes growing wider, to each of us. I feel a little uncomfortable, as if I'm being examined under a microscope! He continues to talk until I'm overwhelmed with information.

Finally, Baba apologizes, saying that he would like to see us again, but must now go to the market. He immediately pops up from his bed and walks out his door, our cue to leave as well. We follow along behind his bowlegged, gnome-like gait for a couple of streets. In front of one house, three children run out and start tugging at his robes. Suddenly he turns around and growls fiercely at them, causing them to shriek and run a few meters away. Then he breaks into laughter and the children laugh with him. This game continues until the children reach the end of their street and run back home.

Ganesh Baba then says to us before we all part, "Those children will benefit greatly from playing with this Baba."

We find a little Nepali restaurant and discuss our meeting with Ganesh Baba.

"What do you think?" James asks.

"I think he's amazing!" I respond.

"He certainly is an interesting man," Jean adds.

James says, "This is the first time I've been with him that he hasn't smoked his chillum. Maybe because he was alone."

"What do you mean?" I ask.

"Well, there are usually four or five other Indians there, all smoking his chillum as well."

I ask, "Do you think we can visit him again?"

"Sure, no problem. Maybe tomorrow."

"I don't know," Jean says. "He's a bit too much."

However, the next day, Jean gives in to my enthusiasm and we find ourselves back at Ganesh Baba's hut. A young Indian man answers the door and, seeing us, says something in Hindi to the room inside. He then lets us in. As my eyes adjust to the dim light of the room, I see Baba on his bed and four young Indian men in chairs facing him. Baba indicates for us to sit on the edge of the other bed.

"Oh, here you are again. And where is your little dog?"

"We left her back in our room this time."

"Interesting," he says.

I have no idea what that means, but don't really want to ask him. Nothing is said for a few minutes. I notice that one of the young men is packing a large chillum with hash. Atop the hash he has placed a coil of twine to ensure the pipe is smoked evenly to the end. He then hands the chillum to Baba, who says to me, "Do you smoke charas?"

"Yes," I respond. "Well, sometimes."

"Ah, we shall see," he replies.

As another young man lights the chillum for him, Baba takes an enormous inhale, holds his breath for several seconds, eyes closed, and then blasts out a gale of smoke, accompanied by deep, racking coughs, shouting, "Om Shiva Shankara, Bom Bom Bolay!" (I learn later that this is an invocation to Shiva who, among other things, is the god of charas.) Baba then repeats his ritual two more times, as the room grows ever dimmer with smoke. He then indicates to the young man to hand me the chillum. I feel that I'm living the same scenario as the rooftop garden in Kandahar again. This time, I take just a small inhale, which causes me to explode in a coughing fit.

Laughing, Baba says, "Yes, young man. Sometimes."

Jean declines to smoke, which seems to amuse Baba. James then takes a large pull from the chillum and coughs out the smoke. Next, each of the young men takes a great pull from the chillum. I can see that they're trying to match Baba's draw, though none of them is able.

Now Baba launches into a lecture on another, more disturbing topic. He says that the decadence of the West is causing the destruction of the world. Of all those in the West, only certain hippies will be saved, finding refuge in the Himalayas. By now, I'm quite stoned from even my small pull from the chillum and am beginning to feel paranoid with this talk of destruction.

Then Baba says to me, "What is the matter? Are you concerned that you're not fit enough to survive? Maybe you are not."

Turning to Jean, he says, "Why do you travel with one so thick-headed, who is headed for destruction?"

Before Jean can respond, I jump up and yell, "Mind your own business, old man! You have no idea what you're talking about!"

I'm furious and hurt. The Indians look shocked, as Baba's eyes widen with amusement. I know that he has baited me, and like a foolish fish, I leaped at the bait. My fury turns to embarrassment. Not knowing what else to do, I storm out of the hut. Jean and James follow, seconds behind me. I have no idea what they could have said to excuse my outburst.

I have a difficult next day: thoughts racing, angry with Jean, the dog, and distancing myself by taking long walks through the streets of Darjeeling. Why did I react so violently to Baba's words? Is Baba just a charlatan? Well, he is definitely no Yogananda! Am I really unfit, not good enough to be a survivor of the coming world destruction? As the sun is setting, it suddenly dawns on me that, in reading just one book, *Autobiography of a Yogi*, I have become bloated with the idea of spirituality. Baba's words cut through my immature view of what a spiritual person is, and how I should act as one when, in fact, I know so little. This last realization brings a sense of release. I realize I have much to learn. I now have a strong urge to see Baba again, to apologize for my outburst, and to tell him of this realization.

I wait another day before going by myself back to his hut. Another young Indian man answers. He ushers me into the room, where several others I have not met before are sitting. He tells me that he and his friends are disciples of the Baba and that they are waiting for him to arrive. In conversation, he tells me that he has just completed a year-long retreat doing Baba's prana techniques and smoking several chillums each day. He says he feels very liberated. Baba arrives soon after. Two disciples help him to his place on his bed.

Looking up and seeing me in the corner, he smiles and says, "Oh, there you are. You have come back."

I say, "I've just come to apologize for my outburst the other day. I realize now that I was so full of myself that I couldn't accept what you said to me."

"And what did I say to you?" Baba asks. I can't tell whether he wants me to repeat this for my own sake, or that he just can't remember.

"That I am unfit to be a survivor of the coming destruction."

Baba bursts out laughing, causing a wave of titters through his disciples. "What is important is that you are learning."

I decline his invitation to stay and smoke a chillum, saying I must get back to my hostel. Saying goodbye to Baba, I thank him for teaching me not to pigeonhole any human being into such a limited view of spirituality, that all shapes, sizes, and lifestyles can be gateways to self-liberation.

We're to see Ganesh Baba again, a chance encounter in Calcutta, where he is sitting in the center of a semicircle of long-haired Westerners. We say hello in passing. He says hello back, but I don't think he remembers us.

While all this was taking place, Scott had been visiting Kalimpong, a small town on the border of Sikkim, where he met a Chinese Buddhist master named Yogi Chen. He says that, although the yogi spoke some English, he would just sit with him for hours, bathing in his "aura of pure joy." Scott's enthusiasm entices us to meet Yogi Chen ourselves. That very day, we acquire permits from the same office where we've renewed our visas. James and I have a final game of snooker and beer with Scott that evening, as he's leaving shortly to Calcutta and Southeast Asia.

The very next morning, a hired jeep driver is transporting James, Jean, the dog, and me on a four-hour journey through Darjeeling tea plantations and down winding, dusty roads to Kalimpong. This town, located somewhat lower than Darjeeling on the southern foothills of the Himalayas, lacks the majestic views of snowcapped peaks but is, instead, verdant with trees and foliage. We locate a small hotel recommended by Scott and settle into two rooms for the night.

The next day, following Scott's directions, James and I leave Jean and the dog in the hotel and climb a small hill and up an outside staircase to the second floor of a white building. Yogi Chen answers shortly after we knock. Short, bald, and clean shaven, his smile is like a sunbeam! We introduce ourselves, saying we are friends of

Scott. He seems delighted, and not at all surprised to see us. He escorts us through a narrow kitchen into his only other room, with a single bed in the corner and every wall lined with books. We sit on floor cushions as he goes to the kitchen and returns with cups of tea.

For a time, nothing is said as we sip our tea. I don't feel at all self-conscious; rather, relaxed and happy to be in Yogi Chen's presence. He then asks us questions in halting English about ourselves, where we grew up, and why we've come to India.

I ask in turn, "Yogi Chen, how did you come be here?"

"I come from China." Looking at each of us with his great smile, he adds, "If you like, I tell you my story."

"Oh yes!" We chime in together.

"Then I say this. Twenty years ago, I leave my wife and children to come to India and follow the path of the Buddha. I do pilgrimage, visit many places that the Buddha go. In Bodhgaya, where Buddha become enlightened, I meet the Buddha himself. He tell me I must go to Himalayas and meditate in cave."

I look at James, who appears to be in a trance of rapt attention.

"There," Yogi Chen continues, "I meditate for two years, eat very little. Then the Buddha come again and tell me I must now leave the cave and come here to Kalimpong, where I live for many years, not seeing anyone but one boy who brings me food from the market. Last year, the Buddha come for the third time and tell me I will soon visit the West, and I should begin to let the outside world in."

"And we are the outside world," James comments.

"Yes. I write many books and want them translated into English. So, these people are the first to come here, the translators. Then some people from universities read my books and come to visit. Later I meet young people from the West. Many, like you," he points to me, "have long hair. They seek to know more about the Buddha, so I write little books to help them. The translators make them into English."

He then reaches into a shelf and produces a small pamphlet that reads, "Welcome Hippies by This Way."

"Yes, I have many more books like this."

I ask, "When do you plan to visit the West?"

"I do not know. I receive mail now from students in New York and California. But, yes, this is in the hands of the Buddha."

Upon leaving, I ask Yogi Chen if I can return the next day with my wife. He says he will be honored to have us come back. James and I practically run back to the hotel, jabbering excitedly about our meeting.

"Man, did you feel his vibes?" James pants.

"Most definitely! My face hurts from smiling!"

Needless to say, our enthusiasm piques Jean's curiosity, and she agrees that she has to meet this man.

After a dinner of samosas and rice at a local restaurant, we hear a loud commotion coming from a nearby street. We turn a corner to the noisy celebration of a Nepali Hindu wedding. A loudspeaker is playing, of all things, Christmas songs by Alvin and the Chipmunks, their high, falsetto voices sounding remarkably like the Nepali music we've heard in Darjeeling. As the bride waits with her family outside the door of a large house, the groom, decorated with royal robes and a crown, is driven slowly toward her in a new car. We can see that this is a very expensive wedding. A man in the wedding party spots us Westerners and invites us to join in the celebration. Jean and I politely decline, but not James, who enthusiastically joins the procession. Jean and I return to the hotel and try to get a little sleep with the dog continuously barking to "… We don't want a hoola hoop …"

The next morning, a Saturday, the streets of Kalimpong have transformed into a big marketplace, farmers and merchants hawking their produce and wares. We're surprised that many of the shops are selling used Western pants, shirts, sweaters, and shoes. We knock on James's door for him to accompany us to see Yogi Chen, but the bleary-eyed person who answers is going nowhere but bed. It seems James has been partying with the wedding crowd until sunrise, so all he can mutter is, "See you later."

Yogi Chen is delighted to meet Jean and the puppy, who is now rarely out of her arms. As we sip tea in his bedroom/library, he begins to talk about how devastated his homeland, China, has become under Mao Tse-tung.

"Yes, I grow up in Beijing. I know Mao since childhood. We go to same school. Even then, he is bad, a bully, power hungry. Now he is splitting families. I am afraid I not see my family again."

As Yogi Chen speaks of this, he cries, and the whole atmosphere of the room changes to one of such sadness, we cry as well. Suddenly, he changes the subject and begins to talk again about the books—pamphlets really—he has written for Westerners. The room instantly, magically, transforms back to an aura of bliss. As he explains the contents of each book, he gives them to us as a gift, until I'm holding a pile of pamphlets.

The hours with him pass quickly. We tell him as we depart that must leave the next morning when our visas expire. Looking sad, he says he still has so much yet to teach us. We respond by saying we hope one day to see him again in the West.

We depart Kalimpong by a previously arranged jeep the next morning. The ride back seems shorter and, before we know it, we round a bend to a wonderful view of Darjeeling and Kanchenjunga.

Back at the Sham Rock, we've barely unpacked when there's a knock at our door. I open it to a woman with curly blonde hair holding a furry puppy in her arms.

"Hi, my name is Bonnie. I'm a friend of the Ungles, the owners on the second floor. I just wanted to say hello."

Jean comes to the door, holding our little puppy.

"There she is!" exclaims Bonnie. "I thought you had a dog. I just dropped by so our two puppies can meet each other."

We invite Bonnie in. The puppies are delighted with each other, chasing each other around the floor.

"I was just given my puppy by Tibetan friends. She's a Lhasa Apso. I was told that, traditionally, these dogs guarded monasteries."

Jean responds, "Ours is a marketplace mutt," bringing chuckles from all of us.

Bonnie tells us something of her life in the hour or so we spend together.

"I've lived in India now for two years, mostly in Darjeeling. Last year, I met a Tibetan *lama* [teacher] whose monastery is just in the next town south. His name is Kalu Rinpoche. After going to see him for some time, he's become my teacher, and last month, I took refuge with him."

"Refuge?" I ask.

"Yes, that's when they say you become a Buddhist. You take refuge in the Buddha as teacher, the *dharma*, the Buddha's teachings, and the *sangha*, those who follow his teachings."

Jean says, "We've just been to see Yogi Chen in Kalimpong."

"Oh, Yogi Chen!" Bonnie smiles broadly, reminding me immediately of the man himself. "I've been to see him several times. What a wonderful man! One of his teachers is my teacher, Kalu Rinpoche."

"Wow!" I respond, "Can we maybe meet Kalu Rinpoche?"

"Sure. I'll take you there myself when you're ready."

Bonnie is quite a bit older than we are but is as bubbly as a teenager. She seems to see each moment as a great adventure. During this last week in Darjeeling, she and her puppy visit us for a cup of tea most afternoons. Our puppy is excited to see them climbing up the hillside street, and so are we.

James leaves the next day to Nepal. He's become a good friend in just a few weeks. We escort him to the train station, all promising to stay in touch but resigned to the fact that, like so many friends we've each met on the road, we probably won't see each other again.

What a fateful event then when, only minutes later on our way back to the Sham Rock, we encounter two new friends! We overtake a man and woman carrying heavy backpacks up the hill. Like us weeks before, they've heard that there are some inexpensive guesthouses further up the hill. They both look exhausted. We lead them to the Sham Rock, introduce them to Mrs. Ungle, who offers them James's vacant room!

In the days following, we become good friends with Ted and Ginny. We learn that they trekked over five weeks from Kathmandu, climbing mountain passes, fording fast-moving rivers, and passing through villages where Westerners had never been seen before. As they never encountered a border crossing, they were in India with no visas, and Darjeeling with no permits. This doesn't seem to trouble them, Ted saying, "We've crossed so many bridges, we cross that one too when we get there."

Ted is a big, friendly, bushy-haired man who worked for two years in Nepal as a Peace Corps volunteer. When his stint ended, he returned to his home in Washington State and married Ginny, his college sweetheart. Ginny is short with short brown hair and is the practical partner in the twosome.

She tells us, "You know, Ted, he's a dreamer. All he could talk about was going back to Nepal to trek the Himalayas. He wasn't interested in settling down, and no way I was going to be left behind. So, here I am, mostly following behind, making sure he doesn't fall off a cliff!"

The days grow grayer and colder, and we spend much of our time indoors learning to play Bridge and Hearts with Ted and Ginny, both avid players, and drinking hot cocoa and delicious gingersnap cookies sold at a nearby shop. Then we bundle up to climb down the hill together to introduce them to our favorite restaurants, and even a movie or two.

Now two other Westerners arrive at the Sham Rock. Ben and Mimi have traveled through Africa and Asia as students of Friends World College, a school based in the Quaker tradition. Mimi is friendly but reserved, preferring Ben be the spokesperson of the couple. Ben, as slight of build as Mimi with an earring dangling from his left ear, seems to be a dedicated charas smoker. Just after arriving, he comes into our room as we're playing cards with a chillum of charas saying, "Anyone interested in a bong hit?" Aside from the one time with Ganesh Baba, we haven't smoked hash since Afghanistan. Both Jean and I take a hit of the chillum. Fortunately, the charas isn't as strong as that of Baba, so I still feel functional. Ted and Ginny haven't smoked charas before but are willing to try with Ben instructing them how to hold the chillum properly. A short while later, card game forgotten, we're all smiles and laughs as we share stories of the road.

Christmas is just days away, and everyone is caught up in the festive spirit of the holiday. We start decorating our rooms, even the outside of the Sham Rock, with pine boughs and holly. Jean and I tack our heaviest "Christmas stockings" above our fireplace. We're determined to share, as Ted puts it, "a wholesome, old-fashioned American Christmas." As Ted and Ginny's room is the largest of the three, we decide that our Christmas Day celebration will be there. Ginny's family tradition included a Christmas duck dinner, and we take her lead, the women shopping for essential supplies in the marketplace while the men wander around aimlessly looking for possible gifts for their partners. Jean and I have made a frugal pact not to spend more than ten rupees on each other, a sum that will certainly limit our choices.

Darjeeling is resplendent on Christmas Eve, with many buildings lit up in Christmas lights. It's obvious that, along with Darjeeling's different cultures and religions, Christianity, promoted by the British Raj, still has a strong hold on this city. Our proprietors, the Ungles, are Nepali Catholics themselves, and have invited us to their church service this evening. We gather together in the early evening in our room. Mimi has made a potent eggnog, and Ben busies himself passing around the chillum. In high spirits, we all enjoy a good meal at our favorite Chinese restaurant. Then we set out to find the Ungles' church, only to be told that the church service has been postponed until Christmas night. On our way back to the Sham Rock, we decide to join a band of Nepali Christmas carolers. We all wander from door to door over the next hours, laughing and singing carols in Nepalese and English. It's well after midnight when we return to the Sham Rock and our beds.

The next morning, Christmas Day, is cold and clear, with Kanchenjunga gracing us once more with its majesty. The men have been assigned by the women to bring back a duck and a bag of coal from the marketplace. They've already arranged with Mrs. Ungle to use her makeshift coal oven upstairs—a tin box with a door—to cook the duck. I'm dreading this expedition as, by now, Jean and I are 90 percent vegetarian. Ben, who tends to swagger with a touch of self-importance, takes the lead. We soon find ourselves at the butcher's pen, where there are several ducks quacking and wandering about. Ben spends way too much time pointing at different ducks and negotiating prices. A deal finally settled, the butcher then chases after and catches an unsuspecting duck. To my horror, he holds the duck down on a block, chops off its neck as its legs quiver, and proceeds to pluck its shiny, multicolored feathers!

Mimi is in charge of cooking the duck, while the rest of us help with preparing rice, potatoes, and vegetables. Jean has remembered that small block of hash she smuggled through the Indian border and decides to make hash brownies. None of us have actually cooked a duck before, so our best guess until its's ready is two, maybe three hours. Mimi continues to check on the duck upstairs, reporting that it is "coming along." After three hours, all the sides and Jean's brownies have been cooked, as we hungrily await the arrival of the duck.

Mimi is close to tears as she returns from her umpteenth trip upstairs, saying, "The damn duck won't cook! I don't know why. Maybe the oven isn't hot enough."

We immediately console and relieve her by taking turns to check on the duck. Meanwhile, most of Jean's hash brownies, reserved for dessert, are consumed with gusto. These brownies prove very potent and, taken on empty stomachs, produce a variety of effects, none of them good. Jean and I get sick, others simply pass out in chairs or back in their rooms. By early evening, the duck, along with the sides, are completely forgotten; certainly not the Merry Christmas we had imagined at the beginning of the day!

The next morning, we find out that Mrs. Ungle had returned from her Christmas service and continued cooking the duck, a process taking ten hours. Apparently one of us told Mrs. Ungle that she could have the duck, so she brought it over to her friend's house. By mid-morning we're mostly recovered when Bonnie arrives with her dog. We tell her about the potent hash brownies but, despite our warnings, she eats one. Shortly later, she throws up and passes out on our bed. Well, she can't say we didn't warn her.

Tues., Jan. 5
Hi Y'All,

I got your "community letter" today and really enjoyed reading all the notes from everybody and sure glad you got the tea. We loved Darjeeling tea! Christmas in Darjeeling was beautiful—there were a few Westerners there, some were Peace Corps volunteers on a holiday break. We made friends with 2 other couples—one couple from Friends World College, and the other couple walked to Darjeeling from Nepal, a trek that took them 5 weeks & that's all through the Himalayan Mountains! So we decided to "do it up good," and on Christmas Eve day the men went to the woods to get pine branches and holly, and the women went to the market to buy the needed goods for our home-cooked duck dinner on Christmas Day. The landlady of the guest house had a makeshift wood oven and we cooked the duck with rice, raisins nut stuffing, sweet potatoes and pumpkin, and I made brownies which never rose but were good. On Christmas Eve, we had cheese fondue and eggnog that we made & then went caroling w/ a bunch of Nepalese. On Christmas morning we opened our stockings. Each of us was allowed to spend ten rupees ($1.00) on the other. Bruce bought me 2 pairs of earrings, lots of candy and two pieces of coal! I gave him a book, candy and incense, also the old Fritts trick of an orange and a banana! It was really a fun-filled time for us. I'm glad yours sounded as fine and as fun as ours—what did you get for Christmas? Did you get my Christmas card? ...

Ted and Ginny depart soon after Christmas for Nepal, this time by train. Their plan is to collect belongings they've left in Kathmandu and then to travel into South India. This is our intention as well, so we promise to leave messages for each other in Madras. A couple of days later, it's our turn to leave too. Bonnie urges us again to visit her guru, Kalu Rinpoche, whose monastery is in the nearby town of Sonada. We agree, as it's just the next station south on the Darjeeling train line. Instead of taking the train, she arranges a jeep ride for Ben, Mimi, Bonnie, and us, along with our two dogs. We reluctantly say goodbye to the Ungles and the Sham Rock. It's difficult to leave Darjeeling as it has become a comfortable, familiar city. We wonder if we'll ever see Kanchenjunga again. Passing through a tea plantation on our way south, we round a corner, and Darjeeling, with its magic mountain, is out of sight.

Journeying South

Upon arriving in Sonada, Bonnie leaves us for a few minutes and returns with a German couple, Tomas, and Rita, his very pregnant wife. They invite us to their small, comfortable house for lunch while Bonnie goes off to the monastery to make arrangements for an audience with Kalu Rinpoche.

While enjoying a rare treat of peanut butter and jelly sandwiches, we ask Tomas why he was living in Sonada.

"Rita and I have met many teachers before, both Hindus and Buddhists. But, when we met Rinpoche, we both just knew he was the right teacher for us."

"Why was that?" I ask.

"Hard to say," Rita responds. "I think it was important for us to meet different teachers and try different practices before we found Rinpoche."

"Or, before he found us," Thomas interjects. He and Rita laugh heartily.

Jean asks, "If you don't mind, how long before the baby is born?"

Rita beams, "Any day now."

Mimi adds, "Are you having the baby here?"

"Of course. Where else would I want my child to enter this world? Here, I have the blessings of Rinpoche and a wonderful midwife who has done hundreds of successful deliveries."

Tomas and Rita have been in the village for months now, regularly going to the monastery to serve and learn from Kalu Rinpoche. I envy these two who are so devoted to him and seem genuinely happy and fulfilled in their lives.

Bonnie returns to announce that Kalu Rinpoche has agreed to meet with us immediately.

"But it has to be a short audience as Rinpoche is just recovering from an illness and needs to conserve his strength."

Rita offers, "We can keep your dog here while you have your audience."

"No, thank you." Jean replies. "We'd like to ask Rinpoche if he will give our dog a name." This is news to me!

No one objects, but I detect secret smiles being shared by Tomas and Rita. Thanking our hosts, Ben, Mimi, Jean, and I follow Bonnie the short distance to the monastery. The town itself is so quiet and devoid of traffic that I wonder if anyone actually lives here. Entering the monastery courtyard, we see several Tibetan monks and Westerners sitting together in a circle, while one monk is standing and lecturing in Tibetan, the back of one hand slapping the palm of the other.

"They're having a *dharma* class," Bonnie explains. "The *khenpo*, or teacher, is slapping his hands to emphasize a point."

I'm immediately struck by the serene atmosphere of the monastery. I've experienced this same sensation in certain Christian churches, Muslim mosques, and Hindu temples; a powerful reminder that spirituality cannot be pigeonholed into any single belief.

Now a tall Westerner in robes, with long blond hair clipped in a ponytail, greets us at the far entrance to the monastery itself.

"Hi, my name is Sherab Tarshin, and I'll be the translator for your audience. Rinpoche understands but speaks no English. Follow me."

He leads us down a dark corridor to a curtained doorway. Indicating for us to wait, he disappears behind the curtain for several minutes before returning and beckoning us to enter. The room is small, faintly lit, and redolent with incense. In the middle is a low table with a teapot and cups, with cushions around it. Two monks are busy preparing tea and conferring with a small, very thin man in robes sitting cross-legged on a raised platform against one wall.

This is Kalu Rinpoche. He sits perfectly erect and still, much like a statue. Yet his lively eyes and beatific smile radiate both interest and kindness.

Sherab Tarshin indicates for us to sit around the table, as the monks serve a sweet mixture of boiled tea, milk, and sugar. There's no mention by anyone of the little dog in Jean's arms. Sherab takes his place at the foot of Rinpoche's platform and confers with him in Tibetan. We sit in silence for a few minutes, sipping our tea, before Sherab says, "Rinpoche is very glad to meet you. He would like to know if you have any questions."

We look to each other for cues as none of us had even thought of a question to ask him. I suppose I thought that he was just going to tell us things. Finally, Ben asks a question about whether Rinpoche ever plans to return to Tibet, which Sherab translates. I see a faint shadow crossing Rinpoche's face, as he responds to Sherab.

"Rinpoche says that the time is not right for him to return now."

Now a question arises in me from nowhere, but one I've been asking myself without realizing it. "Rinpoche, can one attain enlightenment without a guru?"

Rinpoche and Sherab confer together before Sherab answers emphatically, "No."

I'm speechless, shocked at such a clear, definitive response! Although I have just read about Yogananda's relationship with his guru, I thought a guru was of secondary importance to singular discipline and practice; in other words, it's nice to have a guru but, really, one can attain enlightenment all by oneself, much like my image of the "hero's journey" of Jesus, Mohammed, and the Buddha, alone for days in the wilderness. I'm searching for some retort, some rationalization, even a point to argue, when suddenly our puppy pounces out of Jean's arms onto the table, upsetting cups, spilling tea everywhere! The monks silently busy themselves at once with cleanup, as Jean and I utter words of apology. Rinpoche still sits perfectly still, but his eyes are dancing, his smile broadened.

Collecting the puppy in her arms again, Jean remembers her mission in the audience. "Rinpoche, I wonder if you could give our puppy a name." Sherab translates, but Rinpoche leans further toward him, perhaps asking for clarification. Then Rinpoche giggles and, with a broad smile, says, "*Tashi Deleg!*"

Sherab translates, "Tashi Deleg is a common greeting among Tibetans. It has several meanings, such as 'good day,' 'good luck,' and 'Happy New Year.'"

And so, our puppy has been named. We call her Tashi from this moment on.

Shortly after this, Rinpoche leans toward Sherab again, and Sherab says, "If there are no more questions, Rinpoche now has to take his rest. He is very happy that you have come to see him." At that, Rinpoche chants in Tibetan, which Sherab says are his blessings for our safe journey. Then Rinpoche stands and is escorted from the platform and the room by a monk. We follow soon after with mixed feelings: my own confusion regarding Rinpoche's response, and our mutual delight in Tashi's new name, given by Kalu Rinpoche.

Back in the courtyard of the monastery, Sherab introduces us to a smiling, rotund woman in robes with whom he first traveled to India. Sonam Chinso really needs no introduction as she is outgoing, even ebullient, relieving Jean immediately by taking Tashi into her arms.

Sherab asks a favor of us. "My mother is flying into Calcutta in a few days for her annual visit to the monastery. I would normally meet her, but Rinpoche is ill, and I feel my first duty is to his wellbeing. Sonam has offered to travel to Calcutta in my place, but I think she could use some help. A woman traveling alone is not a good idea, and you see," he says, looking at Sonam, "Sonam can be quite scattered and forgetful."

I'm surprised that Sonam doesn't object to this description. Instead, she blurts, "Sometimes I just don't know which end is up!"

"Anyway," Sherab continues, "Sonam has a bus ticket to Siliguri this afternoon and then might need some help in buying a train ticket to Calcutta. I wonder if you two can escort her down to Calcutta."

We readily agree. I'm a little disappointed that we won't be taking the Darjeeling train but reason that a bus will definitely be quicker.

Meanwhile, Ben and Mimi are going to spend the night with Tomas and Rita in Sonada and then embark on the plan they had mentioned in Darjeeling to travel east into Assam. We return to the little house to collect our packs, say farewell and safe travels to Bonnie, Ben, and Mimi, and walk a short distance to the bus station to buy our tickets. Sherab and Sonam arrive shortly later, just as we finish a meal at a station restaurant. Sherab is like a doting father to Sonam, grateful for our help, reminding Sonam not to lose her passport and visa, and not forgetting what time his mother's airplane arrives. Sonam, for her part, seems delighted to be embarking on a big adventure.

The bus trip to Siliguri takes less than three hours, a huge difference from the seven-hour Darjeeling train! We don't have a chance to speak with Sonam on the bus, as our seats are far apart. Our first conversation occurs over dinner at the Siliguri train station as we wait for the evening train to Calcutta.

Jean asks, "So, are you and Sherab a couple?"

Sonam laughs. "Yes, we were when we came to India. We were even thinking of getting married. But that all changed when we came to see Kalu Rinpoche."

"How did you hear of him?" I ask.

"Actually, Sherab had heard of him through his studies in Tibetan language. He came to India with the intention of meeting him." Laughing again, Sonam adds, "I came along for the ride."

"But why did you and Sherab then split up?"

"Oh, we never did, really. It's just that Sherab has focused all his attention on Rinpoche, serving as his translator and assistant. And I'm preparing to take vows to become an ordained nun, which includes the vow of celibacy. We're both devoted to Rinpoche and the dharma. So, now Sherab and I are like brother and sister, rather than lovers, and we're happier than we've ever been."

I see the truth of this in her joyful, carefree personality. At the same time, Sherab's description of Sonam's scatteredness becomes evident as she rummages through her bags for her passport and money, eventually locating them tucked in her robes.

Following Sherab's instructions, and because his mother is paying for everything, Sonam has bought a first class ticket to Calcutta, while we settle for third class berths. Boarding the train, we first escort Sonam to her roomy compartment, with just one other seat. Then Sonam accompanies us to our third class compartment, already occupied by several people. This way, we know where each other is in case of emergency.

Jean and I take turns visiting Sonam throughout the long, twenty-four-hour journey, just to make sure she is okay. The glorious Himalayas change to an endless landscape of farms, plains, and deserts, the cool weather to stifling heat and colorful clothing of mountain people to the drab whites of plains dwellers. We're both in a dark mood, mourning the loss of our lives in Darjeeling. Are we going to see any more Tibetans and Nepalis? We make a pact that, after South India and maybe Ceylon, we'll return to the Himalayas, maybe to Kalu Rinpoche's monastery.

A couple of hours into the trip, a conductor stops in to check our tickets. Seeing Tashi, he insists that we pay a full price ticket for him. We argue that we were never told this when we bought our tickets. This starts our fellow travelers into a heated conversation with the conductor and each other in Hindi. We don't understand the words, but it's evident that battle lines are drawn. Apparently, those on our side win, because the conductor finally throws his arms up and, with a final blast of expletives, goes away, leaving some passengers smiling at us, while others sit in sullen silence. We get away without paying for Tashi this time but realize that we'll have to figure out a solution for our next train ride.

We all sleep fitfully until four o'clock in the morning when we're awakened by the conductor. We have reached the Ganges and now have to deboard the train. We learn that the bridge over the river is still under construction, and we must take a ferry to the other side, where another train is waiting. We help Sonam down with her bags and then have to wait three hours for the ferry to arrive. Sonam has been on this journey several times before. She tells us that the construction of the bridge was begun in the last year of the British Raj and is still not completed. We're to see more evidence in the months ahead of this breakdown of construction and services throughout India since the efficient days of the Raj. We board the next train at 7:00 a.m. and spend the day looking out at a flat landscape of plains, farms, and water buffalo, periodically checking in with Sonam.

In the late afternoon, we cross into the State of West Bengal and, in the evening, pull into a crowded Howrah Station, Howrah being a district of Calcutta. We collect Sonam and struggle our way through a jaw-dropping sea of humanity to a closed horse-drawn carriage, a throwback to nineteenth century England. Our route takes us across the Howrah Bridge spanning the Hooghly River, a branch of the Ganges leading to the Bay of Bengal, and onto Chowringhee Road to the city center. Sherab's mother has reserved a suite for Sonam at the Oberoi Grand, a hotel obviously too expensive for us. We've heard that the nearby Salvation Army has clean beds, so we direct the driver to take us there first. Dropping us off, Sonam suggests we come right to the Oberoi Grand after settling into our lodging so we can enjoy a room service dinner with her, paid for by Sherab's mother.

Unfortunately, the Salvation Army is full so, at the suggestion of their desk clerk, we walk several blocks to the Modern Lodge, a run-down hotel on an alley lined with homeless tents. The portly manager of the hotel shows us a sad room with a deeply sagging bed on the first floor. We decide to take the room anyway as our plan is to stay in Calcutta for just a few days, and besides, he allows us to have Tashi "for no rupees extra."

We take a bicycle rickshaw an hour later to the Oberoi Grand. I marvel at the skill and determination of our driver in negotiating the sheer volume of taxis, rickshaws, and horse-drawn cabs, every vehicle close enough to reach out and touch other passengers. All this while avoiding several cows, the driver mentioning that the increasing number of cows is becoming a traffic problem. We have to cover our faces with cloth from overwhelming dust and foul odors.

The lobby of the Oberoi Grand is magnificent: high ceilings, lush carpeting, stately furniture, and two large fountains. The desk clerk calls up to Sonam's suite on the fourth floor and she immediately comes down to greet us. She has exchanged her robes for a long white skirt and pink blouse, looking every bit the tourist on vacation; a stark contrast to us two dirty travelers with their little black dog! Her suite is as impressive as one can imagine: a large, open-plan living and dining room with floor-to-ceiling windows on one wall overlooking Chowringhee Road; an adjoining bedroom with a king-size bed and, most important of all, a spacious bathroom with an oversized bathtub.

Sonam suggests we take a bath while she orders a "special dinner" on Sherab's mother's tab as thanks for our being good guardians. The bath is big enough for both of us. Hot running water and delicately scented soap—what luxury! Tashi barks to join us in the tub until I splash water in her face, sending her whining to the corner until we're finished. She doesn't get off that easily. We empty the tub of dirty water, refill it a little, then plop her in the tub, clean and dry her until her coat is shiny. When we emerge, dinner is ready, and what food: shrimp, lobster tails, rice, salad, chutneys, and hot buns!

As we dig in, Jean asks Sonam about Sherab's mother.

"Oh, she's coming in tomorrow afternoon. In the morning, I've got some shopping to do for the monks and nuns. The list they gave is as long as my arm!"

Jean asks, "Does Sherab's mother come here often?"

"Every year like clockwork. She has a very interesting story, you know."

"Really?" I mumble through a mouthful of lobster tail.

"Yes. You see, Sherab grew up in a wealthy household in California. His mother, a widow, was so against her son going to

India with me that she offered him lots of money and a house to give up his 'foolish idea.' But he left with me anyway. Maybe a year later, he wrote a letter to his mother telling her about Kalu Rinpoche and how we had changed our names."

"What were your names to begin with?"

"Bob and Elinore, Ellie for short."

We all laugh. Even Sonam seems in disbelief that she was once Ellie.

"Anyway," she continues, "Sherab's mother was horrified and immediately bought a plane ticket to Calcutta to save her son from this 'guru.' She spent a couple of days in Sonada trying to convince Sherab to return with her, but he refused. She then insisted that she meet Rinpoche to demand that he release her son from his 'spell.' The meeting was short, and she came away dissatisfied. But, during it, he gave her a valuable *thanka*, a painting of the Tibetan saint Milarepa. Sherab told me that Rinpoche's head monk was upset that he gave such a valuable *thanka* to this difficult woman. In fact, she left Sonada the day after meeting Rinpoche without taking it with her. When Rinpoche heard about this, he sent a monk all the way to Calcutta to give it to her again. Sometime after returning back home, something told her to hang the *thanka* in her bedroom. She awoke in the middle of the night to see Rinpoche standing at the foot of her bed! Immediately, her anger, fear, and distrust flew out the window, and she has since become a disciple and generous benefactor to Rinpoche and the monastery, visiting for a month at this time every year."

"Wow!" I exclaim. "What an incredible story! How did he manage to do such a thing?"

"Who knows?" Sonam responds. "Sherab told me that Rinpoche could do many things like this. His action came from clearly seeing the benefit his mother would receive."

We sit in silence for a while, contemplating the power of the thin little man sitting on the platform regarding us with his beneficent smile.

We hug Sonam goodnight and goodbye as she'll be too busy the next day with shopping and meeting Sherab's mother.

"We may not see each other again," I lament.

"Oh, I think we will," Sonam laughs, "just maybe not in this lifetime. We might all end up as sacred cows in traffic together!"

Jan. 6, 1971

Hola Familia,

Well, it's been over two weeks since I wrote and many things have happened on our journey south. I hope you all had a Merry Christmas and a happy New Year (incidentally, the last letter I received from you was in Calcutta, dated on the 14th of Dec. and arriving on the 28th—very slow.) This was Nancy's 14th New Year!

From Darjeeling we traveled to Calcutta for mail and rupees. For an overcrowded, filthy city, with 1,000,000 homeless people, a three day stay through New Year's was long enough. A most amazing city, Calcutta: squalid, teeming, colorful, exciting, and so much more. Peace and quiet aren't among its descriptive terms, and it was soon necessary to scuttle off to the beaches of Puri ...

The next morning, New Year's Eve, we wander to the nearby "New Market" where we were told by James back in Darjeeling the black market money changers are located. Down to a handful of rupees, we figure that $300 should be enough for our trip through South India.

Honing my bargaining skills, I settle on two of the many stalls offering the "best price" for our dollars. Jean, meanwhile, sits on a bench with Tashi on a makeshift leash, really a thin rope, investigating the new smells of the marketplace. This whole bargaining thing, which I love, is definitely not for her! I tell the first money changer I want to change $100, and he responds with an offer of 11 rupees per dollar. The second man offers me 11.50. When I tell them that maybe I'll change $200, the exchange goes as high as 12 rupees. Finally, asking each man what I can get for $300, I settle for the first money changer's offer of 13 rupees. So now we have 3900 rupees. The official bank rate remains fixed at 7.50 rupees to the dollar. So, who benefits from such a difference in rates? According to James, some say the money is rebought by Afghanistan, others, China, but he thought the Indian government itself benefits from holding down the exchange rate and then cashing in on the difference negotiated on the black market, with a commission on sales given to the money changers. This sounds feasible to me. How else could this black market thrive with such impunity? The rest of the morning is spent combing the market for a basket large enough to hold Tashi, as we're determined not to pay an extra train fare for her.

I leave Jean and Tashi resting at the Modern Hotel in the afternoon while I taxi to the train station to buy tickets for the next evening to the city of Puri, on the Bay of Bengal in the state of Orissa. The process is hot and tedious, but, in the end, I come away with two third class berth tickets.

That evening, to celebrate New Year's Eve, we leave Tashi in our room and go to an English-speaking movie on Chowringhee Road: *The Out of Towners* with Jack Lemmon and Sandy Dennis. This is about a Midwest businessman and his wife who vacation in New York, only to get beaten, robbed, and generally overwhelmed by the callousness of the city. Supposedly a comedy, the movie leaves us depressed and feeling like two out-of-towners, magnified a hundred times over!

New Year's Day is spent with Tashi at the large "Golden Park" on Chowringhee Road, directly across from the Oberoi Grand. Our spirits are lifted by the airy openness of the park and blue sky above, such a stark contrast to the surrounding dust, traffic, and decaying structures of the city! I think to myself that perhaps Calcutta has always been a city in decay. Now free to wander without a leash, Tashi joyfully pounces on leaves and barks excitedly at nearby pigeons. We've mainly been feeding her hamburger meat since leaving Darjeeling and can see she has put on weight.

An organ grinder comes over to us with three monkeys dressed as a father, a mother, and a baby. For a rupee, the monkeys entertain us by playing out a family scene of father and mother arguing while baby steals their food. Now we hear band music as a parade of

Sikhs proudly march in step in front of a group of officers reviewing them from the steps of the Oberoi Grand.

We come across a strange sight further into the park: a large, fenced area, festooned with flowers, beads, and incense, with hundreds of rats inside busily feasting on rice and a variety of vegetables and fruit! People surround the fence, some performing pujas, or sacred ceremonies.

Seeing our confusion, a man approaches and introduces himself as Narayan.

"I see that you must think this a very strange sight."

"Well, it certainly isn't something you see every day," I respond.

"Yes. We call this 'Rat Park.' It is a special place indeed."

Narayan explains, "Calcutta has more than one million people living on its streets, and many times more than that in the rat population. The danger of hungry rats biting sleeping people was a big problem, you see. Even some babies were eaten alive! Can you imagine this?"

"No," I respond, "I can't even imagine."

"Terrible! The authorities tried every way to get rid of the rats, but nothing worked, you see. Then someone, a forward thinker, suggested a revolutionary plan to actually feed the rats. This fenced area was put up so the rats could come each morning and evening to eat the food offered by the people of the city. And this plan has certainly worked. The well-fed rats no longer attack the people of the streets."

"But," I ask, "what happens when people don't bring enough food one day?"

"No, this cannot happen. You see all the flowers and incense here? This is because the rat is venerated in our Hindu tradition. You can see in every picture of Lord Ganesh, the son of Shiva, the little rat at his feet. This rat is named Mooshika and symbolizes the ability of Lord Ganesh to conquer all obstacles. So, the people, they come here to venerate Mooshika so all their obstacles will be overcome. No, there will always be enough food in Rat Park."

We thank Narayan for his lesson but leave soon after, as Tashi is barking and pulling at her leash to get at the rats behind the fence. She wouldn't have a minute's chance of surviving in there!

Evening finds us at the crowded Howrah Station boarding the overnight train to Puri. Tashi is safely latched into her covered basket, chewing on a meat bone. We find our berths and climb up for the night. As passengers and porters mill around below us, we pass food to each other for dinner. The train slowly pulls out from the station, and in a short while, Calcutta is behind us.

... So here we are in Puri, enjoying warm, sunny weather for a change, living at the Bay View Hotel for $1.00 a day each, including three full meals and tea. This city is noted for the Jaggannath Temple, Lord Jaggannath being the 10th incarnation of Vishnu, a principal Hindu God along with Brahma, the creator, and Shiva, the preserver/destroyer. Puri is one of the ten principle centers for Hindu pilgrimage. (There is a good pictorial article on Puri and Orissa in last October's National Geographic.) The buildings on the beach are huge, hollowed-out shells, one-time luxury abodes of the British-giving them the appearance of a Fellini set. John would love to film here.

Well, we now have a third member of our traveling troupe: Tashi Deleg (pronounced day lay,) a furry black, part everything dog given to us in Darjeeling, and named by Kalu Rinpoche, a high lama in Sonada, a town near Darjeeling. Tashi Deleg, roughly translated, means "good luck." She's been wonderful though, quite active, and fast becoming the fattest pooch in India. What a contrast to the starving beach dogs of Puri!

To devote a paragraph to any one place is negligent, and to devote one letter to a month's stay in India is criminal. But you know me and my writing habits. I hope, though, that I've communicated the general gist of past events, and I promise to write more often in the future. Hello to all and, of course, love. Oh yes, due to the change of weather, we might ship a bundle of warm clothing back to you from Madras. Love and Kisses, Bruce and Jean

I sleep surprisingly soundly and awake to sunrise streaming through the dusty window of our compartment. Jean is already awake, looking the worse for wear as she's had to take a whining Tashi to the bathroom twice during the night.

Our train screeches into Puri Station within the hour. We collect our bags, latch Tashi into her basket, and make our way down the platform, past a conductor suspiciously eyeing our basket, to waiting bicycle rickshaws. The day is already warm and clear, the fresh air a welcome improvement from Calcutta and the dusty train ride. We can just make out the massive Jagannath Temple in the distance. We direct a rickshaw *walla* to the tourist bungalow, again per James's instructions in Darjeeling. We're told by the desk clerk upon arriving, however, that the bungalow has no vacancy, but that we can try the Bay View Hotel, just two kilometers further along the road paralleling the Bay of Bengal. The short ride is lovely, the first time in months that we've seen an ocean. There are just a few beachcombers and fishermen on this stretch of white sand beach. Rising up from the beach, like giant gray ghosts, are a line of dilapidated structures, which we later learn are the remains of mansions built by the British for their seaside resort vacations from their jobs in Calcutta. When the British left, so did much of their wealth, leaving these houses to slowly fall to ruin. The effect is eerie; I've no doubt that the squatters who must live in them now are cohabiting with ghosts of the past.

The Bay View Hotel does have a vacancy. The manager shows us to a small but comfortable room right off its central garden, its trellises dripping with vines and paths lined with colorful flowers. The price of the room is just 6 rupees per person per night, the dog free of charge. We also pay an extra 2 rupees each per meal at the garden restaurant after we're told there are so few restaurants in the area. Jean orders breakfast while I release Tashi to wander the garden and find a good place to pee. In no time, she jumps onto the lap of an older Western guest to his surprise and the delight of his wife.

I apologize for Tashi's exuberance, but the man says, "Not at all. It's wonderful to have a dog jump in my lap. Reminds me of my own dog many years ago."

The couple invite us to join them. They introduce themselves as Roger and Jane, Brits who have been living and working in Nepal on a cultural research project. This is their first vacation in two years. An outgoing, "chipper" couple, they are happy for our conversation. During our stay, we meet regularly for breakfast with them. They even treat us one day to breakfast at the tourist bungalow which, in my opinion, is not as tasty as the food in our restaurant. In one corner of the gardens is a ping pong table with a worn net. Roger and I discover we both like to play ping pong, so we meet each afternoon for a match we call the "British Open," or the "US Open," depending on who won the last game. In truth, neither of us is very good, but we have some good laughs.

It turns out the gardens provide quite the social scene. Tashi makes lots of new friends, gratefully eating their table scraps. We apologize often but come to realize that most guests are delighted to have a pet, if only for a meal. A happy puppy pouncing on a lap and licking a face can make a traveler's day! Through Tashi, we meet two other couples: Tom and Ellen, and George and Lynn. Tom is thin with wispy blond hair. He is quiet, allowing only for glancing eye contact, and preferring that Ellen, his short and pudgy partner, speaks for both of them. I realize soon enough that if I say anything to Tom, Ellen will answer like a mother responding for a child. She explains that they reunited in Calcutta a couple of months before, just after Tom traveled from Vietnam, where he was discharged from the army. I ask Tom what he thought of the war, and Ellen responds, "Not much. Tom is happy to be out of it now." We can see that she's reluctant to say more. Tom likes to smoke hashish, so his days are spent getting stoned in his room or sitting quietly in the gardens. I never see him leave the hotel.

George, a big, bearded fellow with an engaging smile, and Lynn, a petite blonde, are also a quiet couple, but during the days we spend with them, we come to appreciate their subtle humor. They've been apart as much as together in their seven-year relationship, sometimes for a year at a stretch, but always get back together again.

George says, "We brought up the idea of getting married one time but quickly gave it up."

"Yeah," Lynn laughs, "when I go home alone to my family in Maine, maybe a couple of questions will come up about where my boyfriend is. But, if we were married, believe me, it would be a family crisis!"

We spend hours on the nearly empty beach each day with George and Lynn, enjoying Tashi's antics. A mountain dog, she doesn't know what to make of her paws sinking in the soft sand, which we have to keep her from eating. She barks with sheer delight and excitement as she attacks, then retreats from the waves, and she is one sad, drenched sight when a wave wins, washing over her. She could play this game of chasing waves all day long.

> *Hi All,*
>
> *... On New Year's, Bruce gave me a lovely pair of jade earrings as a surprise gift! Now we're in Puri, nice and warm with a beautiful beach on the Bay of Bengal—today we went body surfing for hours & now my sunburn hurts as I sit on my bed underneath a mosquito net. We went shopping today, and temple seeing also. We bought a deerskin ($5.00) and are having our own mosquito net made to take w/ us, as the mosquitos get worse further south. Soon we will head for Madras (write: c/o Tourist Bureau,) for a while to Bangalore & then to Ceylon definitely! We've heard fantastic things of it as we've gone along. Our packs are as heavy as ever, our big paper flower is still w/ us and gets hung up in our hotel rooms & now we have a new family member! We have a dog from Darjeeling 2 months old, black and funny—looks like a Labrador. Her name is "Tashi Delay" given to her by a Tibetan Lama. It means good luck—she's been very good so far—we'll see. Never got your letter #1. Where did you mail it? I'll write more soon. Send Norma's address. Love to all, Peace, Jean and Bruce*

Every couple of days, Jean and I take a twenty-minute rickshaw ride to a small, dark post office near the Jagannath Temple. Jean is concerned that she hasn't received any mail for weeks. Each time, the little postal clerk tells us that there is no mail under "F" for Fritts, her last name. On the third visit, Jean has an idea.

"Could you please check under M?"

"Ah," the clerk announces, "Here are two letters addressed to Miss Jean Fritts."

Of course. Jean's mom has always addressed "Miss" first.

As we're leaving, Jean has another idea. "Could you please check under J?"

Sure enough, there's another letter from home. We just shake our heads at this inexplicable filing system.

Jean is so happy and relieved that we decide not to return to the hotel and beach, but to explore the Jagannath Temple, just a short walk away. Upon reaching the main gate though, we're told that, as non-Hindus, we are forbidden to enter. A small, whiskered man near the gate approaches us.

"Hello, no it is true that you cannot enter the temple, but you can look at it from the balcony of my building, just here, next door. My name is Krishna, and I know much about Jagannath Temple. I can inform you of this."

I comment on Krishna's excellent English. He tells us that he went to fine schools in Calcutta and had a *pukka,* "very good," position in a British company but has fallen on harder times now that the British have left.

After negotiating a small fee for his services, Krishna takes us to his balcony, where we can see into the entrance courtyard of the temple.

Krishna says, "This temple is served by five thousand *pujaris,* or priests. Every year, millions of visitors come to worship Lord Jagannath."

"Who is Lord Jagannath?" Jean asks.

"Jagannath means 'Lord of the World.' He is, in fact, Lord Krishna, after whom I am named."

I say, "In a picture I saw, his image is black."

"Yes, *kilaya*, black," Krishna responds. "This is the true color of Lord Krishna."

"I thought he is blue."

"No, that is only someone's modern representation. His real color is black."

I'm not about to argue the point as Krishna embarks on a discourse of Jagannath Temple. "As you can see, Jagannath Temple is very big. It goes on for over one kilometer. One of its buildings is forty-five stories high. This is considered one of the ten most sacred pilgrimage sites in all of Hinduism, a gateway to heaven. No planes are allowed to fly over it. Also, no birds are seen to fly over the temple either. Interesting, isn't it? Another interesting point is that the temple casts no shadow. Scientists have come from all over to investigate this phenomenon, but no conclusions for this miracle have sufficed."

Krishna certainly has our attention.

"Each day, *prasad*, offerings of rice, dal, and chapatis, are steamed in pots, one pot on top of the other, the topmost pot being finished first. Very strange. After the offerings to Lord Jagannath are made, the food is distributed to the holy beggars you see below," Krishna points down from the balcony, and now to his left, "and to all the people in Anand Bazaar over there. Amazingly, there always seems to be enough food for everyone. Yet another miracle of Lord Jagannath."

Krishna continues, "Each year, during the summer months, the Festival of the Chariots is held here. This is when the three deities are brought out from the temple. These are Lord Krishna, in the form of Lord Jagannath, his older brother, Balabhadra, and younger sister, Subhadra. The chariots, rebuilt each year, are floats on wheels, decorated with thousands of flowers. The festival lasts for nine days, drawing millions of people. Much singing, dancing, and feasting occur throughout the festival. Everyone is extremely happy that Lord Jagannath has blessed us for the coming year."

We thank Krishna with a baksheesh as we leave, appreciating how much we've learned for just a few rupees.

Just outside the Bay View Hotel, Tashi has made a friend of a skinny, shaggy white dog who always hangs around the small shop of a fish *walla*, or "seller." As the dogs play together one morning, the fish walla makes me an offer of 100 rupees for my dog, thinking that I must have brought this big, healthy puppy from America. I thank him for his offer, but refuse, thinking, "If he could only have seen our skinny market dog just a month ago."

Returning from the beach one afternoon on the short stretch of road to the hotel, we become aware of a couple of street dogs following us.

"I wonder what they want?" I say.

Jean retorts, "Food, what else?"

"Maybe they're just curious about Tashi."

It's certainly a contrast, our big, healthy puppy and these bony creatures. In no time, the two become three, then even more, as the snarling, hungry dogs begin to surround us.

"Get out of here," I yell, picking up stones and throwing them at the closest dogs. They're not at all intimidated, edging closer.

Jean picks up Tashi, urging, "Just keep walking, don't stop, don't look at them, and don't yell at them!"

Our walk turns to a dead run as we just manage to hustle inside the hotel grounds with the dogs baying and nipping at our heels. We collapse on our bed, traumatized and exhausted! The hotel manager tells us later that those were just a few of the many wild, hungry dogs roaming the beaches and streets of Puri.

"They attack in packs. Chickens, cows, other dogs, even some children have been killed and devoured."

I ask, "Why haven't people done something about this?'

He replies, "We have. We called out the army. They came and fed them poison chapatis. This killed them off for a time. But more and more appear. Where from, I don't know. I suppose we'll have to call the army again."

I'm just happy we're alive and are leaving Puri soon!

We spend our last day in Puri on the beach with George and Lynn. Safety in numbers! They are off in a few days to Calcutta and on to Nepal. Our direction is south to Madras, where we'll get visas for Ceylon before touring Bangalore, and maybe Pondicherry. It is sad to say goodbye to them as we've all grown close in just a couple of weeks. Roger and I play our last games of ping pong in the late afternoon, with Roger winning the ultimate award of proclaiming all of our games under the banner of the British Open.

Tom and Ellen have decided to join us on the morning train to Madras. We've bought first class tickets, just the four of us in a compartment because the trip takes forty-eight hours, and we know we can't hide Tashi in her basket for that long in third class. This way, we can actually lock our door and let Tashi out of her basket, and Tom can smoke his hashish near an open window.

For ten hours, the train transects endless, flat farmland, and I've fallen asleep when our train comes to a halt at a station. There is a loud knock on our door. Jean scrambles to shove Tashi back in her basket as I open the door to a conductor who informs us that this is the final stop for this train. We must disembark and wait two hours for a "mail train" to take us on to Madras. After two hours waiting on a hard station bench, the mail train arrives. We all board to find all the first class cabins full! I immediately go to the station ticket master, and complain, showing him our first class tickets to Madras.

"Yes, these are first class tickets, but you have no reservations."

"But I bought reservations in Puri to Madras."

"Yes, of course, but only as far as this station. You did not buy reservations for this train."

"Then how do we get to Madras?"

"I will sell you reservations for tomorrow morning's train."

"Tomorrow? So, we just have to sit here all night?"

"Oh no," he replies. "We have excellent first-class accommodations here at the station, and also we have an excellent restaurant for your convenience."

I'm about to explode in frustration, but see we have no choice but to spend the night in the station.

The room, also on the second floor of this station, is comfortable, with two double beds, and the restaurant adequate. (It seems every train station in India has overnight accommodations for travelers.) The station manager finishes his work for the day and leaves, allowing us to unlatch Tashi's basket so she can wander around the station. Groups of Indians gawk at the strange sight of us two hippies and our healthy pet. We sleep well enough and board the morning train, relieved to find an empty compartment. The trip takes all day and night as we pass from Orissa through the state of Andhra Pradesh and into Madras State. Tom and Ellen are pleasant enough companions but share little of their lives, preferring instead to listen to our stories of traveling the Great Hippie Trail.

The northern chai wallas at the station stops transform to southern coffee wallas, still selling their product in disposable clay pots. This coffee, a major export of South India, is laced with chicory, a root that cuts the caffeine content and enhances the flavor. Ironic, then, that we're to discover many South Indians prefer the taste of Nescafé Instant Coffee, perhaps because it's a more expensive foreign product, or maybe they're just tired of the taste of chicory.

When our train pulls into Madras station, we tell Tom and Ellen we'll meet them outside the station and quickly secret Tashi past officials through the exit gate. Outside, we wait in vain for our friends for half an hour. Finally, I return to the station platform and search everywhere for them, including our compartment. Our exit is the only one in the station. Where could they have gone? Returning to Jean, we wait for another half hour, but they've completely disappeared! Bewildered, concerned, we ask a conductor and others if they've seen a Western couple leaving the train, but no one has. Finally, knowing not what else to do, we find a taxi, asking the driver to take us to a "hippie hotel." He takes us down a maze of wide, crowded streets, through canyons of low, nearly identical white structures, to a building with a sign: Hotel Daneshwar. Our room on the second floor is large, with mosquito nets covering two single beds, a ceiling fan, and an attached bathroom. Tired and hungry from travel, we're told by the desk clerk of a rooftop restaurant next door. The dinner is quite good: *masala dosas*, thin pancakes stuffed with spicy rice and potatoes; *raita*, a cooling yogurt and cucumber dish; and *idli*, steamed rice cakes. Back in the hotel room, we have our worst argument since Iran, blame stemming from our worry for our missing friends. Tashi's barking and jumping into our laps help us both to calm down eventually, leading to apologies and admitting to each other that we're lonely and feeling far from home. We agree that we'll stay in Madras just long enough to check mail and get a "dog visa" for Tashi to Ceylon, which is a document certifying that she has no distemper or rabies.

We set out to locate the Tourist Bureau the next morning, a Sunday, where we hope to receive mail and find a message from our Darjeeling friends Ted and Ginny, and maybe even a message from Tom and Ellen as to their whereabouts in the city. Our way by taxi through the sprawling city does nothing to uplift our spirits. The hotel, the Tourist Bureau, the railway station, the port and beaches on the Bay of Bengal, every place a long taxi ride away from each other. There seems to be no city center. Jean receives a welcomed letter from her mom at the Tourist Bureau, but the message Ted and Ginny have left us is disappointing: "Hi Guys, we waited a week for you to show up, but are taking these people up on their offer of a motorcycle ride to Rameswaram, where we'll catch a boat to Ceylon. We'll leave a message for you at the American Express in Colombo, in case you show up. We hope to see you there! Love, Ted and Ginny." After reading this, we're more determined than ever to go to Ceylon. There is no word from Tom and Ellen. I wonder aloud if Tom has not been discharged from the army like Ellen said, but is AWOL, a possible reason for them to disappear to avoid capture. Jean wonders if they were ghosts.

We taxi to a city beach, again several kilometers distant. It's good to be near the ocean, but the day is too hot to stay for long. After Tashi burns her paws on the sand, I carry her to the water edge where she does battle with the gentle waves. The beach is strewn with the litter of discarded bottles, cans, and food scraps—either there has just been a festival, or this is its permanent condition. At another taxi driver's suggestion, we're driven to the city's Natural History Museum. It is blessedly cool inside, but being Sunday, the crowds at each exhibit dictate that we move along quickly to avoid being trampled! We spend the rest of the afternoon and evening in our hotel room, with another good dinner at the restaurant next door.

Thurs. Jan. 14ᵗʰ
Hi Again,

Here we are in Madras—the train trip took almost 2 days, but we splurged and went 1ˢᵗ class, that cost 64 rupees each. It was a good trip, only one change w/ an 8 hr. layover. Tashi Deleg did very well. I hide her in a basket, with a shawl over her head. She is allowed on trains but you must pay full fare. Since she is only three months old, we can still hide her, but one day she will be quite big (her paws are huge,) and that will be soon enough to pay. I've heard though that a woman traveling alone is allowed a dog so we'll try that one too. She looks like a Labrador but also has many Indian dog traits. Here we will get her shots and papers so in a month she can go to Ceylon with us. Before Feb. 11ᵗʰ, we must extend our visas for another 3 mos. And we hope to do that in Bangalore, for it's a small city, and that makes it easier. Then after seeing some of Southern Indian cities, we will go to Ceylon for a while. Mail should be sent to Poste Restante, Bangalore, India up until Feb. 11ᵗʰ or so and then c/o American Express, Colombo, Ceylon. Love to you again. J & B

Monday morning finds us at the veterinary hospital for Tashi's exam. I mention to the attending doctor I've noticed that Tashi has the sniffles and has been sneezing quite a bit. After examining Tashi's chest and limbs, the doctor assures us that Tashi is healthy, that the sniffles are typical of a slight cold or allergy, probably the reaction of a mountain dog coming down to a humid sea-level climate. He estimates Tashi's age at only three or four months old and

128

determines that there is no need for her to have rabies or distemper shots. Then he tells us that the final travel papers will be ready in a few days. This is disappointing news. What are we going to do in this city for three more days?

The clerk back at our hotel suggests a solution. "Why don't you visit Mahabalipuram? It is only a few hours there by bus. Oh, this is a very beautiful place. Many pilgrims go there to see the famous Shore Temple. I myself have been there many times."

We are at the bus depot by late morning, purchasing tickets to Mahabalipuram. There's no way to hide Tashi for long in an open bus, so I negotiate with the driver to pay half fare for her. The trip takes just three hours, including many stops. There are official bus stops, but most just hail the driver from the road, or yell from inside the bus to disembark. We travel through a rich landscape of farms, low hills, and forests. As usual, we attract the attention of the Indian travelers, being the only Westerners, and longhairs with a dog at that.

Mahabalipuram is just a crossroads of restaurants, gift stalls, and hotels. What a change from the crowded city! We settle in the nearest hotel, our room furnished with a sizable bed inside a mosquito net, the ubiquitous ceiling fan, and a large window looking out to a lush countryside. We collapse on the bed, enjoying the blessed quiet and fresh sea air.

After a while, we walk a block to the beach to view the Shore Temple, standing alone with blue sea and sky as a backdrop. The main attraction for pilgrims, it was built in the seventh century, a magnificent Dravidian structure housing two large shrines to Shiva and a smaller one to Vishnu. The temple can only be visited during low tide, as it's nearly immersed during high tide. Fortunately, it is low tide. We join a throng of pilgrims and Indian tourists to explore the inside of the temple. Lining the walls are beautiful carvings depicting the stories of two of the most revered Hindu stories, *The Ramayana* and *The Mahabharata*. I had coincidentally bought these two stories in cheap paperback versions in the New

Market of Calcutta, so I'm generally familiar with these stories of the gods, Rama and Krishna, that the carvings depict. Later, as we walk through the hills and grottos surrounding the village, we see that many of the rock outcroppings have similar carvings of the gods and stories. I feel as though I'm walking through chapters of India's ancient Vedic sagas.

As the sun sets, the day's hordes of pilgrims leave on the last buses, and Mahabalipuram reverts to a sleepy village. Leaving Tashi in the hotel room, we try one of the three vegetarian restaurants. We line up to wash our hands in a long, three-faucet sink and sit down with several others at a long table. Then a crew serves a meal called *thali*, providing, in order, a large banana leaf as a plate, a clump of rice called *chawal*, a cup of dal, a cup of *sambar*, or spicy soup, curried vegetables called *subje*, a cup of *dahi*, or curd, and finally two or three *papadam*, South India's crispy, spicy version of the *chapati*. Then we all set to eating the meal by scooping the food with our right hand, using the left only to break pieces off the *papadam*. At first, I think, "Oh my God, this is the hottest food in the world! I'm going to die of starvation because I just can't eat this." But we find that by mixing the hot curries with the curd and rice, aided by a soft drink of orange soda called Gold Spot, the spicy food is bearable. In fact, over the next days that we're in the village, we come to look forward to the evening *thali*. Jean slips some rice and dal into a little bag each night that she brings back to a hungry Tashi.

Sitting one afternoon under the shade of a large stone carving of a battle scene from the Mahabharata, a young boy carrying a bag approaches us, saying in broken English, "paisa please for seeing live mongoose." I hand him ten paisa, and he produces a sleek, ferret-like animal, tame enough to pet.

"Ten rupees, you can see this mongoose fight a cobra to the death!"

"Uh," Jean responds quickly, "we're not interested."

The boy looks disheartened until I ask him his name.

"Krishna," he beams, "just like the god." Yet another Krishna. (I learn later that, years before, to honor the memory of Mahatma

Gandhi and his *ahimsa* movement, the Indian government initiated a campaign to have newborns receive peaceful names. Within that year, hundreds of thousands of Indians became Krishnas, Ramas, Sitas, and scores of other names symbolizing peace and love.)

Krishna continues, "But you must meet my older brother. He is a great magician!"

"Yes," I reply, "maybe later."

The next morning, as we're eating an English-style breakfast at the one tourist restaurant near the Shore Temple, Krishna appears with a young man carrying a large sack, who introduces himself as Ramamurti. Like Krishna, he is happy and engaging. We agree to see his magic show while we eat breakfast. Ramamurti then produces three smooth stones the size of lemons from his pocket, which he then swallows! Next, he pulls out playing cards and does some impressive card tricks. Then he moves on to coin and ball tricks, all very adroit at fooling us. As he works, he tells us stories and jokes. We can see that he's certainly a seasoned performer. After these tricks, he reaches into his sack and produces a reed pipe, with two small gourds attached.

Ramamurti says, "This is a snake-charmer's horn. With this, I will now charm this cobra!" And with that, he pulls a hissing six-foot cobra from his sack! We watch, awestruck, as he plays a repetitive tune, the cobra rising and swaying to the movement of the horn. The cobra strikes at the horn, but Ramamurti moves away just in time. This song and dance go on for a time, the cobra striking out, Ramamurti deftly avoiding the strike, until one strike gets his hand, drawing blood. I can see Ramamurti is in pain, but he keeps playing.

The snake-charming show over, Ramamurti now opens his mouth and coughs up the three stones we'd forgotten he'd "swallowed" at the beginning of his performance.

We're more than impressed and full of questions. "Did the snake bite hurt you?" Jean asks.

"Oh yes," showing us his hands, scarred from years of snake bites, "but I'm used to it. This snake is young and new to this dance.

Also, he has not yet been slowed by captivity. I haven't completely learned his movements yet. But, not to worry, his poison sack has been removed."

I say, "Ramamurti, that is a good trick, pretending to swallow those stones."

"No, this is no trick. This takes years of training to develop the sacs in the throat to hold the stones. I still have two in my throat now."

That said, he raises his head and taps his neck, causing a clunking sound.

"My father taught me the technique of stone swallowing. He was a great magician and traveled the whole world with the Bombay Circus. He became very famous and wealthy, but he lost all his money because he was a spendthrift. Finally, he died swallowing a large stone. It accidentally went down his throat instead of into the sac, and he choked to death."

This leaves us speechless. After giving Ramamurti a generous baksheesh for his performance, he repeats what Krishna had offered us the day before. "For only ten rupees you can see this cobra and a mongoose fight to the death."

"No thanks," I reply. "Neither of us want to see any animal die."

"This is a relief," he says. "Both Krishna and I grow very fond of our animals, and it is hard to see one die. I don't like to do this, but our family needs the money." He adds, "You two are very different than most tourists. They can't wait to see these animals fight."

Jean says, "The cobra always wins, right?"

"Oh no, not so. A well-trained mongoose will usually beat a cobra. He knows just how to move and when to strike."

We're walking on the beach with Tashi at the far side of the village a couple of days later, when Ramamurti and Krishna run out of a small hut, Krishna yelling, "Please come and have coffee with our family."

We have to stoop to enter the hut and squeeze into a group of six people seated around a central fire. We're introduced to their mother, uncle, and four siblings. I notice that they all have the similar appearance of dark skin, high cheekbones, flat noses, and small, slanted eyes—very different from the village Indians.

When I comment on this, Ramamurti replies, "Yes, we are all from a tribe that are nomads and magicians. We travel throughout South India, performing for money wherever we can. We are not part of any caste, but a caste of our own." (Again, I learn later that Gypsies, or Roma, originally migrated into Europe from South India. Could this be one of their ancestral tribes?)

We're served coffee and *chat*, a mixture of salted and sweet crackers and nuts. The family is curious about us and our long hair. They've all heard about hippies and have a lot of questions, translated from their native tongue, Telagu, by Ramamurti, with Krishna piping in. We share stories and a lot of laughter. Jean and I are touched by their openness and friendliness. They come to a conclusion that hippies are their own caste, just like them. We agree that, in all the important ways, we are just like them.

The following day, Krishna asks if we'll sit with him by the Shore Temple as he awaits the arrival of the day's tour buses. "Two hippies and their dog sitting by me will be good for business. The pilgrims will be very curious and spend good money to talk to us and see my show."

I watch Ramamurti performing his sleight-of-hand card and coin tricks several more times, but his hands are still quicker than my eyes.

We've stayed in Mahabalipuram well past our original plan, charmed by all this village has to offer. We visit the family in their hut once more to say goodbye and give a parting gift of rupees. We say we hope to see them all again someday, all of us knowing that will be unlikely. Hardest of all is to leave Ramamurti and Krishna. We've learned so much from them about how the human spirit can soar even in the poorest of circumstances.

By early afternoon, we're back in Madras, this time staying in the Friendship Lodge, which is a short walk from the Tourist

Bureau. We plan to be in the city for just long enough to pick up Tashi's "visa," check mail and send packages, and purchase bus tickets to the next city south, Pondicherry. We see a couple of hippies in the lobby, the first ones in many days. We don't engage them, but their presence in this confusing metropolis is somehow comforting.

We meet with the same doctor at the veterinary hospital, who hands us the necessary certificate to allow Tashi into Ceylon. I bring up our concern about his sniffles and sneezing again, which haven't abated, but the doctor assures us that her adjusting to sea level will just take a little more time. Then we send and receive mail at the Tourist Bureau, checking in vain the message board for any word from Tom and Ellen. Their disappearance remains a mystery.

The next day, after a breakfast of eggs, fruit, and toast at a nearby restaurant, we finally unburden our backpacks of winter clothes and previous purchases, packaging them and sending them home through the Tourist Bureau.

By the next morning, less than two days after returning to Madras, we're on the bus headed south.

ANANDA ASHRAM

It's late afternoon when we arrive at the crowded bus station of Pondicherry. We choose one of the many bicycle rickshaw drivers vying for our business. We want to connect with other travelers, so I wave my ponytail at him saying, "Please take us to where the hippies stay."

"*Huh Jee*, Oh yes," he says, all smiles and waggling his head in agreement. We hop onto the carriage as he loads our bags and then slowly starts pedaling.

From previous conversations on the road, we know that Pondicherry, originally a French colony, is the home of Aurobindo Ashram. A poet and mystic, Sri Aurobindo founded the discipline known as Integral Yoga. He is considered one of India's great saints. He died in 1950, but the ashram and the large international community associated with it, known as Auroville, continue under the direction of Sri Aurobindo's French partner, affectionately known as "The Mother." Thousands of people from around the world consider themselves *chelas*, or disciples, of Sri Aurobindo and The Mother, and their visits support the economic well-being of Pondicherry.

Our rickshaw driver is still laboring along a half hour later in a direction away from the city center. I'm becoming anxious as the sun is about to set.

Tapping him on the shoulder, I say, "Where are you taking us?"

"To where the hippies are, sahib."

"Hippie hotel?"

"Oh yes, many hippies."

Just as we pass through a village we later learn is named Lawspet, the driver stops and points to a large white structure a hundred yards away, sitting on what appears to be sand dunes.

"Hippie hotel, sahib."

All we can do now is pay the driver and trudge to the building through the dunes and prickly bushes with Tashi and, fortunately, our lighter packs. I notice a number of Indian children playing just in front of the hotel as we come closer and think they might be the children of the hotel workers. Closer still, I see several Westerners sitting on a porch, eyeing our progress. We arrive at an imposing wooden front door, and I knock loudly, wait a minute and, just as I'm about to knock again, a lovely, dark-haired young Western woman in a white sari opens the door.

"Hello," Jean says. "We were told that we could stay here for the night."

"*Namaste*," replies the woman. "You look like you've traveled a long way. Please come in."

She introduces herself as Meenakshi Devi and asks us to have a seat in the hallway.

"Swamiji will greet you shortly." She then glides up the central staircase.

"Swami who," we say to each other. "Where the hell are we?"

A few minutes later, Meenakshi descends the stairs and says, "Please follow me. You can leave your packs here. They will be safe."

She leads us up to the second floor, through a door that opens to sizable, wood-paneled office. A large, barrel-chested man with long white hair, beard, and flowing saffron robes rises from behind a wide desk. Everything about him reads big, so I'm surprised that he's inches shorter than I am. He smiles but says nothing as he ushers us into a comfortable sitting room with a balcony overlooking the sand dunes we just crossed. He is fair skinned, and we don't know whether he is an Indian or Westerner. As a young man, it's impossible for me to determine his age; his long white hair and beard read old, but he radiates strength and health, and he moves with the grace and agility of a young man. He does look the very embodiment of every Westerner's image of a guru. He sits in a large chair, Meenakshi standing just behind him, and indicates for us to sit on a couch opposite him.

Then he asks, "So, are you the ones asking about staying here?"

"Yes," we answer, "but we don't know where we are."

He seems taken aback by this but responds quickly. "You are at Ananda Ashram, where we teach all aspects of yoga."

"Oh ... and who are you?"

"My name is Swami Gitananda, and I am the head of the ash-ram. People just call me Swamiji." He speaks with no discernible Indian accent. (Although I see later that he can affect that accent when speaking English to other Indians.)

Now noticing the puppy in the opened basket, he says, "And who is this?"

"This is Tashi," I respond. "We've brought her from Darjeeling."

"Oh? And what breed of dog is she?"

Jean responds, "Well, her papers say 'nondescript.'"

After a pause in which we think we may not be welcome with a dog, Swamiji smiles, saying, "I see your world has no problems."

"No, not really," I shrug, not knowing what else to say.

"Well, you are welcome to stay here if you wish. You'll find bed-ding on the roof.

"We'll probably just stay for a few days," Jean says.

This seems to amuse him. "The students you saw downstairs have completed the first month of a three-month yoga retreat. If you'd like, you can stay through the rest of the retreat."

All I can reply to his invitation is a weak, "Oh, thank you."

He adds, "Dinner is in one hour, and *Satsang* right after that."

He indicates to Meenakshi to lead us out of his apartment and back down the stairs, we thinking, "*Satsang?*"

Meenakshi leads us to a long room attached to a kitchen where a number of students are already eating, saying that she will see us later. Most are Westerners, and of these, most are young longhairs like us. The service is cafeteria-style, so we stand in line and fill our plates with rice, *subje*, dal, and a puffed bread called *puri*. We make no contact as everyone eats in silence. We notice several people sneaking peeks at Tashi, who's whining to jump from Jean's arms and investigate these new surroundings. Soon a bell rings, and a woman nearby tells us that it is time for Satsang. We line up to clean our dishes in the kitchen, grab our packs, and join others in climbing the stairs to the rooftop. This large space has a thatched roof and is open-sided. The evening is warm, with just a gentle breeze. Rows of mats and blankets face a chair on a raised platform. All the students settle onto their mats, while Jean, Tashi, and I sit against a back wall.

Swami Gitananda soon arrives and takes his seat on the platform. Not for the last time, he reminds me of a proud lion. After chanting Hindu mantras, he begins to talk about the health aspects of *asanas,* or "yoga postures." He throws in some barbs at the decadence of Western diet and lifestyle, a theme we'll hear from him throughout our stay at Ananda Ashram. At the end of his talk, there's a short question and answer period. He then leaves, instructing the students to end their day by sitting for a time in meditation. I sit straight, trying to recall the breathing techniques I read about in Yogananda's book. Then, one by one, the students either leave the roof or simply lie down on their mats, pulling light blankets over themselves for the night. Jean and I find an unused corner of the roof and set up our king-sized mosquito net, shoving our packs, sleeping bags, and Tashi inside.

The sun wakes us up early in the morning. It's already warm, as South Indian winters here are generally cloudless and hot. Just after we've had enough time to get ourselves to the bathroom and walk Tashi in a garden within the ashram walls, a bell rings signaling, we're told, that morning hatha yoga class will begin. The students are assembling on the roof when a loud alarm clock rings, bringing some giggles and low comments. Soon after, a bent old Indian man with a stringy gray hair and beard enters and slowly makes his way to his yoga mat at the furthest place from the entrance. We learn that this is Dr. Rao, a longtime student of Swamiji. He has returned to the ashram having spent years away in the West. Each morning, his routine is the same, appearing minutes after his alarm clock rings. A student tells us that he often brings his alarm clock with him, and it sometimes goes off in the middle of classes and at Satsang. Some believe this is a little joke he plays to irritate Swamiji. Swamiji himself appears moments later and leads us through a series of asanas in an hour-long class. We remain at the back of the room, trying our best to imitate the postures. Jean is quite good at this, while I'm struggling with even the simplest moves. Years of high school and college sports have not been helpful to me in producing a flexible body. Even sitting on my heels is impossible! At the end of the hour, Jean seems exhilarated, while I'm in pain!

We then adjourn downstairs to a silent breakfast of *sambar, idli*, and chai. This is followed by a community cleanup period of the ashram and grounds, during which we begin to meet some of the students. Several students approach to pet Tashi, wanting to know all about her, and about us as an afterthought. Tashi, of course, is happy for the attention, and liberal with her licks. Dick is tall with a droopy mustache. He says that he's in his fourth year of a nine-year commitment to become a full-fledged yogi under the tutelage of Swamiji. We learn that he is the de facto leader of the students. Meenakshi says hello as well. She is also in her fourth year here and serves as Swamiji's secretary. She doesn't have a sleeping place on the roof, so I suspect that she is staying in Swamiji's rooms.

Ron, thin with a wispy brown beard, tells us that he came to Ananda Ashram to find a discipline to work with his chronic condition of pernicious anemia. He's a gentle soul, becoming a good friend during our stay at the ashram. We're to run into him again many months later in Delhi.

We learn that some of the students who have completed their first month of the three-month retreat are planning to leave in a few days. They complain about "King Gitananda," seeing him as an egotistical, intolerant bigot. Most of the others disagree, explaining that Swamiji is completely passionate about the discipline of yoga and determined to instill a proper view and conduct in his students.

We don't know what to think, but agree that, whatever the opinions of individuals, the students as a whole exhibit a sense of serenity and confidence, so different from most travelers we've seen on the road. In short, we're intrigued by this world of yoga.

We spend the next several days feeling out ashram life, taking all the classes offered, and meeting more Western and Indian students. All seem friendly and communicative, making us feel accepted in this community. We now have a difficult decision to make. By staying at the ashram, we may forfeit our ability to travel to Ceylon. Our visas are soon up for renewal, and if we do leave the country, we won't be allowed to return to India for six months. After a couple of days of deliberating back and forth, we approach Swamiji and tell him that we want to stay until the end of the program. He smiles broadly, ensuring us that we have made the right decision. Relieved of any conflicting emotions, we can now just concentrate on participating fully in the program.

Hi Again,

We are now in Pondicherry—4 hour bus ride from Madras— arriving around 5 p.m. We asked the rickshaw driver for a place to stay and he took us out of the city to an ashram (Hindu residency.) Upon arriving there were many young Westerners around & we found out that it was a school (sort of) for Yoga and meditation. So we were given dinner and room on the roof (covered) to sleep. We met the Swami Gitananda (the teacher and head of the ashram) and attended classes for the next two days. They told us of the new 1 month class opening up for Feb. and, after much deliberation, we've decided to stay & learn many healthy disciplines & a lot of yoga. It may mean not going to Ceylon because of visa problems, but we feel this is more important than that. So tomorrow we start our classes—wake up bell is 5:00 a.m., tea is 5:30, and our hatha yoga class is at 6:00. 7:30 is breakfast (all meals here are strictly vegetarian & geared toward health.) 8:30 is optional language class (Sanskrit or Tamil,) 9:00 required yoga/health/diet & relaxation class, 10:00 optional indigenous medicine and yoga therapy. 12:30

140

p.m. is lunch, 2:00 meditation, and 3:00 is Yantra teachings. 5:30 supper, 7:30 lecture & questions & meditation. 10:30 lights out! This goes on for 6 days a week, with Thurs. (after our 6 a.m. class) our day off. Tashi is adjusting to it all—she sleeps a lot during the day and will stay under the mosquito net when told. It costs us 8 rupees each a day (12 Rs to the dollar.) That includes our meals, lodging and classes—so it is quite cheap for us. The address is "Me," Ananda Ashram, Lawspet S.P.O., Pondicherry-8, South India. So write many times up until Feb. 28ᵗʰ, when we will probably leave. I can't wait to teach you & dad yoga & health—if done correctly it can cure thyroid (I'll still take my pill though) & much else—also rejuvenate you 20 yrs. But it's not easy & must be done constantly w/ a good diet. Hope all is well with all—we are healthy and happy. Love and miss you, Jean and Bruce

We'd missed our first month, the "cleansing period," during which students prepared themselves physically and spiritually for the next months of "rebalancing" and "advanced techniques." So at first we find ourselves over our heads in a sea of new terms, ideas, and basic instructions on postures and meditation techniques. After a couple of weeks of following the routine of the daily class schedule, asking and receiving advice from Swamiji and senior student Dick, we become more attuned to the various disciplines.

During that first month of the program, students were encouraged to fast for three days to cleanse themselves physically and mentally for the rigors of the more advanced yoga practices. As we weren't yet here, I decide to fast on my own, mainly to experience any changes in behavior and outlook. Jean opts out, preferring as usual to observe how her "guinea pig" fares with his discipline. The fast begins with a "saltwater purge," drinking many glasses of saltwater, performing releasing stomach exercises, and running to the toilet until nothing but saltwater is expelled. For the next three days, I experience a gamut of sensations and emotions, from dizziness, weakness, feeling false hunger, irritation, and jealousy of those who are eating. At the same time, I notice that my senses—seeing, hearing, smelling, and touching—are increasingly heightened. At the end of the fast, I feel proud of my small accomplishment and can't wait to start eating again. As I'm downing a big bowl of rice and vegetables, Meenakshi tells me that Swamiji once fasted for eighty-nine days!

About a dozen disgruntled students leave after our first week here. This concerns us, but we see two benefits in this: one, the remaining students seem fully committed to Swamiji and their yoga practices; and two, a couple who left offered us their separate bedroom on the second floor. The cost of the bedroom is only slightly higher than the general tuition fee, so we jump at the opportunity. Now we can have some privacy and leave Tashi in our room as we do our rooftop classes.

Swami Gitananda, as the heart and soul of Ananda Ashram, is the focus of everyone's attention. An amalgam of different influences, he was born in Maharajganj, in the state of Bihar, to an Indian father and Irish mother, which accounts for his light skin tone. He is a revered holy man and medical doctor who has practiced throughout the world. His knowledge of physical and spiritual disciplines is unassailable. We learn that he spends several hours each day treating local patients, primarily with traditional Ayurvedic medicine, at his medical clinic on the first floor. (The children we saw playing upon first arriving at the ashram were either waiting for their parents being treated, or patients themselves.) Particularly striking is Swamiji's concern for others, including ourselves, and his remarkable energy. Evening Satsangs are opportunities for all of us to absorb Swamiji's encyclopedic knowledge of all disciplines of yoga and traditional medicine. At the same time, his emotions are volatile; he can become angry and intolerant in an instant! His two main complaints seem to be the decadence of Western society and the corruption of the Aurobindo Ashram, and particularly Aurobindo's partner, The Mother. Suddenly, in the middle of a lecture, Swamiji will switch to a harsh accusation of something or someone he is opposed to. Question and answer periods following his lectures can sometimes degenerate into an argument with his students. I can understand why some students were so upset with him that they left the ashram.

When a student asks him one night about why the disgruntled students left, he declares, "I am not here to make money or gain your votes. Therefore, I do not have to please you. My job is to help you grow. And to grow, you have to shed all this false conditioning which binds you back."

During the afternoon rest periods before evening meals, many of us enjoy playing volleyball in the main courtyard. Tall and athletic Dick is always a team captain. Swamiji joins us sometimes, displaying good skills. Dick tells us that Swamiji was quite an athlete when he was younger and supports all kinds of community sports activities in the nearby village of Lawspet. I appreciate these light, relaxing moments, just having fun with Swamiji, our only focus helping each other hit a ball over a net.

As the days pass though, Tashi's sniffles and sneezing are increasing, and she's exuding ever more mucus from her nose, eyes, and tips of her ears. She's still her friendly self but has noticeably lost weight. Her energy has steadily dwindled to a point where she walks with some difficulty.

Swami says to us one morning, "I'm very concerned about Tashi. I think you need to take her to a veterinarian. There is a good one in Pondicherry."

"We saw one in Madras who told us Tashi just has allergies."

"Doctors make mistakes." I wonder if he is speaking from experience.

We're on a rickshaw with Tashi that very afternoon to the veterinary clinic a few kilometers away. During this first visit, the vet examines Tashi perfunctorily, quickly checking her eyes and nose and listening with an ancient stethoscope to her heart and lungs. The vet concludes that she has some fluid in her lungs, but this may just be the result of a bad cold. He gives Tashi an injection of penicillin "just in case," and asks us to come back the following day to see if her condition has improved. I don't feel confident in this diagnosis. The vet mainly works with cattle and farm animals, rarely with dogs, seen by so many locals as competitors for food and therefore unworthy of help. We ride back to the ashram in silence, lost in our own fears.

We've now visited that clinic seven days in a row, each time the vet giving Tashi a shot of penicillin. Tashi's condition has only deteriorated. She can no longer walk and is as limp as a rag doll. The mucus streaming from Tashi's eyes, nose, and ears has steadily increased.

Finally, the vet says, "The penicillin shots should have improved her condition. There is nothing more I can do."

We arrive weary and disheartened back at the ashram with our sick puppy. By now, Swamiji and all the students are awaiting news of Tashi's condition, and then give us condolences and some words of advice and encouragement. We're just too tired to participate in the afternoon classes, and retreat to our room.

The days pass slowly. Tashi won't eat but is constantly thirsty. Jean and I exchange times going to classes and sitting with Tashi, giving her glucose water, and cleaning out the fluid pouring from her nose, eyes, and ears. Nothing really helps, and our hope steadily fades for her recovery. We are spent emotionally and physically.

When Tashi begins convulsing, all we can do is hold her. She's lost all recognition of us, and during one convulsion, nips Jean's finger. We're finally too exhausted to continue the struggle. We can no longer deny that Tashi is dying. Jean is so overcome that she lies on the bed and falls into a deep sleep.

I go to Swamiji and say, "Tashi's dying."

"Yes," he replies, "I fear she has distemper. She cannot survive much longer."

"Can you give her something to speed up the process? She's in such agony."

"If this is what you wish, I can give you something. But you must administer this yourself, as I won't take on the karma of killing her."

144

We go together downstairs to the clinic and Swamiji gives me a hypodermic needle.

"This is a combination of methedrine and adrenaline. Inject her anywhere and she'll soon be out of her body."

I hold Tashi for a long while, searching in vain for a last sign of hope, before injecting the needle into her side. Her convulsions stop almost immediately, but she now begins to spin on her side, eyes closed and yapping as though she's chasing or running from something in her sleep. I hear Swami just beginning Satsang upstairs. I wait an hour for the drugs to take effect, but the puppy just continues to spin and yap. Finally, I can't bear it anymore, go upstairs and interrupt Satsang and tell Swamiji that the drugs aren't working. He seems perturbed by this, saying that he'll be down in a little while.

I return to our room. Jean is still sleeping, perhaps not willing to wake to this nightmare. I sit and watch Tashi spin and yap. Another hour passes and Swamiji is still talking upstairs. I go through a gamut of emotions: anger at Swamiji for not coming down, despair for our dog, and worry about Jean. All I can finally feel is numb.

Swamiji comes into the room at last and is surprised that Tashi is still alive. "Those drugs should have shot her out of her body immediately. She's a very strong soul to hold on for so long."

I'm in tears, words streaming out of me from a place I've never known. "I don't care. She just needs to die!"

Swami leaves, returning a few minutes later with another needle of adrenaline and methedrine that he administers himself. Then we both sit and watch Tashi spin and yap.

After a long while, Swamiji says, "Bring the dog downstairs."

Just as I carry Tashi down to the ashram gardens, dogs in nearby Lawspet begin to howl, sensing, I think, this tragic loss of one of their own. I'm amazed by how light my dog is, just flesh and bones. At Swamiji's direction, a couple of participants have already dug a shallow grave under a Banyan tree. Swamiji now reappears with a large needle of strychnine that he says he uses only for horses. Just as he injects the needle in the base of Tashi's skull, the howling of dogs grows even louder. It takes only a minute for Tashi's weak movements to slow down and then stop. At this exact moment, the howling ceases! Swami and I look at each other, a moment of understanding beyond words. We lay Tashi in the garden grave, cover her and say words of prayer for her great spirit. It's midnight, seven hours since I gave Tashi that first injection.

Standing at the grave, I remember something. "Swamiji, Tashi nipped Jean's finger during a convulsion."

This seems to worry him. We stand in silence a while longer.

Then he says, "There is no way of knowing for sure what Tashi died of. I think that it was distemper, but it might also have been rabies. The only way of determining whether Tashi had rabies is to cut off her head and send it up to the veterinary hospital in Madras. This could take two weeks, and by then, if it is rabies, Jean will be dead."

Now fear for Jean creeps in and mixes with my grief for Tashi. Swamiji concludes that Jean will have to go the very next day to the medical clinic in Pondicherry to receive rabies shots. I'm too tired to process this at the moment. I thank Swamiji and the participants for their help, return to our room, and fall into a deep sleep.

Jean awakens the next morning feeling better, until I recount the details of the previous night and Swamiji's insistence that Jean undergo the anti-rabies treatment, a shot each day for fourteen days, administered in a circle around her navel! We cry together as Meenakshi makes arrangements for a rickshaw to take us to the local hospital in Pondicherry.

Jean and I spend the following sad days riding bicycles and rickshaws to Pondicherry for her painful shots, which we alleviate afterward with coffee and ice cream. At some point, we recall how ironic it was when Swamiji said to us upon first meeting him and introducing Tashi: "I see your world has no problems."

Feb. 27

Dear Dad, Mom and Nancy,

We received your letter of this month—always good to know that we're being thought of. I hope everyone is feeling better and looking forward to a well-deserved Spring. Please convey our love to Grandma Tillie, Uncle Harry, Tanta Karen and our various friends. Our life in Ananda Ashram this past month has, for the most part, been a happy, productive one. We've learned a lot about many aspects of yoga living, including: Hatha Yoga, Yoga Therapy (can't wait to get back and work on your bodies a little,) relaxation, meditation, Yantra (an ancient mathematics system that works with life cycles through a basic pattern of nine,) and Satsanga, the nightly talks of everything under the sun by Swami Gitananda. We've become so attached to this way of life in fact, that we'll stay through March, the end of the course.

Last Thursday, after a two-week downhill struggle, we were forced to put Tashi to sleep. As a result of the damp southern climate, Tashi caught pneumonia. This was further complicated by spinal meningitis, a hopelessly fatal condition. In 17 days, she changed from a healthy, chubby dog to a living skeleton, convulsing every half-hour. So it was time for her to leave her body, just a short period on this earth. Her karma is good and we hope to see each other again. Amen ...

Everyone at the ashram is excited about the upcoming South India temple tour, an annual week-long trip Swamiji takes his students on to visit famous Hindu temples. Dick tells us that Swamiji is also excited as he considers this tour essential to his students' understanding and appreciation of the breadth of Hindu culture and the depth of its adherents' devotion. As it's scheduled just a week after Jean has begun her shots, we've resigned ourselves to staying behind.

Swamiji approaches me one day and asks, "Do you two want to join the group on the temple tour?"

"Yes, of course," I reply, "but I don't see how we can. Jean is only halfway through her treatment."

"Oh," he smiles, "I think we can arrange something."

We find out that evening that Swamiji has gone to the hospital and convinced the doctor to give him enough anti-rabies serum to finish the last seven days of shots. He has also arranged for a young doctor at his clinic to join us for the sole purpose of administering Jean's shots. All the students who have lived with our loss of Tashi express their happiness that we can join them on the tour. Swamiji seems satisfied as well. Now nobody will be left behind.

Early in the morning, Swamiji and his thirty students load onto a bus headed south through the state of Tamil Nadu. The plan is to visit the most famous temples; perform pujas, or devotional ceremonies; eat in nearby restaurants; and rest in *dharmsalas*, the hostels provided for pilgrims. The route and schedule are well-planned as Swamiji has been leading this excursion for a number of years.

Most of the temples we're to visit, Swamiji tells us, are built in the Dravidian style: pyramid-like structures displaying elaborate sacred carvings inside and out. Our first stop is Chidambaram, a city of temple complexes. The main temple, Nataraja Temple, with its golden dome and intricate stone carvings, is one of the oldest temples in India, dating back 1,500 years. The temple and its surrounding area are teeming with *pujaris* (priests), pilgrims, and vendors selling food, incense, red powdered vibhuti, mementos, and statuary. Bell ringing, incense smoke, and fried food assault the senses. Only a few people seem surprised to see us, and no one questions Swami Gitananda as he leads us into one of the inner chambers to perform private puja. He is considered a revered personage, and besides, many have seen him and his annual gaggle of young Western students before.

The central figure in the temple is Nataraja, the "dancing Shiva," who dances on the head of the demon Muyalaka, the embodiment of ignorance. A pujari leads us all in performing an offering puja of flowers and incense while we repeat the requisite Sanskrit mantras. Afterward, we find a restaurant large enough to accommodate our group and enjoy the South Indian cuisine of *dosai*, thin pancakes filled with assorted vegetables, rice, and dal.

After lunch, we visit nearby Thiruvetkalam Temple, dedicated to the goddess Kali. She is an aspect of Shiva's consort, Shaki, who destroys everything that prevents *moksha*, or "liberation." Her image is terrifying: blue-black in color, eyes fiercely gazing, tongue extended, she has four arms, one holding a sword and another holding the severed head of a demon. She stands with one leg on the passive body of Shiva himself. The puja we perform is similar to the first in the Nataraja temple, but the chants are louder and more forceful.

The next day, we visit Sri Ranganatha Temple, this time performing pujas to the god Vishnu. Vishnu is one of the triumvirate of Hindu gods, along with Brahma, the Creator, and Shiva, the Destroyer. Vishnu is the Preserver, specifically of Brahma's creation of the world, and is worshipped as the one who protects mankind from destructive or evil calamities.

We travel farther south in Tamil Nadu to the city of Madurai. We arrive on the eve of Shivaratri, the annual celebration of Shiva's "birthday." Thousands of pilgrims from all over South India have already arrived. The air is thick with incense and ceaseless bell ringing as hundreds of pujas are in session. We spend an entire day at the Meenakshi Temple, dedicated to Meenakshi Devi (after whom our ashram secretary is named), an aspect of the goddess Parvati, a consort of Shiva. This is considered the largest temple in India, consisting of a great network of passages and shrines, bordered by four two-hundred-foot-tall *gopurams*, ornate pyramid-like structures, and is served by five thousand pujaris and their families. A pujari leads us into an inner sanctum, where we perform pujas to the consort Meenakshi Devi. Dick tells us that only teachers of the highest status, such as Swamiji, are allowed into this part of the temple. Even some of the pujaris who live within the temple grounds are not allowed in this area!

Dick says, "Here we are, all of us Westerners with just a short introduction to Hinduism in our time at the ashram, now allowed to accompany Swamiji into the most sacred chambers in every temple we visit, and all because of how venerated he is."

For Swamiji, overseeing the travel, temple tours, and arranging for meals and accommodations at dharmsalas for thirty students is a full-time occupation. He's a stickler for punctuality, and the inevitable wait for stragglers to enter temples or show up at restaurants makes his blood boil! Aside from the young doctor administering rabies injections for Jean, his only official aide is an older Indian "ashramite" named Mister Vajranath, charged with making the necessary arrangements. He is ill-suited for the job, often becoming confused and forgetful, and so is a regular recipient of Swamiji's wrath. The rest of us steer clear of Swamiji during these moments, knowing that, as quick to anger as he is, he is also quick to let the anger subside, often with apologies all around.

At dusk, we settle into our rooms at a nearby dharmsala. Swamiji instructs us to break up into small groups and find our own food for the evening before gathering together at the temple at 11:00 p.m. for a grand puja to celebrate Shivaratri. Jean and I find ourselves hooked up with Sheila and Tom. Sheila is a wealthy young Brit, self-described as a "jet-setter," who decided to try out yoga "as a lark." She's been at the ashram since the beginning of the course but confides that she's no fan of Swamiji. "For a supposed holy man, he certainly can lose his shit!" Tom has been in the Peace Corps in South India for two years and came to the ashram to study a "body–mind" discipline before returning home. We can see that he and Sheila have hooked up as a couple, but they're so different from each other, we wonder how long their relationship will last. Then we both smile, realizing just how different the two of us are! We spend the evening walking the streets, caught up in the festivities of color and music, as more and more people converge around the temple. We meet up with the rest of our party at 11:00 p.m. and enter the temple with Swamiji. This time, there are a dozen pujaris assisting Swamiji in performing puja, a ceremony with more incense and vibhuti than we've ever seen before! We're all exhausted at the end of the night. This whole day of celebrating Shivaratri, the most sacred day in and around one of the most sacred temples, has been fascinating, so dreamlike.

Upon awakening the next morning, many of us climb up to the top of one of the temple's four gopurams to watch the sunrise. How peaceful to be sitting atop this ancient structure, viewing miles and miles of awakening earth and sky! Returning to the dharmsala, however, I find that Jean isn't feeling well and has developed a slight fever. She has started her period and is having a reaction to the daily rabies shots. The young ashram doctor who is charged with giving her the shots is very shy and nervous about having to inject Jean's exposed belly. As a result, his awkward shots are much more painful than those administered at the Pondicherry hospital, causing hard lumps and angry red rashes at his injection sites. His technique does improve toward the end of the trip, but Jean continues to feel ill, often staying behind on the bus during our temple visits.

Our next stop is the city of Rameshwaram, at the southernmost tip of the Indian subcontinent, where boats regularly cross a narrow channel to the country of Ceylon. We have to leave the bus at one point and take a shuttle train across a bridge to the sandy island of Pamban, where the city is located. Arriving in the city at night, Swamiji splits us into two groups with orders to find dinner for ourselves and then locate the dharmsala where we'll be staying. This proves not to be the best instruction as each group splits into factions based on food preference, and most get lost trying to find the dharmsala. Eventually, we all arrive safely and bed down for the night.

Sunrise the next morning finds us all on a nearby beach practicing hatha yoga. After breakfast, all but Jean, who doesn't feel able to join us, head off to the city's Ramanathaswamy Temple.

This temple is dedicated to Shiva as the Lingum Ramanathaswamy. There are actually two *lingums* in the inner sanctums: one created by Rama, the seventh *avatar*, or "incarnation," of Vishnu, and one brought to the temple by his loyal general,

151

Hanuman, also known as the Monkey God. (Both of these deities appear in the Indian classic, *The Ramayana*.) Again, of Dravidian architecture, the temple's gopurams are connected with corridors, reputed to be the longest in India.

The most avid of us to visit the temple is old Dr. Rao. Bent with his eighty-six years, the tour has been difficult for him, and he has often stayed on the bus when we've gone into the various temples. But this is the very reason he has made such a big effort to come. Rameshwaram is where he was born, and he hasn't been back since he was a teenager. With the help of a strong student on each arm, he slowly makes his way into the temple, down a long corridor, to perform a private puja in an inner sanctum.

A carnival atmosphere is taking place outside the large entrance to the temple. Vendors are everywhere, even inside the temple itself, all hawking food, mementos, vibhuti, and incense. An elephant blesses some students on their heads with his trunk for a few paisa. Several ash-covered, skeleton-thin saddhus approach us seeking alms. One, who actually has a long dagger piercing his cheeks and running through his blood-stained mouth, charges us 20 paisa per each photograph we take of him. Swamiji escorts us into the temple to an inner chamber where once again we perform puja.

We return to the dharmsala with just enough time to pack up and catch the train back to our bus. The train is so crowded, some of us have to stand. Swamiji is in a bad mood after having to yell at some ashramites for almost missing the train. Swamiji is seated, but now an Indian with a long, dusty bedroll stands next to him. Seeing a spot on the luggage rack above Swamiji, he throws his bedroll up, its dust and dirt falling on Swamiji's head. This is the last straw! Yelling at the skinny man in Hindi, 250-pound Swamiji grabs him by the collar, lifts him off the floor, and bounces him up and down. His act of violence shocks everyone! His anger quickly spent, Swamiji apologizes to the poor man, and spends the next several hours expressing sorrow for what he had done.

The long ride back to Pondicherry takes two days, with wayside stops for food and rest. We pass the hours on the bus sharing life stories and singing group songs. On the way, we stop at our final site, Thiruparankundram Murugan Temple. A Shiva temple, it was built into granite rock in the sixth century, its fascia marked by dozens of colorful, life-sized sculptures of the hero Muraga, who slayed a demon who had imprisoned Indra, the god of the celestial deities. Families of monkeys are seated on the sculptures and the temple walls. Swamiji tells us these monkeys are cared for by the temple pujaris and the many pilgrims who visit each day. "But, don't get too close to them, and hold tightly to your bags, as they can be very aggressive!" Some of the larger, alpha monkeys strutting confidently along the walls, do seem to be sizing us up for a quick "grab and run." As always, the pujaris are deferential to Swamiji and his students as we enter the temple to perform puja.

We finally arrive back at Ananda Ashram in the evening, our bus met by the ashram staff and some villagers from Lawspet, who are abuzz with questions of our trip. A meal has been prepared for our return. Exhausted, most of us eat quickly and go right to bed.

Dear Mom, Dad and Nancy,

... We've just returned from a week-long tour of South India with Dr. Swami Gitananda. We visited a huge temple in Madurai for Shivaratri, Shiva's birthday, journeyed further south to a Vishnu temple on the island of Rameshwaram, then next to Trichingopoly. We finally returned, a weary crew, last night. All in all, we had fun-filled, informative excursion.

So we continue to learn in hopes of progressive evolution, and trust you are doing the same. We plan to send letters soon to John and Marcia, and Randy and Merle. We think of you every day.

Love, Bruce and Jean

It's business as usual the next morning, with hatha yoga to begin the day. I'm a bit surprised that the alarm clock rings as, minutes later, Dr. Rao slowly shuffles his way to the mat up front. He looked so spent upon arriving from the trip, I thought he might allow himself to sleep in. The daily schedule proceeds as before, with Thursdays our day off after morning hatha yoga. Early Friday mornings, the hatha yoga class, minus Dr. Rao, bikes to a nearby beach to do our asanas at sunrise.

I become fascinated with our daily afternoon study of *yantra*, an ancient method of determining characteristics defined by *chakras*, the twelve psychic centers in and just outside the body. An in-depth study of yantra takes up volumes of information but, in general, this is an explanation through numbers, one through nine, of a person's life cycle as determined by their date of birth and spelling of their name. The date of birth is one's "Birth Path" number, and the spelling of one's first and family names determine the numbers defining one's "plane of mind," outer appearance, expression, and destiny. These numbers can be interpreted as positive and negative in relation to the Birth Path number. Jean's birthday is an eight in the Birth Path, corresponding to the eighth chakra, outside the right ear of the body, while mine is a three, the third chakra in the solar plexus. Each number has specific characteristics, with associated colors, animals, and so on. Jean, as an eight, embodies characteristics that include: justice, authority, integrity, charity, and grace. Her color is dark blue, and her animals are hippos and rhinos. As a three, my characteristics are expressive, artistic, magnetic, ambitious, argumentative, and intolerant. The colors are yellow and royal blue, and the animals are large cats. (I'm told that Swamiji is also a three in the Birth Path, which makes sense, as he's magnetic, but can certainly become intolerant and argumentative!) However, an analysis of my name indicates that it does not line up well with my Birth Path number. In fact, my destiny reads, "bankruptcy in all fields of action"!

I approach Swamiji and say, "The destination for my Birth Path number is terrible! How can I change it?"

"Just change your name," he replies.

"But I don't want to return to my home as a Rama or Krishna. I think it would devastate my parents."

"Well then, just change the spelling of your name."

"Really? That will make a difference in my destiny?"

"Of course it will. Any change will produce a different result."

Thanking Swamiji, I return to my notes to work out a different spelling. At the end, I'm satisfied. I'm now Brus, pronounced the same way, and my destination is favorable. Jean is amused by my new name at first, calling me Brush, but I'm determined and further encouraged when our friend, Ron, changes the spelling of his name to Ronn. Others in the ashram have also changed their names. One doesn't study yantra materials for hours on end without being affected by its interpretations, particularly for us young and impressionable Western students. My name change has stuck with me to this day.

Just as the final month of the program begins, Dr. Rao dies. According to Swamiji, he suffered two major heart attacks in the middle of the night, the first one straightening out his bent body, and the second shooting him out of his body.

In the early morning, several Indian ashramites lay his body out on a table on the front porch, while others adorn him with flowers. Then we all gather around the body to perform a puja to help him on his transition from life to death.

Before beginning, Swamiji tells us Dr. Rao's life story. "Years ago, Dr. Rao was a yogi, renowned throughout South India. Following a calling for missionary service, he left his wife and children and traveled to America to teach yoga and diet. He was gone for many years, so long that he was unknown to new generations of Indians. He ran into bad times in the 'Promised Land' succumbing to alcohol, losing his practice and his money. Old and dejected, he returned to his home in Bangalore to find, to his amazement, the wife he had left fifty years before waiting for him! Several years passed, enjoying the company of his wife, children, and grandchildren. When his wife died, he knew that he must return to the spiritual path. He approached me and supplicated to be able to come here and reestablish the yogic disciplines he had forsaken. His present to me were these *sannyasa* beads," he touches coral beads around his neck, "as a tribute to my degree of attainment. He told me then, 'When I have finally reached the stage of *sannyasa*, I will ask for these beads back.' Dr. Rao has been here for more than a year now, practicing daily and participating in all of our special events. He came on our temple tour knowing he didn't have much longer to live. Now that he is free of his body, he is ready to advance to the degree of *sannyasa*."

At Swamiji's direction, Dr. Rao's body is positioned to face the rising sun. We all participate in a sannyasa ritual, chanted in Hindi. At the end of the ceremony, Swamiji declares that Dr. Rao is now renamed Sita Rama Rao, and removes the sannyasa beads from his neck, placing them around the neck of Dr. Rao.

Following the ritual and throughout the day, many villagers, young and old, come to lay flowers and pay their respects. The mood of the day is joyful, for the belief is that his *atman*, or "soul," is finally free of the old body and can now continue freely on its journey. We're also excited about the plans to cremate Dr. Rao that very afternoon as, by law in hot and humid South India, a body must be disposed of in twenty-four hours to prevent the spread of disease. A cremation pyre is already being built on a dune in front of the ashram. All classes are suspended as we participate in the cleaning of the building, a customary act following the death of a family member.

We spend the afternoon sitting on the porch with Dr. Rao. Dick tells us of his conversations with Dr. Rao, who was always insightful and had a wicked sense of humor. Meenakshi relates that, just this morning, as she was gathering Dr. Rao's possessions in his room, his alarm clock went off, causing her to jump. "I almost had a heart attack myself! Dr. Rao was already laid out on the porch, but maybe the alarm signaled the moment when his soul was finally free."

"Or maybe," Dick adds, "this was Dr. Rao's last joke!"

In the early afternoon, we see a car slowly making its way over the dune toward the ashram. Four Indian men emerge and ask to see the Swami. Meenakshi asks them to wait and then returns to lead them to Swamiji's quarters. A half hour later, she comes downstairs to inform us that these men are relatives of Dr. Rao's wife, and they've come to take his body back to Bangalore immediately as the trip is long and they're also charged with having to dispose of his body within twenty-four hours.

She continues, "They have all the necessary legal papers, so they are within their rights to take Dr. Rao away."

Everyone's mood changes suddenly from joyful to sad, even angry, as it seems so unfair that these men are just going to take Dr. Rao away, depriving him his opportunity to have a proper sannyasa cremation. We all watch the men pick up Dr. Rao from his dais and carry him to the car. They have a difficult time getting him into the back seat as rigor mortis has already set in. Finally, they bend him in sitting position and position him in the back seat. Then, without another word, they all climb in, with two men on either side of the body, arms around his shoulders. This would be very funny if we aren't so sad. Farewell, Sita Rama Rao.

Sat. March 6
Hi Again,
... When you get a headache, tell Dad to massage the deepest part of the inside of your hands, with good pressure, using his thumbs. Then shake out your hands, doing some deep breathing (slowly) while lying down, and relax! It works! One of the students (an 86 year old man) died yesterday morning from a stroke, so we had the day off, and a Hindu-style death ceremony went on. He was lying on the porch for the day waiting for the sunset and cremation on the back grounds. Swami spoke to us of death & tried to teach us the difference between Eastern & Western thought. He quoted an author's words, "Tell us what happens after death. I say sunrise." A very meaningful quote for me. No more room—both well and happy and learning. Miss and love you, Jean and Bruce

As the days move on in the third month, our practices become more involved. We're now introduced to *Laya Kriya* practices to harness the energy of the chakras from the first chakra, *Muladhara*, at

the base of the spine, to the seventh chakra, *Sahasrasa*, at the crown
of the head. Jean becomes so proficient in opening the Muladhara
chakra that her body shakes with vibrations and starts spinning like
a top! At one point, Swamiji sits behind her, wraps his arms and legs
around her body, and breathes deeply. Within minutes, her shaking stops, causing the unleashed power of the chakra to become
centered. Other students concentrate on levitation techniques—
our friend, Sheila, lifting from the ground enough to bounce along
the floor! Our diet now is restricted to raw foods, which actually
increase our energy. Many students are fasting entirely. We all experience, to varying degrees, great energy and heightened senses. We
practice throughout the day, whether we're in formal classes or not.
No one sleeps more than a few hours a night.

During this last month, our daily routine is interrupted by special events. The first is the *darshan*, or "blessing," for the ninety-
third birthday of The Mother, the Italian partner of Sri Aurobindo.
After his death, she remained in Pondicherry, overseeing his estate,
including Auroville and many properties and businesses within the
city. She is well loved and considered a saint by many. Although
Swamiji is no fan of hers, he allows us all to go for a few hours
to Pondicherry for the darshan. We join a throng of pilgrims in
the street below a large office building, waiting excitedly for The
Mother to appear. Suddenly, someone points upward, and the
crowd immediately quiets. Appearing over a wall on the building's
rooftop above us is an unsmiling, tiny, and wizened figure, a dark
scarf wrapping her head. As we watch, she systematically scans the
crowd with penetrating dark eyes and then seems to float to another
part of the roof to scan some more. Is she somehow on wheels? Is
she looking for someone in particular? Many pilgrims around us
offer prayers, with some weeping openly. I suppose I'm looking for
something spectacular, perhaps an aura emanating from her, but
all I see is an old woman. Just a few minutes after appearing, she
disappears behind the wall of the roof. The darshan is over. We
return to the ashram and our not-so-mysterious teacher.

Swamiji announces during one evening Satsang that he is reviving the "Horse Festival" in the village of Lawspet. "The Horse Festival was held every year at this time to ensure good crops and good fortune for the upcoming year. A statue of Lord Shiva in the village temple was placed on the back of a special horse, groomed all year for this purpose. The statue is then carried through the village as a blessing to all, before being returned to the temple. But one year, a mistake was made. The horse chosen for the festival was promised on that same night for a wedding financed by a wealthy landowner to carry his son, the groom, to his bride. There were many protests, but the wedding planners insisted that they had the first right to use the horse. But just as the groom was hoisted atop the horse, the horse dropped dead! The temple pujaris proclaimed that this was a bad omen and that the Horse Festival must be canceled indefinitely. The temple was locked. That was twenty years ago, and the temple hasn't been opened since. So now I have been meeting with the pujaris to revive this three-day festival, and I will need your help with all the details."

To prepare, we work with the villagers to gather food and flowers, as Swamiji, with the help of senior student Dick, scouts around the area to rent a horse. The temple is opened again and the pujaris labor to clean years of dust and mold from the building.

When all is prepared, Swamiji leads a procession to the temple, with Dick holding the reins of a big brown thoroughbred bedecked in flowers, followed by villagers and ashramites. Swamiji holds an elaborate puja to open the temple. Then the Shiva idol is taken down from the central shrine and placed on the horse's back. However, the horse wants nothing to do with this, bucking wildly to remove whatever is on his back! It takes all of Dick's strength to hold onto the reins, as several villagers struggle to balance the idol on the horse's back. Finally, the horse calms down enough to be led throughout the village streets. The villagers are ecstatic, many praying and singing while their laughing children run up to touch the nervous horse, whose wild eyes signal that he is one step away from bolting altogether. Two villagers even fall to the ground, screaming that they have seen God! Swamiji, undeterred by all the hoopla, calmly leads the procession back to the temple, where the idol is removed from the horse's back and replaced on the shrine. He then declares the ceremony successful, ensuring that the signs are favorable for good crops and fortune for the village of Lawspet. This signals the beginning of festivities: three days of feasting, music, and dancing. The highlight for me comes on the first evening, when the renowned "Katha Kali" dancers display their remarkable acrobatic skills under the lights of tall torches. After this first day, we students return to our daily schedule, as the villagers continue to celebrate for the next two days. Meenakshi tells us later that the entire festival has been financed by Swamiji.

Still another event is the bathing of the gods in the sea. The day-long procession of gods—idols placed in carts decorated with flowers—include all the major and minor deities of the people of Pondicherry. The procession ends at a sandy beach, where each idol is carried into the sea and ceremoniously dunked numerous times, depending on the rites accorded that particular deity. Swamiji maintains that the best way to observe these ceremonies is from one hundred yards offshore, so many students spend hours treading water. Jean and I remain on the beach, high and dry.

Finally, an unscheduled event occurs when a number of us are late to yantra class because we were playing music after lunch and lost track of the time. Swamiji becomes so angry that he orders all students out of the ashram and stomps off to his apartments. With no place to go, most of us bicycle into Pondicherry and spend the afternoon in the coffee shop. Finally, Meenakshi arrives and tells us that we can now return. At evening Satsang, Swami walks in and just continues with a subject started the previous night, as if nothing had happened.

The end of the course is approaching quickly, and many of us are practicing double-time to gain as much experience and knowledge as possible. As each practice instills energy, no one is exhausted. The combination of our regular activities, combined with our participation in special events, has melded us into a cohesive, caring community. The atmosphere is charged with great appreciation of Swamiji and all we've experienced, along with the sadness of imminent departing from one another.

On the last full day of the course, Swamiji calls for a special *"guru puja,"* a traditional ceremony to honor the ashram guru, and to ensure his long life for the benefit of all of his past, present and future students. A raised dais was set up in the garden the previous night, and now Swamiji, bedecked in rich ceremonial dress, ascends the dais and settles on a cushion. One by one, we approach the dais, his older students prostrating, and offer our gifts of flowers and rupees to this lion of a man who, with all his knowledge and passion, has taught us so much. We'll be forever grateful to have received these precious teachings of yoga from Swami Gitananda.

We remain at Ananda Ashram a few days after the course has ended, saying goodbye to new friends, all leaving to different destinations, and preparing ourselves for the journey north. We're anxious now to return to the Himalayas. We've been able to extend our visas for three more months in Pondicherry and really don't want to leave India. The irony of first skipping Nepal and now Ceylon to stay in India is not lost on us. So much has changed since we arrived at this "hippie hotel" with our sweet puppy. A couple at the course, Richard and Zena, are full of praises for Manali, a small town at seven thousand feet in the northeastern state of Himachal Pradesh, where they were recently married in a Hindu ceremony. This seems like a good destination for us, at least for a while.

We say goodbye to Swamiji, who reminds us to continue to study and practice yoga. He tells us that he is also leaving Ananda Ashram for a couple of months on a lecture tour throughout India, accompanied by Meenakshi and Dick. (We're to find out much later that Meenakshi has given birth to a baby boy, his son, who they name Ananda Balayogi.)

Our final tearful goodbye is to Tashi at her gravesite in the ashram gardens. We've often reflected how much our dear puppy gave us in her short life. Through her, we experienced a great depth of joy, loss, and sorrow. She was our beloved catalyst in helping us to further mature and bond together.

We decide to bus to the city of Bangalore on our way north. We've heard that this is the home of Satya Sai Baba, a Hindu guru to many Indians and Westerners. We're curious to see him as he is reputed to have psychic abilities and produce miracles. Many consider him to be among the greatest saints in India.

A taxi takes us through the city center of modern office buildings and boulevards to a funky little hotel striped in a riot of colors, with an attached restaurant, its sign reading "Pancake and Hamburger House." A Western woman named Sarah shows us to an adequate room. We tell her that we're here to see Satya Sai Baba.

"Oh," she says, "I'm a devotee of his. There are many of us here from all over the world."

I ask, "Is he near here?"

"His ashram is in Whitehall, a town about twenty minutes outside the city. But buses leave to there from just down the street all the time."

"So," Jean asks, "can we go to his ashram anytime?"

"Of course. Everyone is welcome, but the best times to visit are during his darshans. There are two a day, one in the morning and one in the afternoon."

We decide to spend the day exploring Bangalore. After a tasty pancake breakfast, we lose ourselves wandering through streets until we happen upon a zoo. The rest of the day is spent observing animals, particularly the amusing baboons. We return to the hotel for a passable hamburger and fries before an early bedtime.

We catch an early bus the next morning to Whitehall, thinking that, if we enjoy the morning darshan, we'll stay for the next one in the afternoon. From the Whitehall bus stop, we walk along a high white wall encircling the ashram grounds until we reach the entrance. More than a hundred Indians and Westerners are milling around in the lush, well-manicured ashram gardens, waiting for the guru to arrive.

We must look a little lost because a large bald man with a heavy New York accent approaches us and, without introducing himself, says, "You know, you two are among the most fortunate people on earth."

"Oh?" I ask. "Why is that?"

"Because you are about to see the Avatar."

We don't know how to respond to this as he takes me by the arm and leads us to a shady place under a low tree in the garden.

"This is the best place to see *Guruji*," he beams. Then, apparently noticing Jean following close behind for the first time, he says to her harshly, "This area is reserved for men only. Women sit over there," indicating an area to our left, and slightly behind.

Now we notice that, indeed, the women and men are split up. What's more, the women, both Indian and Western, are wearing full saris; all, that is, except Jean, who's wearing a thin skirt and sleeveless blouse, her regular dress at Ananda Ashram, clearly inappropriate for this occasion.

Just then, we spot Richard and Zena from the ashram entering the gardens, giving us an excuse to escape our brash New York devotee. We're happy to see each other, familiar faces in a sea of strangers. They've just arrived on a night train, coming directly to Whitehall. Zena is dressed like Jean, but now she pulls two light shawls from her travel bag so they can at least cover their shoulders. Richard and I go to the shade tree with the rest of the men. A silence now falls over the crowd in anticipation of Satya Sai Baba's appearance. Suddenly, Baba appears in the gardens! Even though I was looking exactly in that direction, I don't know how he got there! Dark-skinned, with a large ball of afro hair, he glides silently though the crowd, his long white robe trailing behind him. Receiving a gift from one person, he gives it to another. His eyes move from one person to the next, seemingly looking for someone or something. I see several people shouldering their way through others to get closer to him as he continues gliding through the gardens. He then touches three people on their heads, two men and a woman, and slowly leads them to a large house at the end of the gardens. Why and where is he taking them? The darshan is over, having lasted no more than ten minutes.

The crowd now mingles, talking excitedly about the darshan. I hear people talking about the "miracle" they witnessed when Baba produced vibhuti from his mouth. None of the four us from Ananda Ashram saw this.

Although the morning darshan has been interesting, we don't feel the need to stay for the afternoon one. Besides, having just arrived, Richard and Zena are hungry and in need of lodging. We all bus back to the hotel and assure Sarah that the darshan was wonderful as she shows Richard and Zena to their room. We all go to the Bombay Circus in the evening. No Ringling Brothers, this little two ring affair features several tired acts. We leave before the finale, laughing that they should have paid us to sit through those performances.

Jean and I spend the next morning buying food for the evening train to Delhi. We spend the afternoon with Richard and Zena, who will stay in Bangalore another day before heading north. We all see the humor in our mutual influence; after speaking with us, they are now considering a visit to Darjeeling, just as, after speaking with them at Ananda Ashram, we are considering Manali. We engage in a group *Laya Kriya* meditation before parting and wishing each other safe travels.

MANALI

By nighttime we're settled into our third class berths on the train. The journey from Bangalore to Delhi via Madras lasts fifty-five hours, passing through the states of Mysore, Tamil Nadu, Andhra Pradesh, Rajasthan, finally into Haryana, and its capital, Delhi. Although we're traveling north, the April heat of the plains seems to intensify. At first scrutinized by our fellow Indian passengers, hours through similar landscapes, eating together, with frequent naps all around, breeds a bond of bored familiarity. The train stops are infrequent as this is an express train. Most of our fellow passengers get off at a stop on our second day, leaving us with a vague sense of loss. The new passengers converse loudly, apparently excited to be on their new train venture. That night, a passenger insists on keeping the compartment door open, despite the loud noise of the engine and cold air coming in. I ask him nicely twice to please close the door. Other passengers urge him to do the same, to no avail. Finally, I leap down from my berth and slam the door shut, yelling at the man to leave it shut. Nobody says a word. I climb back up to my berth, feeling surprised and a little ashamed of my action, mixed with some pride in my boldness. I've roared like a lion, like Gitananda! The compartment door remains closed for the rest of the night.

We arrive in Delhi on the morning of the third day. Intense heat assails us on leaving the train, even this early in the morning. Hot and dusty, our first priority is a bath. We've decided beforehand not to return to Colacco's Guest House, but to save money by staying at the Youth Hostel Camp recommended by Ronn, our friend from the ashram. A full hour's search by taxi brings us to a dusty, treeless encampment high up on a hill overlooking Delhi. A sleepy chowkidar collects four rupees and shows us to two bunk beds in a long metal Quonset building.

I ask him, "Where is your bath?"

"Oh, I am sorry, sahib," he replies. "There is no running water here during the days, and only a little in the early mornings."

"What?" Jean exclaims.

"Oh yes, it is true, sadly. The water reservoir is just there," he explains, pointing to a nearby large cement structure on the hillside. "We are too high up here for the gravity to bring us water."

Jean demands, "Well, how can we get a bath?"

"Oh, there are very nice baths down below in New Delhi. I can direct you there."

"Is this what the other guests do?" I ask.

"Not at all, sahib. You see, there are no other guests right now."

Sure enough, all the other cots in the building are empty. At another time, we wouldn't consider such accommodations, but we're healthy and strong from our time at Ananda Ashram and decide to at least give this a go.

For the next few days, we awaken to the heat of the morning sun beating down on the hostel's tin roof, do a few minutes of hatha yoga, and wash and brush our teeth in a trickle of water before heading down by taxi to New Delhi. We spend each day wandering from one air-conditioned shop and restaurant to another, and sitting through forgettable movies, mostly Westerns, in air-conditioned theaters. Sipping banana lassis in a shop off Connaught Circle, we overhear a tourist saying that the temperature at noon is 113 degrees Fahrenheit! Tired and hot, we return after sunsets to our cots at the youth hostel. We figure that, by trying to save money on our lodging, we've spent twice as much as we would have if we'd just stayed in an air-conditioned hotel! At least we've managed to receive and send mail at the American Express, change more dollars for rupees on the black market, and buy train tickets to Chandigarh, a city 265 kilometers north of Delhi, where we'll then bus to Manali.

The night train to Chandigarh is uneventful and, by morning, we're sipping chai as we wait to board the bus to Manali. We take our seats behind the driver, a Sikh who seems anxious to leave and irritated by his diminutive ticket conductor, who keeps reminding him to wait until all the passengers board. The journey is long, taking us through the plains and along narrow, winding roads of the foothills of Himachal Pradesh. At noon, we reach the small town of Mandi, where we stop for a quick lunch.

Just as we set off again, the front tire of the bus blows, causing the bus to careen off the road onto a side street. The cursing driver swears at his hapless conductor, who announces that we must get off the bus again until the tire is fixed. This takes two hours while the conductor labors to remove the tire and carry it to a nearby car repair shop. The driver, meanwhile, has fallen asleep under a tree. The tire finally repaired and remounted, we're on our way further into the mountains. Several hours later, we stop for a rest in the town of Kulu, at the base of the Kulu Valley, a lush farming area between high Himalayan peaks and just two hours from Manali. Jean and I are delighted to be back in the cool, fresh air of the Himalayas, with the colorful dress and distinct languages of its peoples, and marvel again at breathtaking views of distant peaks. Kulu is the destination point for most bus passengers. We reboard after an hour. Others have joined us, including an Australian named Michael. He's perhaps ten years older than I am, paper-thin, with earrings, a nose ring, and strings of beads around his neck. He seems stoned out, but friendly enough.

"I'm just up from Calangute Beach in Goa. Lots of us travelers there now, more each year. Most go up to Kathmandu when it gets too hot, but my mates and I prefer Manali. Smaller, less of a hassle from the government."

We've been sitting in the bus now for almost an hour, waiting for the driver to show up. The conductor and a couple of passengers go looking for him. They reappear shortly with the driver, who now seems to be stumbling drunk. He clambers into his seat and, before anyone can protest, honks the bus horn twice and is off. The two-hour drive to Manali is a living terror as the driver careens around narrow mountain roads! Jean and I silently chant prayer mantras while passengers continue to yell at the driver to slow down. The driver just laughs, sharing the big joke with his conductor, who looks about to throw up. We nearly collide with an oncoming bus on one bend! The road is too narrow for both vehicles to pass. Both drivers emerge, yelling at each other, and it looks as though they'll come to blows. The conductor, to the rescue again, intercedes, convincing our driver to back up and slightly off the road so that the other bus can pass. Crisis averted, our driver sneers at the conductor before resuming the wild ride. The relief of every passenger is obvious when we finally arrive at the bus station in Manali. I want to kiss the ground! Several passengers now shout at the bus driver, who just walks away, probably to find another drink.

It's long past sunset by now and cold enough to don jackets. Even though we can't see much of the town, the fresh mountain air mixed with pine fires lift our spirits. Michael tells us that he knows of a great hotel; he can't remember its name, but it's just a short walk away from the bus station. We follow behind Michael. After what seems like a long while stumbling through apple orchards, we finally come upon a lighted porch. Sure enough, it's Michael's hotel! The *malik*, or "owner," remembers Michael and is happy to show us to two rooms. Then he and his family prepare a much-appreciated supper of vegetable pakoras, rice, and chapatis.

After supper, Michael asks if we want to shoot morphine with him. We respectfully decline but observe his practiced procedure of tying up his arm, finding a vein, and injecting himself. Our conversation with Michael subsides after a few minutes as he enters a world of his own.

We awaken to a rooster's crow on a frosty morning. We've decided we want to stay closer to the town. Also, Michael has told us that he's waiting for his friends from Calangute Beach to arrive, and we really don't want to be part of their drug scene. We pack our bags after breakfast, thank the malik and his wife, and tell Michael we'll see him around town. He looks more weathered than ever but gives us a cheerful hug goodbye.

Manali this morning resembles a small logging village. After months in heat, the cold, fresh mountain air is a welcome change. Kulu Indians, Tibetans, and Nepalese fill the shops and streets, all dressed in colorful wools. A number of travelers sit in chai shops, several looking as worn out as Michael. We ask a longhair about hotels, and he points down the street, saying the best place is down the first alley we come to. We find the hotel easily and, after a short financial negotiation, the manager shows us to a beautiful wood-paneled room with a parquet floor, a queen-size bed, a writing desk and armoire, and large windows on three walls overlooking Manali and its vast sweep of the Kulu Valley with its surrounding snow-capped mountain peaks! We just lie on the comfortable bed for an hour, basking in our "luxury apartment." The rest of the day is spent in exploring the town, where we see several good Indian, Nepali, and Tibetan restaurants we plan to try out in the days ahead. There's even a couple of Western restaurants advertising pancakes and hamburgers. We spend a long time perusing a lively Tibetan market down one alley. All in all, Manali seems a lively, welcoming place.

We make further discoveries over the next several days: a Tibetan *chang* (barley beer) shop, an ornate Tibetan temple with a ten-foot prayer wheel at its entrance, a cidery in the middle of an apple orchard and, most important of all, hot sulfur springs! These are located across a river and up a two-mile path. There are two springs: one is a small, natural pool, free of charge and therefore packed with people throughout the day; the other is the government-run pool, which costs one rupee a person. There's a considerable wait to get in, but once in, you have the use of a private pool and shower for forty-five minutes. The smell of the sulfur pool takes a little getting used to at first, but we can take a freshwater shower afterward. The pool proves to be therapeutic as well. We'd just received smallpox vaccinations in Delhi, and as a result, Jean developed a reaction of a large swollen and discolored infection around the vaccination site. Just two trips to the sulfur springs and the infection has completely disappeared! We quickly become "converts," making "pilgrimage" to the government pool each day.

April 16, 1971
Dear Dad, Mom and Nancy,

Several days and many more travel hours later and we find ourselves in Manali, a tiny logging village in Kulu valley, north of Delhi and Chandigarh, 7000 feet into the Himalayas. That's right. After the hot, humid plains climate of South India, we've made a beeline right back to the mountains for some fresh air. This side of the Indian Himalayas proves to be as impressive as the Darjeeling side, and we've already moved into a large house on a wooded mountainside (if only for a little while.) Again, the area is filled with Tibetans, so the atmosphere is charged with excitement, color and music. I've never seen a grander race of people (you know of course how easily I get carried away.) The town of Manali Bazaar is small—one long street—giving the impression of a 19th century western/logging/cowboy town, a good John Wayne set. We try of course to continue our "sadhanas" or yoga practice, but the area is pleasantly distracting to the newcomer. Also, back into cold nights and warm days makes it difficult for the old 4:00 a.m. hatha Yoga class. Here is the clincher—at a thirty minute walk from here is a hot sulphur springs, where for 1 rupee (12 cents) one is able to spend his day immersed in a hot water bath—we stand a chance of becoming the world's cleanest, most water-logged people, but well worth it.

O.K., that's all. I hope you had a good Easter, much chocolate and food. Say hello, love to all and forgive the rambling letter as my fingers are cold and I feel so bubbly/good. Love, Brus and Jean

We meet new friends at our hotel: Englishman David, his German friend, Ulrich, and Americans, Pam and Georgeann.

Bearded David is a hash smoker, spending hours practicing his sitar; Ulrich is young, plagued by dysentery, and bemoaning ever having left Germany. Pam and Georgeann, both short and thin, have been in India for years studying Tibetan Buddhism. They look so alike, we at first think they're sisters. Their stories of adventures and meeting high lamas fascinate us. In turn, we share our experiences of meeting Kalu Rinpoche and studying with Swami Gitananda. David reintroduces Jean and me to charas after months of a healthy yoga lifestyle. We now spend days doing morning asanas and meditation, then sharing food, stories, and smoking charas with our new friends.

David returns to the hotel one day, saying, "I just spoke with a guy who wants to rent his house for 200 rupees a month."

"Really?" Pam replies, "That sounds cheap. Where is it?"

"He says it's just up the mountainside, about a kilometer from here. He says it has seven rooms."

"Wow!" Georgeann exclaims, "That's big enough for all of us!"

Jean and I are reluctant to leave our beautiful hotel room, but the excitement of our friends convinces us to join in the adventure. Besides, we can save a lot of money in rent. The next day, bags packed, we all pile into a hired jeep and make our way up a winding road and past a small, ancient Hindu temple to the house. Situated in a pinewood forest on a small stream, the house looks either under repair or in complete disrepair. We're dismayed to find that a family is already living there!

An Indian man comes to the door to greet us. "Hello. And who are you?"

We introduce ourselves and explain that we've agreed to rent the house from a young man for the month.

"Yes, that is my son. I am Kumar, and I own this house. As you can see, we are still in the process of restoring it."

"So," David asks, "this house isn't for rent?"

"Oh yes, but only the four rooms on the first floor. The upstairs rooms are not yet habitable. Also, my wife, daughter, and I must stay here for three more days to finish the work we started. Then you may have the house for one hundred rupees a month."

We agree to return in three days, happy that we'll only have to pay half of what the son asked. True to his word, Kumar and family leave in three days, and the house, at least the four rooms on the bottom floor, is ours. Shortly after we arrive, Kumar's son walks up and demands that David give him a 100-rupee baksheesh for finding the house for him. David refuses of course, and the son, muttering expletives, skulks away. We realize that we'll have to be on the lookout for him to ensure our belongings are safe.

Our "kitchen" is our small primus stove and a dishwashing bin on a spacious balcony overlooking a small meadow stream and a forest of deodar trees beyond. We must haul water from the stream to wash ourselves and do dishes. This balcony is where we congregate each morning to make plans, and each evening to share the day's adventures.

Pam and Georgeann settle into the largest room that unfortunately has a big hole in the ceiling. Ever the optimists, they figure it's not yet the rainy monsoon season and they'll have a great view of the stars at night. David's room is spacious, with a single bed, a large fireplace, and writing desk. Ulrich's room is the smallest, just a single bed and closet. Our room is adequate enough, with a fireplace, small table, and a serviceable queen-sized bed. The only problem is that Ulrich's room is directly behind ours, and he must pass through our room to get to the rest of the house. Oh well, we think, nothing's perfect. Speaking of which, the house has no bathroom, leaving us each to find a tree or bush in the woods to relieve ourselves. This becomes nightmarish for Jean and me when Ulrich's frequent dysentery attacks cause him to clomp through our room, cursing and slamming doors throughout the nights.

Ulrich's constant complaints about his bad stomach are wearing on us all. His rants include those people in his past who "backstabbed" him, and his concern for his friend in Germany who has become addicted to heroin and is heading for destruction. All attempts to calm him only generate arguments. After we all go to bed one night, Ulrich apparently takes a trip on some acid he brought with him. We find him in the morning, sitting in lotus posture on the balcony, saying that he has at last found Jesus Christ and knows for certain that those who don't believe in Him are damned. He now sees his mission as bestowing Jesus's blessings upon all whom he meets. So now we're all living with a Jesus Freak, the same Ulrich, but with a new set of fantasies. After several days, however, he packs his bags and walks away, claiming that he must return to Germany to save his friend from damnation. His departure is his true blessing.

Pam's boyfriend, John, appears just a day after Ulrich leaves. Soft-spoken, with a beet-red face and hair blown in ten directions, he looks as though he's survived a hurricane. We learn that he has just been with Swami Muktananda at his ashram in Ganeshpuri, below Bombay. There, he received the practices of *Shakti pad* to open all the chakras at once. We were told by Swami Gitananda that this is one of the most difficult practices in yoga because it demands perfect control and discipline. Muktananda is reputed to be able to bestow Shakti pad by a simple touch but will only bestow this to serious adepts. John moves in with Pam and Georgeann in their room.

This leaves Ulrich's old room vacant, becoming a perfect little den for Jean and me to do our yoga practices. Pam invites us one morning to drop acid that John has brought. David, Jean, and I decline, so Pam, Georgeann, and John go off into the hills. They return at dusk, very happy and relaxed, saying they've had a wonderful trip together. John gives Jean and me two tabs of acid that night, suggesting we take our own trip when the time is right.

John's arrival changes our little community. Pam, Georgeann, and John often go off together, not returning until after dark. Jean particularly feels the sting of this as she was beginning to bond with the two women. We find ourselves hanging out more with David, who slowly reveals something of his background. Well-educated from Cambridge, he's been in India over a year. He traveled for months with a young Indian boy whom he met in Benares, and even considered legally adopting him. One day, the boy stole his money and disappeared, an action that left him devastated and leery of new friendships. He cautiously counts our friendship as part of his healing process. David and I often walk down the mountain to town for something or other, but mainly just for the company.

We walk downstream on several occasions to spend time with a bearded, matted-haired sadhu, usually sitting on the same flat rock and playing a flute, a small brown dog at his side. There, we share a bowl of David's charas. We don't speak each other's language, mostly sit in silence, but certainly appreciate sharing the time together in this restful environment. Before we part, David always gives the sadhu a *tola* (11.6 grams) of charas, receiving his toothless smile as thanks.

April 27th—Morning
Hi Y'all,

Got your letter yesterday here (Manali)—never thought it would make it—the post office is only a wooden shack. This town is lovely—like out of a western set—one street mainly, w/ fruit & veg. stands and dark wooden restaurants. Off of one street is a Tibetan market and restaurants. It's so interesting to browse around and look at their stuff. They are "far-out" people—so friendly and interesting. Yesterday was like a birthday for me. I bought velvet, very dark brown, and had a native dress made—you will love it! It's lined in emerald green at the cuffs and gold trim all around—w/ a printed (flowers) brown velvet vest to go w/ it. It wraps around & it's pleated all around the skirt w/ one side pocket. It's about midi-length and you wear Indian pants under it...The native women here wear it doing everything from road construction to washing and house work, never minding the velvet, it's very comfortable. Also, we found a little jacket, all embroidered with many colors, fitted with puffy shoulders ... it's lined in silk & and is used and old—really groovy! Also a silver amulet a finely worked silver chain w/ a green Tibetan turquoise, that matches beautifully. And a silk Tibetan rug

or blanket, and silk hair tassels and woolen socks. Really on a spend-
ing spree—but such lovely things here. We have about $700 left—
and as I said in my 7 page letter (maybe it will come yet) we possibly
will head west in the late summer or fall. But we go to Delhi in 5 days
(May 2ⁿᵈ) and will apply for another Indian visa extension & see if
we can come back to Manali for the summer mos. & then maybe to
the ashram again. If not, we go to Nepal for 1-2 mos. & then get an
Indian transit visa and head back west ... When I know, so will you!
We will see the Taj! Don't know next address yet ... wait for my next
letter to write—also will ans. more questions. Both well & happy,
Love, Jean and Brus (notice new spelling)

A group of French hippies has moved into a nearby house, one
even more dilapidated than ours. Now they start coming around,
in pairs at first, asking if we have any charas and, if we can spare
it, some food. David shares a bowl with them initially, and we offer
them some bread and cheese.

This opens a floodgate of French visitations, usually around
lunches and dinners, until our generosity is tested to the maximum.
David tells us that many of these guys are second and third sons in
a family and have suffered from the French custom of the first son
being the only heir of the family's estates, leaving them to fend for
themselves. Many land in Goa, Kathmandu, and here in Manali,
scrounging food and drugs whenever they can. Finally, we have to
tell them they are no longer welcome in our house and watch their
manner change from gratitude to spite. Now we know we not only
have to protect our possessions from Kumar's son, but from these
French moochers as well!

I hear a knock on the front door one day when I'm home alone.
I open the door to a woman in her sixties with a carefully coifed
hairdo, wearing designer blue jeans and a flowery top. She looks
every bit the tourist.

"Hi," she smiles. "My name is Maji ... well Marjorie, but everyone here calls me Maji."

"Nice to meet you," I carefully respond. "How can I help you?"

"My friends and I have just arrived. We met a young man in the bazaar who said we could rent some rooms here."

I instantly know that she has encountered Kumar's son. I invite her in and explain how we were also duped by this guy. We climb the rickety stairway to the upstairs rooms she was interested in renting, and both come to the immediate conclusion that every room is indeed uninhabitable. She is surprisingly more amused than upset by this. I invite her to have some tea. For the next two hours we get to know each other, and I come to realize as she's sharing her life story just what an amazing person she is!

"I'm from Atlanta, a southern belle who grew up with all the trappings of privilege: mansion, servants, private clubs, you get the picture. Everything for me seemed easy, predictable. I went along with it all, but somehow I knew I never fit in. I was an artist, and some of my paintings sold at exclusive galleries, but my family was completely unsupportive. They all considered my art a whim that got in the way of my real job; that is, to get married to just the right man and have babies. For years, I believed there was something wrong with me. I was taken to psychiatrists and given pills, some to calm down, others to cheer me up. I followed the family plan and married Johnny O_____, a force in Atlanta society, having made his money by inventing cardboard shipping boxes, and had two babies: Penny and Mary. Penny fit in right away. Daddy's little girl, she was 'groomed to be doomed,' just as I was. Mary was a rebel, all energy and fun, and wanted nothing to do with conventional expectations. She was Daddy's vexation and my joy. As the girls grew, Johnny and I were a couple in name only. He spent more time at his clubs than at home. I would have divorced him if I thought I had the choice, but that was strictly taboo at the time. Instead, I just took more pills, sinking so low that, on several occasions, I had to check myself in to psychiatric hospitals."

"Wow, what a life!" I exclaim.

Maji laughs, "Yes, it was, but it goes on. Anyway, Johnny died of a massive coronary, leaving me with the children and his fortune.

I made sure that Penny met the right people and got into the right schools because, well, that's who she was. Mary, on the other hand, was headed in an entirely different direction. When she turned eighteen, she announced that she was going to India. India! Of all the places she could go, she chooses the poorest, most dirty country in the world! At least, that was my thinking at the time. Well, Mary did go to India and has stayed here ever since. She and I have been writing each other the whole time, but she's moved around so much, a lot of letters were lost. When she told me she was living in a place called Goa and had just given birth to a girl she named Dolma, I immediately got on an airplane to Bombay and took a taxi to her house in Goa.

"Mary was overjoyed to see me. She introduced me to her 'husband' David. I doubt they're really married, but he seems like a very nice man. But, my God, her house was filled with the strangest people I'd ever seen: tattooed, nose, eye, and ear rings, wearing tons of jewelry and very little else. They smoked hashish and played music, wrote poetry, and painted bizarre pictures, none of which seemed very good to me. They were all very nice to me, but I felt so out of place, I made plane reservations to leave after a few days.

"Then I met Blue, Mary's outrageous gay friend. He took me under his wing, insisting I accompany him to meet all his friends up and down Calangute Beach. He helped in introducing me to, and explaining, this utterly different lifestyle. Blue was sensitive enough to introduce me to life on Calangute slowly, so I wouldn't bolt away in fright. I began to relax a little more, started smoking some hashish with Blue and his friends. Then Blue introduced me to LSD. This was the turning point of my life! In the middle of the acid trip, I realized that, all my life, I had thought something was wrong with me, something crazy and broken. Now I saw clearly that I was fine just as I was. I could never fit into rigid Atlanta society, and never would try to again. I was reborn on that trip, and I've been on a great adventure of self-discovery ever since.

"I immediately canceled my flights back to Atlanta and, soon after, rented a jeep for Blue, two other friends, and me to drive across India to Calcutta, smoking hash the whole way. That's when Marjorie became Maji."

I think all I've said is "wow" over and over as Maji unfolds her remarkable story.

Maji continues. "That was my first trip to India. This is my second. Once again, I'm in a jeep with good friends, exploring everything I can."

Just then, Jean and David return and, after introductions, David passes around a bowl of charas, which Maji gratefully accepts. We spend a lot of time together over the next few days, Jean happy to have met a woman she can talk with. Maji and her friends find a charming little place, not far above ours, called the "Rose Cottage." At night, we can hear the music of guitars, flutes, and *tablas* (twin hand drums) from the Rose Cottage. And, although Maji sometimes complains about needing to take a break from the "hippie music scene," she always exhibits the vitality of a younger woman.

We must leave Manali at the end of our month's rent and to return to Delhi. Our extended visa, allowing for a total time of six months in India, has run out, and we either have to leave the country or figure out another way to remain. We have an emotional farewell with David and Maji, promising each other to stay in touch. We continue a correspondence with David for several months, learning that he has returned to England with a raging case of hepatitis, perhaps from the same source that is soon to affect me. This goodbye with Maji is only a temporary separation; our strong bond with her is one that will endure through many years and adventures to come.

A blessedly safe bus trip down beautiful Kulu Valley to Chandigarh, and an uneventful overnight train to Delhi, lands us in Jain's Guest House on Jan Path Lane, off Connaught Place. Our only interest now is to take care of business and determine our next destination as soon as possible. First, we must see if it's possible to legally stay longer in India. In the Foreign Registration Office, we meet with a military officer sporting a thin mustache, carefully waxed into curls at the ends. We hand him a letter written by Swami Gitananda stating that we are students at Ananda Ashram studying yoga and the Vedic texts, and we ask him to consider us eligible for one-year student visas.

He states, "Oh, I know of Swami Gitananda, but issuing you these student visas is not possible from this office. You must apply at the office in Pondicherry, where you extended your first tourist visas."

"But," I argue, "You can see that we only have two days left on our current visas. For us to return to Pondicherry now is impossible. Our visas will have expired!"

"This is not my problem, you see. I am not permitted to issue student visas at this office."

Now a tearing up Jean asks, "What can we do? Please help us to find a solution."

I can see that this plea by a pretty Western woman is having an effect on the officer. We all sit in silence as he ponders our dilemma.

Finally, he says, "I will write to Pondicherry with your request for student visas. Meanwhile, I will issue you temporary visas until I receive their reply."

The tension in the room lifts immediately. He readily writes out and stamps a "temporary extension" on our visa cards, happy to have come up with a solution, albeit temporary. And we are secretly elated to know that, with mail service as it is, a response from Pondicherry may take months. In effect, we can stay in India as long as we want! We celebrate our good fortune over fruit juices at the nearby Mohan Singh Market.

We go next to Shankar Market to cash traveler's checks on the black market. A Sikh offers us the best deal, but as we're cashing our checks, I notice his eyes are furtively darting to the door of his shop. Leaving, I look back at his shop and see him talking to a policeman, then both men looking at us. Our walk becomes a run; rounding a corner, we run smack into Roslyn, of Roslyn and Candice, our friends from Iran and Afghanistan! We haven't seen each other for six months, but there's no time for hellos as we tell

Roslyn that we think the police are onto to us for using the black market. She runs along with us until we feel we're in the clear.

We're overjoyed to see each other and catch up over banana lassis. She and Candice had been in India for a month when they received a telegram from Candice's parents that they wanted to have a family reunion in Australia immediately. So both women flew to Sydney thinking that they'd be reimbursed by the parents when they arrived.

"But, when we got there, Candice's parents were pissed off that I came with her. Her father told me to my face that the reunion was for family only! The cost of the flight left me almost broke, and that bastard refused to reimburse me. So, there I was, dependent on people who didn't want me around."

"So, what did you do?" Jean asked.

"What could I do? I was stuck. We were stuck. Candice was torn between being with me and being with her family. Finally, after several weeks of this, we decided to leave. Candice hassled with her family until her dad agreed to pay our fare back to India. We stopped in Bangkok on the way, just to chill out from that horrible experience."

I ask, "So, where's Candice?"

"Well, when we got to Calcutta, we decided to split up for a while. We'd been together for a year and a half nonstop and thought we needed a break. I guess it was a mutual decision," she said, her sad eyes conveying a different truth. "Candice went to Kathmandu and has become involved with Hog Farm people there. Even hooked up with some guy. A man! Can you imagine? I came here through Benares and have been here ever since."

The Hog Farm is a well-known hippie commune from the States. They fed thousands in the rains at the Woodstock Festival, and we ran into them at an "Alternative Media Conference," at Goddard College, where they'd set up their food kitchen. I will always have this image of a naked, round girl, standing on a stepladder, biting off chunks of carrot and spitting them into a giant cauldron of something. This "happening" was also headlined by Richard

Alpert, the former Harvard professor and LSD cohort of Timothy Leary, who'd just returned from India for the first time with a new name, Baba Ram Dass. Jean and I went to his outdoor workshop, and basically spent a couple of hours *Aum-ing* with him on a hillside. We count this experience as a factor in confirming our decision to go to India.

Roslyn tells us that she's living in the suburbs of New Delhi at the house of a man named Sherry.

"Sherry has invented lots of children's toys, and I've just helped him open up an alternative elementary school called Why Not?"

We visit the school with Roslyn the next day. The resources seem limited, but the Indian teacher is attentive, and the children are definitely enjoying themselves.

Roslyn says, "We get no aid from the Indian government, so Sherry has to finance everything. He's running out of money and might have to return to the States and patent more inventions, leaving his wife and me to run things here."

Roslyn invites us to Sherry's house, where we have dinner with Sherry, his wife, and another young man, Matthew. Although only twenty-two, Matthew is an aspiring Tibetan Buddhist scholar, having helped with the translations of a number of sacred texts. Questions I ask of him about Tibetan teachers and teachings are met with a flood of information; so much so that he confesses with a laugh that, when it comes to his work, he has a hard time turning off his mind.

At the invitation of an Indian friend, Roslyn brings us and Matthew to a dinner party the next night at the impressive home of the Belgian ambassador to India. Two servants usher us into a large living room already filled with guests, where we're greeted by the ambassador and his wife. They're both friendly enough, but after inspecting our very best clothing from South India and listening for a short while to our story of Ananda Ashram and third class trains, they move on, signaling that we're really not their type of people. In fact, we feel as though we've just materialized in a different world ourselves! But the cocktails, appetizers, and buffet dinner are delicious; we separate from Roslyn and Matthew, and we find ourselves in good conversation with an Indian artist named Om Pradesh and his friend Kumar, who owns an international art gallery in New Delhi.

The next day, at his invitation, we visit Kumar's gallery with Roslyn and Matthew. Prominently displayed on a central table is Baba Ram Das's "Box," consisting of a book titled *Be Here Now* and recordings of chants. We relate to Kumar our one encounter with Ram Dass, and he tells us that Ram Dass is in India now with his guru, Neem Karoli Baba, in a city called Almora, six thousand feet in the Himalayas in the state of Uttar Pradesh. When we hear this, Jean and I look at each other; this is the sign we've been waiting for! Our destination is clear; we're going to Almora to find Ram Dass!

The next few days are a whirlwind of change. Roslyn tells us two days later that, after months of Kumar's prodding, she has finally met his guru, a *yogini* living near Delhi's burning ghats. She's completely taken with her, is overjoyed to have at last found her guru, and is planning to accompany her on a tour of Europe, leaving with the blessings of Sherry and his wife. Matthew is interested in going to Almora and promises to join us when he's completed some business in New Delhi. A last dinner together and still another goodbye; we part with Roslyn, promising as always to stay in touch.

ALMORA

Along bus journey—eight hours on the plains and five more along windy, dusty mountain roads—and we arrive in Almora, a central trading town in the Kumaon hills, named after an ancient kingdom. It's nighttime, and there's little of the town to be seen other than the usual commotion surrounding a bus station. We book a cozy rooftop room in the nearby Alka Hotel. Just as we settle in our room, we hear a great "Ba-Room!" We spend the next hour observing through the room's large windows a dynamic thunder and lightning show over the entire Almora Valley, a sign we take to be an auspicious welcome to our new home.

We stay at the Alka Hotel for the next few days, exploring the town's large bazaar, encompassing numerous streets down three levels of hillside. We're met with puzzled looks when we initially inquire about Baba Ram Dass. Finally, we're disappointed to learn from an English-speaking Indian that he had been in Almora but had left weeks before to do a retreat in a town called Kausani. We're not fated to meet Ram Dass during the rest of our time in India.

We also mention to the hotel manager that we're surprised we haven't seen any Westerners in town. He tells us that most Westerners live up on the ridge road, about three kilometers above the town. He suggests that we visit Mary Op_____, who knows everyone on the ridge, and gives us directions to her house.

I set out to find Mary's house the next day. Jean is having some stomach problems and decides to stay behind. After a good hike along a packed dirt road, I come upon another bazaar, this one just a single street long. I learn later that this is called Narayan Tenali

Daval, more commonly known as Chota (little) Bazaar. The ridge begins from here. I hike a steep, winding road, barely wide enough for a single car, until I come to a gate marked "Op_____." I ring a bell hanging above the gate, bringing a German Shepherd barking and growling his greetings.

"Timi, cut it out!" yells a voice from inside the house.

Timi slinks away as a gray-haired woman with a bright smile on her wrinkled face comes to the gate.

She asks, "Oh, and who might you be?"

"I've just arrived in Almora and was told to come and say hello. My name is Brus ..."

"Brus!" A familiar voice yells from inside the house and, moments later, another older woman comes running to the gate.

"Oh my God! Maji!" I exclaim. "How did you get here?"

"Well, dear," Maji laughs, "I didn't walk from Manali. Where's Jean?"

"She's back at the hotel in Almora. She isn't feeling great, and anyway, she tends to let me explore new places first."

Maji and I bask in our mutual surprise as Mary serves tea on a table on the front porch of her sweet, one-level, vine and flower covered house. We just can't get over how, when we left Manali, neither of us had any idea we'd find each other in Almora just weeks later. It seems Maji had Mary's name in her address book for some reason and decided to visit. Just an hour after she arrived in Almora, she runs into a Western woman in the bazaar and inquires of her about Mary Op_____.

"Look no further," she replied. "I'm Mary."

Mary immediately invited Maji to stay with her. This was just several days before.

I ask Maji, "What happened to the friends you were with in Manali?"

"I got tired of the same old music and hash scene, so I struck out on my own."

I explain to her how we came in search of Ram Dass.

Mary interjects, "Oh, Ram Dass visited me when he was here with Timothy Leary. He was very nice, had kind eyes. I can't say the same for Mr. Leary."

"Oh? Why?" I ask.

"Well, he seemed, I don't know, edgy. He talked a lot and his eyes were constantly darting around, as if he had other places he needed to be. He made me nervous."

Morning becomes afternoon as we sit around the table and share our lives. Mary has lived in Almora for many years. She's a homeopathist. She knows all the Westerners and Indians who live on the ridge and treats all who come to her house with various aches and complaints. She seems particularly interested in my experiences at Ananda Ashram, as she's heard of Swami Gitananda; she expresses that she is planning a trip soon to South India and would like to visit him. (She never will go there, but Maji does a year and a half later, spending a "delightful afternoon" with Swamiji.) I mention the study of yantra and how it influenced me enough to change the spelling of my name. This leads to my "reading" the Birth Path and supporting numbers for each woman. I'm surprised that I can remember so much without notes. I promise them I'll return the next morning with Jean and bring my notebook on yantra.

I return to the Alka Hotel to find Jean sitting on the roof garden with Matthew. He'd arrived on the morning bus and booked another room on the rooftop. He and Jean surprised each other by stepping out of their rooms at exactly the same time. I relate my day's adventure, and Jean can't wait to see Maji the next day. Matthew tells us that he tried to coax Roslyn into coming with him, but she was just too taken with her new guru and the prospect of traveling with her to Europe. The rest of the evening is spent at a bazaar restaurant talking about Buddhism. Matthew's knowledge astounds us, taking us through the different Buddhist schools of Hinayana, Mahayana, and Vajrayana, their similarities and differences, and some of the renowned teachers of each school. This is the first time we've heard these teachings, and we pepper Matthew with questions. The result of this and later conversations with Matthew is that a seed of curiosity has been planted; Jean and I want to learn more about Buddhism.

Matthew joins us the next morning as we make our way up the ridge road through Chota Bazaar to Mary's house. Maji and Jean are delighted to see each other again, and we all enjoy a wonderful day together, eating cheese sandwiches and cookies and talking about everything from yantra to Buddhism. Toward the end of the day, we ask Mary if she knows of any house available to rent.

"I don't know of any right now, but maybe my friend Reverend Massey does. He's the head minister of the Methodist Church, and also the district superintendent of Lands and Public Works in this area. I know he is in charge of several houses here. Perhaps we can visit him together." We enthusiastically agree and set a date to go with Mary to the home of Reverend Massey.

We see Maji several more times before she takes a taxi directly to Delhi and a plane back to Atlanta, Georgia. We're all confident that we'll see each other again soon. We do keep in touch and see each other often in the States and, later, back in India. Matthew leaves a few days after this, bound for Russia for a short while, where he has research to do, and then on to England. (We've since visited with Matthew in California, where he was immersed in Tibetan studies at the University of California at Berkeley. Without any previous college education, he so impressed his professors that they immediately offered him two years of university credit with a track of completing the entire baccalaureate in just one year. Since then, he has become an eminent translator for visiting Tibetan lamas.)

On a clear morning, we walk with Mary up a nearby hill to Reverend Massey's house. Mary explains to us on the way that his name, Massey, is anglicized, as Indians call Christ, "Esmassey." On the top of the hill sits a rambling one-level stone house with surrounding vine-covered veranda and a jeep in the driveway. Mary knocks, and we enter, finding Reverend Massey and his wife sitting together in a small office. They seem delighted to see Mary and meet her two young friends. Reverend Massey is a slight, soft-spoken, middle-aged man with thinning gray hair, while a chubby Mrs. Massey is more outgoing. They insist on serving us tea on their veranda. During tea, and after sharing news of mutual acquaintances, Mary brings up the topic of availability of any houses for us.

"Oh, I'm afraid I know of no houses that are available right now," the reverend replies.

After a small gap in the conversation, when we must look disappointed, Mrs. Massey pipes in, "But, our back room here will be available in a few days. A young woman named Caroline has occupied the room for the past few months but is leaving shortly back to America." In further conversation, we reveal that we have both been raised Methodist, and that my father is a trustee of our local church. This seals the deal, and the Masseys offer us the room for as long as we want, free of charge!

May 12th
Dear All,

We are in Almora, another hill station in the Himalayas. After Manali we went to Delhi, where I got your letter I missed before. We were given temporary [visa] consideration. The final [student visa] one must come from Pondicherry—but that could take months. At any rate, we have permission to stay in India a while more, and that's what we wanted. So we came right back to the mts. (Delhi was 101 degrees every day!) where we look again for a house for 1-2 mos. We met the District Superintendent & he offered us to stay in his home. We'll see—he is very nice, a Methodist minister of sorts & a beautiful home overlooking the whole valley and mts. Then Swami will be in Kashmir in July, & we would like to go there & be w/ him again for the summer mos. Then we have no plans after that. As for coming home, not yet—we still have much to see and do. I miss you all—think of you almost every day—many times I wish you were with us, seeing the sights too! Write me c/o Mary Op_____, "Haimavati," P.O. Almora, U.P. India. I will write again soon (1 week or so)—Until then Love and Kisses, Jean & Brus

In a couple of days, we're comfortably settled in the Massey's house on the top of, what Mary calls, "Christian Hill," overlooking the Almora Valley and a 360-degree vista of surrounding snow-capped Himalayan peaks. Our room itself is *pukka*, or "first class," complete with a separate entrance, a queen-size bed with mosquito net, a large fireplace, and an attached, Western-style bathroom.

We spend the next several days buying supplies in Almora and Chota Bazaar, including a new primus stove and small table, and getting to know the family. The Masseys have five children. The oldest is a young woman who is already married and has moved away. The two young teenage girls are Usha and Pushpa. Both are quite shy and remain so for our entire stay. However, the older boys, Vinod and Vijay, are curious about our backgrounds, America, and what we think of India, often coming to our doors with more questions. Reverend Massey and his wife regularly express what an honor it is for them to host visiting Methodists from America and insist that we share their meals, urging us to consider their house as our own. We're a little concerned about all this attention, as our preference would have been to settle in a house of our own. After a week though, we all relax into a more neighborly lifestyle where we don't have to engage constantly with each other. I know the Masseys are as relieved by this arrangement as we are.

May 19, 1971
Dear Dad, Mom and Nancy,

At this point, I'm sitting on a hill's peak overlooking two valleys and the town of Almora proper. I'm relaxing in a warm, hazy sun after completing the early morning chores of starting a fire and making coffee, preparing breakfast—which were chapatis, a wheat flour dough rolled into "pancakes" and cooked on a fire; India's national bread—and cleaning both body and dishes. Jean is asleep within our room. Sitting by me is Curly, an Indian market dog who we've somehow adopted—or she, in her affable manner, has adopted us—at least for the time being. The sounds I hear as I write are the wind, the "caw" of a crow flying high above Almora

Valley, and the cackles of chickens nearby. Nothing else. Very quiet. Later, we'll have a walk down the mountain through one of the forests, come back to have the ritual afternoon tea while preparing dinner (usually some preparation of rice and "dal" (lentils,) "subje" (vegetables) and, after dinner, sit around the fire, with Curly at our feet and read aloud from Tolkien's Hobbit Trilogy. Finally, we go sleepily to bed and bundle up from the cold night air, to sleep and dream, to awake tomorrow to the same, or similar, peaceful routine.

We've been in Almora for slightly longer than a week and have already made a bevy of friends. We've become very close with Mary Op____, an American lady of 60 years who has lived in the same home in Almora for 17 years. A remarkable, charming woman who, I'm sure, never fails to leave a tremendous, beautiful impression on anyone she should meet. It was through her that we became acquainted with Reverend Massey and his wife, both Indian. He's the Superintendent of the Almora district and Methodist minister. Besides living in the highest peak in Almora, they are open and generous. They invited us to live in part of their house, a large stone room with big fireplace—reminds me of a castle tower room—and with a separate entrance from the rest of the house. Needless to say, we accepted and moved in several days ago. Aside from the occasional "family meal" with the Masseys, we're left to our own devices (aside from the boy who brings "pani" and "lakri," water and wood, twice daily,) which is exactly what we want. So, for the first time since we left the States (nay, before,) Jean and I are together, alone, in a beautiful rural setting.

Well, I'm finished rambling. Write to us soon—return address on the back of the aerogramme. Nancy, please write and tell me how it is. I think of you often. Love, Brus & Jean

The days go by quickly, occupied in cooking, cleaning, and taking walks. Sometimes I spend long hours just sitting and watching the chickens pecking around the coop just outside our door, and the horny rooster going through his twilight sexual rigors, not stopping until he covers every hen. The Masseys are proud of their chickens, raised on wholesome grains and producing large eggs. Jean has managed to attract two dogs during her walks—Curly, a shaggy white mutt, and Jack, larger and leaner, the color of corn—and we soon become a "family" of four. At night, we all sit around the fireplace while I read another chapter of Tolkien's trilogy. (There are days when we can't wait for the sun to go down so we can rejoin the adventures of Frodo and his companions.) We visit with Mary occasionally, and she sometimes treats Jean with homeopathic remedies for recurring, but mild, stomach troubles. We learn more about the Western inhabitants on the ridge, some of whom have lived there longer than Mary. It seems they're an eclectic lot, mostly keeping to themselves.

Mary laughs, "People refer to our area as "Cranks Ridge" because we can certainly be a cranky bunch. Who knows, I just may be the crankiest one of the lot!"

Although Mary offers to introduce us to some of the residents, we're not that interested in meeting more people. It's enough for the time being to just enjoy our quiet life on "Christian Hill."

Three weeks after moving in with the Masseys, the reverend and Mrs. Massey come to our door. From the looks on their faces, we sense that something is wrong.

"Excuse us, but we must talk with you."

"Oh?"

"Well," the Reverend starts, exchanging nervous glances with his wife, "I have been contacted by two ministers who need accommodations for two weeks. As this room is, by church rule, reserved for these ministers when needed, I must make it available to them."

Mrs. Massey interjects, "We are so sorry, but it is only for two weeks, and then you may return."

I ask, "When would you like us to leave?"

"They are coming in two days' time."

This is disheartening, but Jean says, "No, that's okay. We'll find another place to stay right away."

Reverend Massey brightens at our acquiescence, repeating, "Yes, we are so sorry to do this," and then adds, "but I have located a temporary place for you to stay."

We pack up most of our belongings the next day, leaving some things locked in a closet in the main part of the house, and an apologetic Reverend Massey drives us in his jeep to a dilapidated structure on the ridge, close by Mary's. He then introduces us to Mr. Joshi, who shows us a dark room with a wooden platform for a bed. After the Massey's, this room is depressing, but at least it has a big fireplace. Mr. Joshi proves to be unscrupulous, charging us an outrageous price for the room. When we tell him that the bed has no mattress and the room no light, he brings in a thin, dirty mattress and kerosine lamp, saying that the charge for these items is extra.

We try to make the best of a bad situation, consoling ourselves that we'll be back at the Massey's in no time. We both start itching after the first night, our scratches opening tiny wounds on our bodies. We air out the ratty mattress, thinking this must be the problem, until Jean discovers that the platform itself is harboring between its slats hundreds of bedbugs and "earwigs," named for their propensity to crawl into sleepers' ears! A reluctant Mr. Joshi changes our platform for one without bugs. We sleep without incident from then on, aside from the nocturnal rustling noises that sound suspiciously like the scampering of rats. The house seems haunted, a dreaded feeling that something or someone is watching us. So, we spend a lot of time away from the house, visiting with Mary, shopping, and taking long walks in the woods. We're to learn later that the local Kumaon Indians do consider this house haunted, inhabited by *bhuts*, or "ghosts," the result of a murder committed there years in the past!

After two weeks, Reverend Massey drives up in his jeep and tells us that his Methodists guests have left, and if we'd like, we're more than welcome to return to his house. He doesn't have to tell us twice! In just a few minutes, we're packed up and driving back to his house on the hill. Mrs. Massey greets us with open arms, cookies, and tea. Without her overtly saying so, we glean that she didn't much care for the visiting guests.

Life with the Masseys continues as before: serene days spent in doing yoga practices, reading, walking, and making meals. In a conversation with Reverend Massey, we find out that his lifelong dream has been to go to the United States to visit the iconic sites of the Methodist church.

"As a younger man, I was accepted on a full scholarship to a religious studies program at the University of Michigan at Ann Arbor but couldn't afford the travel expenses. Recently, I was one of the candidates vying to attend the upcoming World Methodist Conference in America but was not chosen."

I reply, "What a shame. You would have been a good representative from India."

"Yes, I think so," he says. Then, after a pause, says, "But I have not given up hope. Someday I will go to America. The Lord will provide."

This conversation prompts me to write a letter to my father, a trustee of our local Methodist church in New York, asking if he knows of any Methodist organization that would be willing to fund the reverend's visit to the United States. Two weeks later, I receive a letter from my father. In his precise handwriting, he assures me that he will do all he can to help Reverend Massey realize his dream. His love and humor come through his words. I tear up as I read his letter, missing him and my mother more than ever. Reverend Massey is tearful himself when I tell him that my father will try to bring him to America for a visit.

With few distractions, we decide the time is right for us to utilize the gift given us by John in Manali and drop acid together on my birthday in early June. Jean wakes up with stomach pains on this day and doesn't want to ingest anything other than water. But she encourages me to drop a tab, offering to "chaperone" me through the trip. An hour later, we're both laughing hysterically at the chickens scratching about in their coop, Jean apparently getting a contact high from me. Soon after, I enter my own world, with Jean making sure I'm comfortable. Reverend Massey knocks on our door in the late morning, asking if Jean will evaluate some children's books he plans on distributing to his congregation, as he knows she has been involved with preschool education. I sit quietly, literally watching the flow of words coming from both their mouths.

Otherwise, there's very little in the way of hallucinations or distortions as the day progresses; on the contrary, the world seems powerfully ordinary, everything in its place, perfectly so. I'm imbued with a strong sense of well-being and, along with this, investment in the welfare of others. I see myself as a caretaker of the world, beginning with the people and animals on Christian Hill. My mind seems to touch the cosmos itself as my body simply moves from a chair inside our room to one outside on the veranda, and back to the inside chair again. I feel so alive and at one with everything! At the same time, my body is putting out tremendous heat. A fly keeps buzzing around me, landing on my sixth chakra, the area between and above my eyebrows. I whisk it away, but it just keeps coming back. Jean looks concerned, but gently refers to me as her "human furnace." As day becomes dusk, the intensity of the trip ebbs, and I slowly return to a more mundane consciousness by the evening fire.

Dear Dad, Mom and Nancy,

I received your letters—one from Mom and one from Dad and thought, now that's a first! Thank you very much. First of all, congratulations Mom on copping third place in the Garden Club's Annual Show! As we say in "Inja," "First-Class!" As for your wanting to meet some of our new friends from India, if everyone we've given our Bayville address decided to drop in for a visit, you'd have nothing short of a zoo on your hands. So next year could prove to be a social scene to end all social scenes. We'll see. I'm glad to hear that Grandma Tillie is well; we think of the Olsens often enough and really should get around to putting thoughts to ink. Nancy, thanks for getting it together to write us; we enjoyed the letter, particularly the poem. I'll try to write soon. Meanwhile, don't walk into any open manholes, Blinky. And Dad, thanks for considering and bringing up the case of Reverend Massey. He's happy to know that someone is trying to help him on that side of the world. Seems you've been having a hard time physically and business-wise this past month or so. Doesn't seem to affect your humor at all. After reading your letter, Jean turned to me and said, "truly the sire of the Westby clan's humor." Please keep me informed on South American activities.

We're still in Almora. Very difficult to leave. Jean and I argue about whose mom makes the best spaghetti sauce, and whether the morning breakfasts we both grew up with are called Norwegian pancakes or German pancakes, so I think we've both been struck with a touch of homesickness. What to do? We'll just have to come back home. If things go according to the present scheme, we'll visit Kashmir in July, leave India sometime in August and be home in late September, early October. Our purpose in going to Kashmir is to meet up with Swami Gitananda and take a month's yoga course, mainly to prepare ourselves for the tedious journey overland. I hope this letter arrives before you leave to G.B. We're thrilled to hear of your upcoming journey and will be anxious to hear how it turned out. Love, Brus and Jean

P.S. IMAGINE, an entire letter written with just one Indian refill!

Several days after my acid trip, I begin to feel pain in the right side of my body, just under my lower ribs. I'm also very tired, even upon waking in the morning. I have no desire to do yoga or walk in the woods. Even eating becomes a chore. I walk down to Almora Bazaar one morning for necessary supplies, and I almost can't make it back up the hill, stopping often to rest. Jean thinks I should see a doctor, but I say that I'm probably just tired from all the energy I put out on the acid trip. The next day, I can't get out of bed, my eyes and skin have turned yellow, and the color of my pee has turned an odorous brown!

Reverend Massey contacts a doctor, who comes to examine me and concludes, "Well, this looks like a hepatitis A virus."

"How could this happen?" Jean asks.

"It is a disease of the liver, contracted through water or food contaminated with feces. He could have contracted this anywhere from two to six weeks earlier."

"So, what can we do? How can he get better?"

"The only cure for this is bedrest for a least two months. Also, he must maintain a healthy diet, high in glucose and low in fats. No fried foods."

Before the doctor leaves, he tells Jean that this is a highly infectious disease, giving her instructions to wash her hands constantly and not eat food from the same dishes.

For the next three weeks, I leave bed only to go to the bathroom. I'm running a low-grade fever and have joint pains throughout my body. I sleep eighteen hours a day, and when I'm awake, I'm in a foul mood, mainly self-pity and anger usually directed at Jean, whose patience with me is tested to the max. Because I'm so depleted of energy, she calls me her "wet noodle."

Mary visits often, entertaining us with stories of the "cranks" on the ridge; always some drama among them, whether it be bitter enmity or not-so-secret trysts. She also checks my eyes, tongue, and pulse before placing homeopathic pills under my tongue. She brings me Nero Wolfe mystery books, although I can't really read more than a few pages at a time.

My appetite begins to return after three weeks, and I feel well enough to take short walks. Mary insists that I receive regular vitamin B12 shots at the local clinic for leprosy patients, so every few days we pile into Reverend Massey's jeep and drive to the clinic. The waiting room is really a hallway with patients lining benches on each side. Being a white sahib, the doctor sees me right after he's finished with his current patient. I never hear objections from those who've been patiently waiting their turns to see the doctor. This mentality is, of course, a holdover from the days of the "me first" attitude of the privileged white British Raj but, in my weakened state, I certainly don't object.

Although the Masseys have been very supportive throughout our stay, both Jean and I are feeling bored with the long days of my illness. The summer monsoons have already begun, further restricting us to our room, particularly during the afternoons when the clouds build up and burst into torrential rain. We become antsy to find a more vibrant living situation. We ask Mary to keep an eye out for any vacancies on the ridge and, just a day later, she tells us that she's learned that a couple is about to move out of their large apartment at Epworth Estates, just a kilometer above Mary's house.

Mary tells us, "Epworth is beautiful. It has seen many well-known people pass through its apartments: Allan Ginsberg, R. D. Laing, Baba Ram Dass, and Timothy Leary to name just a few. Most of them came to see Lama Govinda. There are never any long-term guests at Epworth. Most either leave after a few weeks or months, some even finding more permanent and cheaper housing further up the ridge."

We've both noticed that Mary has looked drawn and tired recently. When we ask about her health, she confides in us that she will be going to the nearby town of Nainital for a while to see a homeopathic doctor about a tumor in her gall bladder.

"The doctors here want to operate to remove the tumor and have it biopsied. But I first want to see this doctor for his opinion. Maybe he can offer me a better option than surgery."

We wish her well and promise to say mantras for a good outcome.

We approach the Masseys about wanting to move. They say they understand and offer to help us with the move, as I certainly can't carry bags. Epworth Estates is an old Methodist missionary house, now used solely for paying guests. In his capacity as district supervisor, Reverend Massey says he will charge a reasonable rent for our new apartment. Jean tells me back in our apartment that she detected a sense of relief from Mrs. Massey. Even though we have all had a good neighborly relationship, now the family can finally have the whole house to themselves once more.

Reverend Massey and his son, Vinod, pack our belongings in the jeep a couple of days later, drive us up to Epworth Estates, and deposit us on the doorstep of our new apartment. We say our good-byes, and I promise the reverend that I will keep him informed about my father's fundraising efforts to bring him to America. (As it turns out, the necessary funds are raised, and Reverend Massey will go to America by himself a year and a half later. Jean and I will meet him at LaGuardia Airport just before we leave for California and bring him to my family home in Bayville, Long Island. My parents are delighted to finally meet him and spend hours over the next weeks sharing stories of their lives in two very different parts of the world. My father introduces him to the clergy and elders of the Bayville Methodist church, and in no time, he is delivering his first sermon. My father writes me saying, "He's just what our quiet, sedate church needs, an old-time 'fire and brimstone' preacher! Who knew? He's such a quiet and reserved gentleman. But give him a pulpit!" Reverend Massey is to spend four months traveling throughout the States, being well received by numerous church groups and giving fiery sermons wherever he goes.)

Our apartment is in the front of Epworth, facing a large lawn ending in a steep drop to the valley below. The view of the Himalayas is mind-boggling: many twenty-three thousand to twenty-four-thousand-foot peaks, including the famous Nanda Dev and the Trishul range of three peaks, through which we can see the old trading pass from India into Tibet. A bay entrance opens to an apartment almost as big as the Massey's house, with high ceilings and three spacious rooms. The living room is dominated by a massive fireplace, with a knee-high round oak table that is to become the center of our daily and evening activities. The room is filled with furniture: a dining table, desk, and numerous chairs, all built of sturdy oak and deodar wood in the days of the Raj. A door off the living room leads to a large bedroom, with three rope-strung cots, an armoire, and a bathroom with a Western-style toilet. A sizable screened-in porch is just off the bedroom. Another door from the living room leads to a kitchen lined with cupboards, a sizable wood stove, and long work counter. As there is no electricity or running water, the apartment is filled with kerosene lanterns. Mary has told us that kerosene, water, and wood wallas will keep us supplied every day for a couple of rupees. We like this apartment immediately and settle in quickly. I can already feel the weight of my illness begin to lift in our new life here.

The next morning, we hear a whining at the kitchen door. One of the dogs, Jack, from the Massey's house, has apparently followed us here. He looks hungry and tired, so we find some beans and chapatis for him. Jean decides to walk to the Massey's later in the day to tell them that one of their dogs is at our apartment. She returns with a big smile an hour later, telling me that the Masseys said that they don't consider the dogs theirs, that dogs always go where there is food.

"Well," she concludes, "we have plenty of food here."

Jean is always happy to host a dog.

The next day, two Kumaon locals appear at our kitchen door— an older man, Mohan Singh, and his nephew, Herat Singh. Mohan Singh explains to us that he is the *chowkidar*, or main caretaker, for Epworth Estates, and Herat Singh is the servant for this apartment.

"Oh?" I respond, "We didn't know the apartment comes with servants."

"Oh yes," he says, "Epworth has always had a servant for each apartment. My nephew is a very good servant. He will cook and clean each day and will shop for you as well."

The nephew looks quite young to me. I ask him, "How old are you, Herat Singh?"

He looks to Mohan Singh, who responds, "He is fourteen and has been servant here for two years."

"Does he speak English?"

"Just a little, but he understands what you want of him."

Jean now says, "What do we pay him?"

"Just two rupees a day, not too much."

Herat Singh proves an invaluable support for both of us. Every day, he appears at our kitchen door at 8:00 a.m., washes the previous night's dishes and pots, and prepares breakfast, usually a mild semolina porridge as I'm still recuperating. After cleaning the apartment, he often goes shopping at the Chota Bazaar, returning with rice, dal, *subji*, and chapatis for lunch. When not shopping, he's buying supplies from the daily wallas, being sure to stack the wood next to the stove and fireplace, fill all the kerosene lanterns, and the water jugs for the kitchen and bathroom. After lunch cleanup, he is done for the day. We come to appreciate this quiet, serious, hard-working young man and, after a couple of weeks, are all able to communicate quite well. Herat Singh takes pride in running the household, and we never have any fear that he will steal even a chapati from us.

Our apartment is one of four—the two in front larger than the ones in back—connected by a long central corridor lined with bookshelves filled with years of travel books, religious texts, and mystery novels. We discover that every apartment is occupied and soon begin to meet our neighbors. Across the hall, in the other front apartment, live Wynn, Sally, and their three-year-old twins, Sammy and Ninny. Wynn, in his midforties, gained a reputation as a painter of nude portraits and as a movie director. His loft apartment on the lower east side of New York was the center of activities for famous beatniks and hippies, such as Alan Ginsberg, Jack Kerouac, Timothy Leary, and Abbie Hoffman. Sally grew up in New York with wealthy parents who were close friends with the Astors and Vanderbilts.

Douglas is another American who lives in the back apartment behind theirs. He's been studying yoga for the past four years, mainly in Madras. Behind our apartment is a Tibetan lama and several members of his retinue. Wynn's friend, John, has recently arrived from New York. He's well known as the poet who created "Dial-A-Poem," an enterprise where anyone could dial a phone number and hear recorded poems by many different poets. This became wildly successful, boasting more than a million subscribers until the FBI began to investigate complaints about the "lurid language" of certain poems. Finally, his funders balked, and he had to shut down the operation. Coming to Almora to regain some serenity, he now walks down each day from his abode up the ridge called Snow View to study Tibetan language and Buddhist philosophy with the Tibetan lama.

Thurs. July 29th
Dear Mom and Dad,

    Got your letter today from the postman as we were sitting down to lunch. Was beginning to get concerned as it had been too long since I heard from you. Mary has still not come back from Nainital (a nearby town) where she went to see about a tumor in her gall bladder (the hospital wanted to operate but she doesn't and so is treating it with homeopathy—a natural herbal kind of medical treatment.) Since she's been away, I've been down to her house 3x looking for her servant to get my mail (of which there was none) but he's never home! Looks like we'll stay here thru Aug.—it's so comfortable and beautiful. The weather (although it's monsoons) after the rains is fantastic! We can see an incredible mt. range called "The Snows." Some are in India and some in Tibet & some in Nepal—we are right on the border. All around us are huge pine trees & grass & mt. flowers. Our house is very large, completely furnished. Up to the cut crystal sugar bowl. There is no electricity, but it's not needed—we have many kerosene lamps for night. Our "servant" comes every day to shop, do dishes, clean house and wash clothes for $5 a month. Our rent is less than $10 a month—and although everything is cheap we are living higher than ever before in India. It's just one huge house (before it was a mission house for the Methodist church) w/ 4 huge apartments and nothing else around it. Brus is better, still a little weak—yes, it was quite an attack (not mentioned to his family because of needless worry)—hepatitis really knocks you out! But he's doing fine now. We got a letter from Swami yesterday & he will be up in the northern part of India in Sept. so we will try to see him then. I'll try to send gifts before we leave India—can't do it before. Do you like sarees? I've worn mine 4x and they're uncomfortable! Send Christmas cards to: Reverend N.

Massey, District Superintendent, Methodist Church, Pithoragarh,
U.P. India. Send as printed matter—that's as cheap as possible.
They of course had to think we were married (which could happen!)
so my last name is Westby to them. Write soon—love to all—keep
buying lottery tickets for us!! Love, Jean & Brus

As the monsoon days settle in, we get to know our neighbors.
Douglas drops by, for only a few minutes at a time, with some tid-
bit of new information. He's very knowledgeable but at the same
time opinionated, constantly expressing his likes and dislikes. A few
minutes with him is all we can stand! He brings us a newspaper
from Delhi one morning. The front-page headline reads, "Worst
Monsoons of the Century!" with photos of cars and rickshaws half
immersed in water. The article goes on to say that this year's monsoons are breaking records for the amount of flooding and destruction. We're happy to be in the mountains, away from the floods.

We become close with Wynn and Sally, sharing stories over long
hours by our fires. We are much younger than they and often just
listen to their fascinating lives.

Sally tells us, "I grew up in a wealthy household, where the men
were expected to follow my father into business. Nobody expected
anything of me, so I was very shy; I had no friends. Really, I was
just a shadow passing through our mansion's hallways. When I was
sixteen, I was raped by my older brother and became pregnant. My
mother refused to let me out of bed for the entire pregnancy, telling her friends that I had pneumonia. When my baby was born, my
mother immediately put the girl up for adoption. I didn't object,
being so cowed by my mother. Later, my parents arranged a "suitable" marriage for me to a wealthy man, who turned out to be a
homosexual and drunkard. He would disappear for weeks at a time
with his boyfriend and then show up with a $50,000 "forgiveness"
necklace, or bracelet, whatever. To make matters worse, he got
into a serious car accident and became crippled, which meant he
depended on me to feed and clean him. After years of this, I had
enough and left him.

"This is about when I met Wynn. He was a hip young artist," at this, Wynn lets out a guffaw, "who offered to paint my
portrait. I knew nothing about him but agreed. I was surprised
he wanted me to wear jeans and a sweatshirt for the sittings but,
of course, said nothing. When Wynn told me he was finished,
I made a big deal out of arranging a show, inviting all the best
people in New York to the gala unveiling of my portrait. After an
hour of schmoozing and champagne toasts, Wynn unveiled my
portrait. There, as big as life, sat a naked fat man, with a little
me in sweatshirt and jeans in the corner, looking up at his penis!
Everyone was speechless, made excuses, and disappeared, leaving
me and Wynn all alone in the gallery. This was the beginning of
our relationship."

"Wow!" I exclaim. "Why did you paint her that way, Wynn?"

"Well, that's how I saw her."

Sally adds, "That's really how I saw myself too: unimportant,
unworthy, just a shadow. But, with Wynn's help, from that night I
changed. That was the beginning of my awakening."

Wynn continues to say that he and Sally lived together for a year
in his downtown loft. He'd just finished directing a movie, *Brand X*,
with Abbie Hoffman, and was getting over a mild case of hepatitis,
which he claims he contracted in Amsterdam on location for the
movie. Sally adds that she had to put up nightly with a parade of
friends reading poetry, playing music, and arguing politics until
early in the morning. At Timothy Leary's direction, Wynn spent
the previous summer experimenting with LSD. Specifically, each
week he'd begin by dropping a quarter of a trip, the next day half,
a whole trip each of the next two days, followed by a half-dose day,
then quarter-dose day, with the final day, a day of rest.

"Just like God," Wynn laughs.

It does seem to me that all those trips have had their effect.
Wynn is an enigma, sometimes present, at others, far away in his
own world. Sally seems to carry the brunt of responsibility when
it comes to relating with the children, but we never hear her
complain.

Sally learns in a letter one day that her brother-in-law, and dear friend, has committed suicide. At the urging of friend John, she asks the lama behind us if he will perform a ceremony to direct her brother-in-law's soul toward a beneficial reincarnation. The lama agrees, and a ceremony is arranged on Epworth's front lawn. Hours of chanting, horn blowing, and cymbals clanging ensue while John explains to us the symbolism of each part of the ceremony. At the very end of the ceremony, the lama goes to light a candle, which John says will ensure the successful passage of the deceased. However, no matter how many times the lama tries, the candle refuses to light. He finally gives up, announcing that the successful passage of Sally's brother-in-law is not ensured. Devasted, Sally walks away in tears, Wynn following with the children.

One reason why so many visitors have come to the ridge is to meet with Lama Govinda. A German Buddhist scholar, he traveled and studied extensively in Tibet, and is well known for his two books, *Way of the White Cloud* and *Foundations of Tibetan Mysticism*. We're told that he and his wife, Li Gotami, welcome visitors on Sundays, so Jean and I decide to go. A half-hour walk on the path up the ridge from Epworth brings us to a small house nestled in a pine grove on a hill, known as Casar Devi. (We learn later that the house occupied by Lama Govinda is the hermitage of the late W. Y. Evans-Wentz, the renowned editor of the Tibetan opus, *Bardo Thodol*, which he titled *The Tibetan Book of the Dead*.) We join several other visitors, seating ourselves in a circle of folding chairs under a vined arbor in the house's garden. We are ten in all. After a few minutes, Lama Govinda and Li Gotami emerge from the house and take their seats. He is a small, thin man with a long white beard and high-peaked yellow lama's cap. She is Indian, heavyset, dressed in a traditional Tibetan *chuba*. She looks as though smiles don't come easily for her.

After thanking us all for coming, Lama Govinda reads from a dissertation he wrote regarding the distinction between the meditative experience and LSD. His contention is that both these experiences are mutually exclusive, and that those who take LSD should not think they are experiencing true meditation. In fact, he reads, the result of taking LSD is just the opposite of meditation, fragmenting the mind, leading to further confusion about one's basic nature. Li Gotami scans each person as he reads, watching our reactions to his words. Having just experienced a recent acid trip, as well as others in the past during which I always felt a sense of peace and wholeness within myself and with nature, I can't entirely agree with his conclusions. I also notice a couple of visitors fidgeting uncomfortably, as though they don't like what they're hearing. In particular, a young Frenchman keeps grumbling to his friend until Li Gotami asks him to stop talking. Lama Govinda's reading is long, and as it begins to get windy and cold, Li Gotami suggests we all come back next Sunday for a follow-up session of questions and answers.

All the same visitors, and a few more, come to Casar Devi the next Sunday. This time the circle of chairs is arranged at a promontory of the property with a magnificent view of the Himalayas. As before, we all settle before Lama Govinda and Li Gotami arrive. As soon as Li Gotami asks if anyone has questions, the young Frenchman stands up and begins to read a long rebuttal of Lama Govinda's dissertation. His English is halting and difficult to understand, but I think I get the gist of what he is trying to say—that is, if one approaches an LSD trip with the right incentive to explore more about oneself, then it will be a meditative experience. He continues to read that many young people (like ourselves) have come to India searching for spiritual teachings as a result of taking LSD.

Just as he's finished, Li Gotami asks him, "Have you ever tried to meditate on LSD?"

"No," he replies.

"Then have you ever meditated while not on LSD.?

"Very little."

"Then how can you say that both meditation and LSD are the same when you really haven't experienced meditation?"

Now it is the Frenchman's turn. "Excuse me, madam, but have you ever tried LSD?"

"No, I haven't," she replies.

"Then how can you say that LSD is not the same as meditation when you haven't tried it?"

They've reached an impasse. The Frenchman smiles smugly while I can almost hear Li Gotami growling. Lama Govinda seems distraught but says nothing. The rest of us visitors begin debating among ourselves until Li Gotami announces that this Sunday's session is over and grudgingly invites us all back next Sunday for another dissertation by the lama.

That night, after Sally puts the kids to bed, we share our experience with her and Wynn about the past two Sundays at Casar Devi.

Wynn laughs, "Li Gotami may not have taken acid, but she sure has an experience of it."

"What do you mean?" I ask.

"Well, one day, when Li Gotami was away, Tim Leary and Ralph Metzner (another LSD pioneer) convinced Lama Govinda that he should take an acid trip. Govinda lost his mind, rolling on the ground, laughing uncontrollably, and yelling crazy stuff in German. By the time Li Gotami returned, he was curled up in a ball, grinning and giggling. She didn't know what happened to him until Leary told her. She went ballistic, yelling at her husband for being so stupid for taking dangerous drugs. She kicked Leary and Metzner out, calling them vicious hooligans, and telling them never to come back again."

"Holy shit!" is all I can say.

"So, you can see why she's so opposed to acid. Him too, I guess."

This experience of the past two Sundays quell any interest in us to visit Casar Devi again.

Mary returns from Nainital. She looks older and more drawn, a sickly pallor to her skin. She's still resistant to surgery, saying that she knows she can cure herself with the right combination of homeopathic medicines. She just has to find the right remedy.

She'll return to Nainital in a few days. Reverend Massey kindly continues to bring me down to the leprosy clinic every few days for vitamin B12 shots. We visit his family on Christian Hill again, but regular visits soon ebb away.

In keeping with the transient nature of Epworth Estates, the next weeks see changes in occupants. Douglas moves out, heading toward Kathmandu. Jennifer, a single, eighteen-year-old woman, moves in. She has been living by herself in different places in Almora for the past two years, including the *"bhut* house" we occupied for the two weeks the Masseys hosted the Methodist ministers. She avoids talking about her past, but fits right into our scene, baking bread and cookies daily to offer at our evening gatherings. Our large apartment, with its great fireplace, is a natural choice for group get-togethers.

The lama and his retinue, along with John, leave soon after, bound for Sarnath, the site we visited of the Buddha's first teachings after attaining enlightenment. In their place, Rogan and Jim, friends from Liverpool, move in. They lived in the very same apartment months before traveling into Nepal and Southeast Asia and are happy to "be home."

Rogan and Jim prove an entertaining twosome, telling endless stories of past adventures in their unique Liverpudlian accents. Over a shared supper by the fire, they tell us of their most recent ordeal.

Rogan begins, "Me and Jim were looking for a new adventure. And we found one in Darjeeling."

"Yeah," Jim adds, "did we ever!"

Rogan continues, "We were told that there was an old trading route directly from Darjeeling into Assam, so we naturally thought this might be just right for the two of us."

Jim: "A Nepali gentleman sells us two horses and throws in a dog."

Rogan: "Mind you, we'd neither of us ever been on a horse before. Then we buy a map of the route we're to take, and off we go."

"Did you have a guide?" I ask.

Jim: "No guide. Just the map."

Rogan: "So there we are, setting off to Assam, two cowboys that never rode a horse, and dragging a dog by a rope, its feet digging into the ground to break free."

Jim: "Probably knew already what we were in for."

Rogan: "Anyway, the dog runs away the first night we set up camp. Useless anyway. We decide to name our horses Stanley and Mary."

Jim: "Yeah, maybe they didn't like their names because they were a pain in the ass. Stanley particularly. He refused to cross streams or climb steep hills no matter how hard we pushed and tugged at him. I finally had enough. One hill too many. When he refused to climb, I got off him, held him tightly by his reins, and punched him squarely in the mouth. Yeah, he cooperated after that, I tell you. But my hand hurt for a week."

Rogan: "Anyway, the whole journey lasted three weeks. Mary just dropped dead on a mountain pass. Maybe a heart attack, I don't know. All we could do was leave her there."

Jim: "Then we ran out of food."

Rogan: "Jim was in charge of provisions."

Jim: "How the hell did I know the trip would take three weeks."

Rogan: "And we brought zero food for Stanley and Mary. Thought they'd just live off grass and stuff. Problem was, there wasn't any grass for most of the time."

Jim: "Probably why Mary dropped dead. So, Stanley's starving when we finally reach Shillong, the capital of Assam."

Rogan: "Hell, we're starving too! After a couple of days of food and sleep, we give Stanley away to our hotel manager to pay for our room."

Jean interjects at the end of their story, "Hmm, sounds like a smart dog." This breaks us all up.

We discover that one of the reasons Rogan and Jim are always seeking new adventures is as a deterrent from shooting opium. They still keep their "works" in the bottom of their packs, "just in case the urge gets to be too much." When they find out that I'm driven periodically to the leprosy clinic for vitamin B12 shots, Rogan offers to do the job himself. Jim will have nothing to do with it, fearing that, "once my works are out of my pack, they may never find their way back in." We add ampoules of vitamin B12 to Herat Singh's shopping list, and "Dr. Rogan" gives me daily injections, more professionally done and less painful than those I received at the clinic. I can feel myself growing stronger by the day.

8/5/71
Dear All,

At this point, Dad and Mom, I bet you're wondering if your trip to the U.K. wasn't all a dream. I know you enjoyed yourselves and are trying to settle back into Bayville life. Please give us a report of your adventures in your next letter. John and Marcia, thanks for the letter. Your confusion concerning the future gives us hope, as we ourselves have no idea what's what. We do know that despite certain visa difficulties that have arisen this week we'll stay in Almora until Sept. 1 or thereabouts. It still looks as if we'll be back sometime in the late fall, so it'll be nice to visit you in Vermont.

Right now I'm waiting for the dough to rise so we can eat home-made bread for dinner. Life is slow here, but never dull, always spontaneous. We've developed a good set of friends here. There's plenty of music—Eastern and Western—and someone bakes a cake at least every other day. We have another dog, Jack—a little scrapper—love him dearly but will probably leave him in the care of a good family when we leave.

Nancy, if you haven't already, try to get hold of the latest Baba Ram Dass literature. It's good. Write and tell us the dirt about Fiedel School! Love, Brus and Jean

The monsoons settle in with a vengeance, every day cloudy and cold, with only occasional breaks of clear skies blessing us with a view of the Himalayas. During these short periods, Jean and I stroll a couple of kilometers up the ridge to a small chai shop, where we enjoy viewing the entire Himalaya range from Anapurna to Mount Everest. On the way back, we walk through the deodar woods, sometimes getting caught in the rains, picking chanterelles, the large, "floppy-eared" mushrooms growing prolifically in the monsoon climate. They become a delicious staple in omelets, soups, and rice dishes.

An emaciated dog shows up at our kitchen door one day. Herat Singh tells us that her name is Shanti (Peace) and that she often comes around looking for a handout. Jean feeds her some leftovers each day, while I refrain from objecting, knowing how Jean magnetizes dogs wherever she goes. Meanwhile, Jack doesn't seem too happy to share our attention, growling whenever Shanti comes near. What I take for her distended stomach due to worms turns out be a pregnancy. Herat Singh tells us that she's been pregnant before but always lost the puppies because she couldn't produce enough milk in her chronically weak condition. Determined not to let this happen again, we feed her table scraps and milk each morning when she appears at the kitchen door for her handout.

Sitting on our front porch one morning, we see two Indian gentlemen in white shirts and ties, carrying briefcases, walking our way. Both are winded from the walk, but the determined look on their faces alert us that something serious is on their minds. After checking a book to ascertain our names, the one man tells us that our applications for student visas have been rejected. Therefore, our temporary visas are invalid, and we must leave India within a week! I'm speechless, feeling an upsurge of panic, but Jean stays calm and offers the men tea, which they gratefully accept.

We all relax a little during tea and light conversation of our families, our travels, and their jobs.

Finally, Jean says, "As you can both see, my husband is not well." I still have a yellow pallor. "He has infectious hepatitis. Traveling right now during the monsoons will severely affect his health. Also, he may possibly infect others."

This brings looks of concern from the men.

"Is it possible for us to extend our temporary visas until he is well enough to travel?"

One man responds instantly, "This is not possible."

But the other says, "This is not our decision. You must take your case to the Foreign Registration Office in Almora. Perhaps they will help you there."

We thank the men for coming and tell them that we will follow their good advice. Even before the men have walked out of sight, we send Herat Singh to Mary's and the Masseys with word of our plight. The next day, Reverend Massey and Mary accompany us to the Foreign Registration Office. It's obvious from the deferential attitude of the officer in charge toward Reverend Massey that the district superintendent holds considerable influence. After we hand over our temporary visas and explain our circumstances, the officer agrees to call the Delhi office. We wait while he converses on the phone in Hindi. Hanging up the phone, he announces that he has permission to extend our temporary visas for two more months, stamps our papers, and expresses his hope that I'll recover quickly from my illness. We leave the office, elated that we have a reprieve. Once again, we have Reverend Massey to thank for his kind help.

We'd been entertaining vague plans to leave Almora and join Swamiji, Meenakshi, and Dick in Nepal for a month-long yoga program during the final leg of their tour. Now, with my continued illness combined with our not wanting to travel down to the plains during monsoon season, we decide to remain in Almora for most of the duration of our two-month visa extension. Besides, we're not ready to leave our friends. We're excited to hear from Dick that Swamiji is considering visiting us in Almora after the program in Nepal.

Rogan and Jim may have given up opium, but they are dedicated hash smokers. Each night, they make elaborate "spliffs," long joints, sometimes cleverly connecting the joints to resemble candelabras. Wynn and Sally are avid participants, while Jean and I sometimes partake. I know that ganja and charas deplete my energy right now, and I have precious little to spare.

A friend of Rogan's and Jim's, Chris, a South African who lives in a nearby cottage, now comes by regularly with his guitar and plays popular tunes. Rogan pulls a harmonica from his pack, while the rest of us sing and drum on pots. We'll never find an audience willing to listen to such a racket, but we have fun!

Mary now joins us most evenings when she's back in Almora, dispensing homeopathic remedies to those with minor maladies. She looks so much healthier than the last time we saw her!

When I comment on this, she says, "This last time in Nainital, I met a young saddhu who wanted me to see his guru, Gan Gotri Baba. Baba took one look at me and prescribed a mudpack of medicines, which he applied to my liver area for two weeks. At the end of two weeks, my pain was entirely gone! I'd finally rid myself of this disease! But the best part, having gotten such a magical cure from Gan Gotri Baba, I feel like I've finally found my guru after living all these years in Almora!"

Mary tells us that Gan Gotri Baba is a Shivite and a chillum smoker, always having disciples on hand to prepare exotic mixtures of tobacco, spices, and charas for his bowl.

"The very first day I was with him, he passes me his bowl of charas, which I decline."

"Oh," he asks, "so you don't smoke charas?"

"Never," I told him.

"Well," he said, "you should."

"From now on, I smoke from his chillum whenever he passes it to me."

So, for the times she is in Almora, Mary, now well into her sixties, avidly partakes in making music and occasionally smoking chillums.

8-24-71

Dear Family,

I've been waiting for a return letter for mine of Aug. 5, but as yet haven't heard anything from the Western hemisphere. So I'll write now quickly in order that this gets in the post this morning. HAPPY BIRTHDAY NANCY! Fifteen and covered with zits I bet.

There's a girl here now, 18, who's been in Almora since she was 16. Her name's Jennifer and she's quite remarkable. She could write her autobiography at this point. You're not getting anything from me now; you'll most likely get a load of stuff when we return. Say hello to Gina and all from us. Write and tell us how trainee living is at the Fiedel School this summer.

How's the political situation in America? The U.S. seems to be bungling again out here. Supplying arms to Pakistan, indeed! That's very silly. There's now a lot of talk of impending war between Pakistan and India after the monsoons end, or sometime within the next month or so. If such a struggle occurs, the U.S. will have to back Pakistan or suffer "loss of prestige." In any event, the American in India is becoming increasingly unpopular, while there's talk of many new difficulties in traveling to and from here overland. So we'll wait here and see what occurs within the next month or so. Perhaps we, and every other American, will get a free plane ticket back to the States, compliments of Mr. Nixon. Ah well.

Life continues here quietly, although there's an ever-increasing influx of travelers entering Almora. We've made many new friends, and now have two dogs and five newborn pups in our care. Each day is filled with new adventures and time passes so quickly.

Hello and love to the Brooklyn chapter. Also, if you see them, say hello to the Fiedels and David and Maggie Hawkins for us. Love, Brus and Jean

Wynn and Sally have another friend visit for a month. Donny is short and pudgy, has a thick New York accent, and brings with him the speed of that city. Adjusting to our slow lifestyle is initially difficult for him, and he spends his first days hiking up and down the ridge. Jean's mother would say that he's "chasing his tail around the block." Determined to use his time at Epworth to lose weight, he embarks on a ten-day fast, drinking only water mixed with glucose. Lack of food causes him to slow down further and let go of his urge to find something to do. At the end of the fast, he does look slimmer and stronger.

We're invited to join Wynn, Sally, their children, and Donny on a three-day visit to the village of Jageshwar, a site of over one hundred temples built between the seventh and twelfth centuries, for the annual celebration of Lord Krishna, called Krishnaratri. Wynn tells us that a friend of his named Nik, who was in Almora the year before, strongly recommended visiting this village.

"He told me that there are fields of weed near the village, and temple pujaris spend hours rubbing the crops into the finest hash he's ever smoked. The pujaris are stoned all the time, and they're more than willing to sell the stuff. That's how the town makes its money."

A bus from Almora Bazaar takes us to within a couple of kilometers from the village. We then walk the rest of the way along a ridge path, the children taking turns riding on Wynn's shoulders. Just as we descend from the ridge on a narrow, serpentine path, a storm hits, thoroughly soaking us. Rivulets of water from the surrounding hillsides funnel into the single main street of Jageshwar, creating a morass of mud. We slog into the village, a wet band of Westerners certainly attracting attention! Men sitting on their haunches measure us, merchants call to us while children run excitedly alongside. Sammy and Ninny take all this in stride, not showing any fear. Indeed, we don't detect any aggression in the attention, just curiosity. The village is surrounded by deodar trees and dominated by ancient temples. Though we are over seven thousand feet, the humidity and denseness of foliage feels like we're in a jungle. Following his friend Nik's directions, Wynn leads us to a hillside tourist bungalow overlooking the village. After some bargaining with the chowkidar, he unlocks the door to a large room with a central fireplace. Several bedrooms lead off the room. The dark, gloomy main room is soon transformed by lit candles and a roaring fire. It turns out this is a *pukka* bungalow, with three well-furnished bedrooms and an indoor bathroom. Wynn, Sally, and the children take the largest, Jean and I the next largest, and Donny the smallest. There are at least eight empty kerosene lanterns throughout the bungalow.

While Jean, Sally, and the children settle in, Wynn, Donny, and I walk down the hill into town for provisions and kerosene. Wynn also wants to connect with Krishna (yet another Krishna), the man who did business with his friend Nik the year before. After some frustration in inquiring about the whereabouts of Krishna (turns out the village is full of Krishnas), we find our man in a chai shop. Wynn tells him over chai that we're here to see the temples and experience Krishnaratri. We agree to Krishna's offer to be our guide for the time we're here. Unspoken, but clearly understood, is the sale of hash. Krishna is delighted to help us. Not only will it bring much-needed money to the village, but his own standing as our chosen guide will be elevated among his people, in particular the temple pujaris. He immediately sets to work showing us where to buy kerosene and groceries, which are mainly potatoes and onions, along with *atta*, or "wheat flour." Back at the bungalow, we set about making a simple soup and pan-fried bread, a tasty repast for hungry travelers. It's surprising how many different dishes we can make over the next couple of days with bare essentials!

Krishna guides us through numerous temples the next day. The pujaris are happy to see us, the only visitors for a long while. Pujaris lead us through puja ceremonies in each temple for a few rupees each. Ninny, quiet like her mother, seems to take it all in stride, but Sammy, every bit as impulsive and energetic as his dad, has little patience for these ceremonies. Wynn and Sally must take turns entertaining Sammy in the street during the ceremonies. All the while, Wynn and Krishna are discreetly negotiating over hash. Charas is illegal in India, but the danger of being caught with a large amount doesn't come from the local police. Rather, because the government has no tax control over this prohibited business, excise agents are on a constant lookout for Westerners coming to Jageshwar to buy hash. They have the authority to inspect body and home without a warrant and to arrest offenders. The price of a full kilo is finalized; it seems like an awful lot of hash to me, and I wonder if Wynn and Donnie are planning to smuggle the stuff into the

States. Krishna tells Wynn that he will personally bring the charas to Almora with payment upon delivery.

The following day is Krishnaratri. The temples are cleaned and bedecked with flowers. Several busloads of Indian tourists arrive throughout the day, and soon the quiet village is transformed into a carnival atmosphere. Vendors hawk their wares while Hindi music blares from competing stalls and radios perched on men's shoulders. We join the throngs of happy pilgrims parading through the temples.

Then, in the middle of the crowd, Wynn produces a bag of LSD pills. Sally looks upset.

"Why did you bring those with you?" she demands.

"Well, I thought it might be fun to drop here in the middle of the party."

"How many do you have?"

"Fifty or so, I think."

"Oh, Wynn, how could you be so foolish?"

We witness this impulsive and reckless side of Wynn come out, as he offers Krishna two trips, which he swallows immediately. He then asks Wynn if he can have a few more to share with his pujari friends. As Wynn reaches into his bag, other people now surrounded him, demanding his pills. They have no idea what acid is and does. Without understanding and preparation, they can easily become dangerously unbalanced. A besieged and intimidated Wynn now surrenders the entire bag of acid! Several fights break out over the bag, and I see one pujari swallowing a whole handful of pills! The crowd that just minutes before had been so carefree and happy now seems dark and menacing.

Krishna urges us to return to our bungalow right away and lock all the doors. "This will be a crazy night!"

We all huddle together by the fire this night, listening to the steady beat of drums mixed with yelling and screaming. We hear people running just outside our door, then an eerie silence, before more running and screaming!

We're upset by Wynn's impetuous act, but Sally is really fuming. "How could you put us all, especially your children, in danger?"

Wynn tries to make light of the situation, but we can see that he's embarrassed and ashamed of himself. Not one of us gets sleep on this night!

In the morning, we walk down to an eerily quiet village. Krishna is waiting for us at the chai shop. Normally quite animated, he is unusually quiet and distant. He tells us that the village went crazy after we left. Some wrecked temple property, some ran screaming through the village all night, some tore off their clothes, while others just lay on the ground weeping. He adds that the pujaris are very angry at Wynn for creating such a disturbance, so we should leave the village as soon as possible. We need no further prompting. We immediately return to the bungalow, pack our bags, walk back up the ridge and along the path to catch a bus back to Almora.

A week later, Krishna shows up at Epworth with a kilo of charas, for which Wynn pays him. He tells us that things have quieted down in the village and that the anger the pujaris felt toward Wynn is gone. All that remains are the many tales of when the world went crazy on the night of Krishnaratri.

Monsoons are slowly coming to an end, the snowcapped Himalayas becoming more visible for longer periods each day. Months of rain have caused such growth in plants and flowers that Epworth has become a garden paradise. We've settled into a pleasant routine of morning yoga before Herat Singh's breakfasts, plenty of rest for me during the day, afternoon walks, and making dinners and enjoying evenings with friends. We're sitting around the fire with Rogan, Jim, Chris, and Jennifer one night when we hear the loud roar of what we think is an approaching truck. We all rush out to see what it could be. A big white Mercedes van pulls up on the front lawn, and out steps James, Shelley, and their two children, Jasmine, nine, and Matteo, two. We make room for them around our fire. Wynn and Sally join us as well, leaving Sammy and Ninny to play with the new children in their apartment. Introductions made, James pulls out a large chillum, fires it up, and passes it around, insisting that everyone smoke "the best Afghani in the world." It certainly is powerful! Both Jean and I are done at one pull of the chillum, as James continues to load the pipe, until a dense cloud of smoke hovers in the rafters above. It seems as though James is intent on establishing himself as the alpha male chillum smoker, continuing to smoke after everyone else has had enough. He reminds me of some of the hippies back in Hayatullah's rooftop gardens in Kandahar competing to see who could take the largest pull from the giant hookah. His intense energy sits in stark contrast to our slow, mellow pace of Epworth. Shelley, meanwhile, is quiet but seems nervous, perhaps as a survival response in balancing James's intensity while trying to raise two children on the road. James and Shelley are excited to be back in Almora, where they lived several years before. They're anxious to see old friends in Almora Bazaar but tell us their primary purpose is to see a Dr. Bindu Joshi, an Ayurvedist, in hopes that he can cure Matteo's amoebic dysentery.

The children come running into the room before we can find out more. Sammy's in tears, and Ninny yells that the big girl hit him. Shelley is immediately on it, gently pulling Jasmine aside and questioning her until Jasmine says she's sorry to Sammy. That seems to pacify Sammy, and the children run back to the other apartment.

Shelley explains, "Jasmine is a tomboy. She plays hard, and sometimes a little too rough when it comes other children."

I notice two things about this last scene: one, Shelley is the active parent, and is good at it; and two, little Matteo does look sickly, his stomach abnormally distended. James and Shelley excuse themselves soon after and retire with their children to the van. The rest of us stay up a little longer, wondering aloud who these new neighbors really are and why they've chosen to camp out at Epworth.

James invites all of us to visit his van the next morning. Wynn said at the end of the night before that he was turned off by "macho man" James and declines to come along. The van is more like a traveling apartment: a large enough living and dining area to fit us all comfortably, with a sizable bedroom and bathroom. The children sleep in a loft above the front cab, which itself has two front and two rear swivel seats. It's only nine o'clock in the morning, and James has already fired up his chillum, showing a flash of irritation that none of us will join him. When we all comment on how spacious the van is, he tells us it only cost him $500!

"What?" I ask, "How can that be?"

So, James relates the story of how he came to buy the van. "We had been living in Afghanistan for the past six months, mainly because Matteo was too sick to travel. Also, the hash was really good. Our money was running out, so I arranged with my buddies back in New York to line up people to buy sweet Afghani hash. I strapped six kilos to my body, covered it all with loose clothes, and flew directly into JFK."

"Six kilos?" Chris asks. "That's some heavy shit!"

We laugh as James continues. "It's not as much as it could have been. I wanted to take in eight kilos, but Shelley said that would be over the top. As it was, I looked like some weird fat guy with a limp. Anyway, nobody stopped me, and through my connections, I unloaded the stuff in two hours flat. I came away with $12,000. I flew into Amsterdam two days later and ran into this guy who needed to dump his van and get home to Florida. He never told me why, and I didn't ask. I offered him $500, and he took it without a second thought. Two weeks later, I'm back in Afghanistan. Matteo is looking better, so we decide to come back to Almora to see if Dr. Bindu can help him."

James also tells us that every Sunday, he likes to take "one or two" tabs of acid, "depending on how I feel." It seems James just can't help living on the edge to feel alive. Shelley adds that he still smokes chillums on Sundays, but she knows he's also tripping because he's a lot quieter and calmer than usual.

I ride with James later in the day to see Dr. Bindu in Almora Bazaar. I'm feeling stronger but think that it wouldn't hurt to see if the doctor also has some treatment for me. As we walk through the bazaar, a number of people greet him along the way. It's obvious that James has left his stamp on Almora! Doctor Bindu is sitting in the doorway of his shop, with its sign overhead in Hindi and its English translation, "Ayurveda." He's delighted to see James again, and as they discuss Mateo's illness, I can see they have a close bond. I realize in that moment that I do like James. I sense a vulnerability in him that he shrouds in layers of bravado. Dr. Bindu tells James to bring Matteo to him, along with his son's stool sample.

Then, turning to me, he says, "But I can see that you're not well."

I explain that I'm recovering from an attack of hepatitis. I'm still weak but feeling so much stronger than before.

After looking at my eyes and tongue, he says, "If you give me 37.50 rupees, I will prepare the medicines you need."

Two days later, James, Matteo, and I return to Dr. Bindu's office. There are other patients in the room, so he has little time for small talk. Taking the stool sample and quickly examining Matteo, he tells James that, by the next day, he will concoct a mixture of medicine that will produce a cure.

To me, he hands three packets of medicines. "The first packet has ten smaller packets inside that you take each day for ten days. You must mix its contents with curd at night and hang it in a mesh cloth so that the whey drips out. Then you eat it in the morning, before breakfast. The second packet also has ten small packets for your second ten days. You simply take the medicine with water before lunchtime. The ten small packets in the third packet you take each day with water just before bedtime. At the end of this one-month cure, you will have regained all the energy you had before this illness, maybe even more."

"What is in these packets?" I ask.

"Oh, so many ingredients. Too many to remember."

For the next month, I follow Dr. Bindu's directions to the letter and do feel better, if not fully restored. Matteo doesn't seem to have responded as well to the first medicines he received. He still looks pallid, his stomach distended, and has very low energy. James continues to return with new medicines from Dr. Bindu.

Fri.-Sept. 17ᵗʰ—Almora
   First "Happy Birthday to you Mom, Happy Birthday to you!" By the time you get this, it should be right on your day. We are still in

219

Almora but going to leave approx.. on the 20ᵗʰ. Swami was going to come here today but due to the worst monsoon of this century the roads to here are bad. These last three days have been fantastic though—not a cloud in the sky, just 20-25 thousand foot, snow-covered Himalayas and the sun ... we are shooting for Christmas season to reach N.Y. That's only 2 1/2 mons. And time flies by when you're happy and moving. No? So I hope you're happy ... summer is almost over there, must be nice now. We hear various reports about the conditions of the States—we must see for ourselves. Hope you write ans. to my letter about sending me my money. We will need about $400 to return. We are shipping some shawls, etc., home which, after presents, we hope to sell to smaller shops on Long Island. That should help us live after we return—also a job w/ Ivan. Have heard from no one but you of late—wrote Carole for her birthday—no word though. Hope everybody is well & Margie is feeling better. Say "hello" to all for me. It's now dusk & a beautiful sunset. Brus is cooking pumpkin soup & he made bread—he's so good. Write soon to Delhi. Love, love, kiss, kiss ... Peace Jean & Brus

The final visitor during our stay at Epworth is Bhole Baba Shankar, a bearded, "Rasta-haired" saddhu who appears with a retinue of several Indian chelas one Sunday and holds court on our front lawn. Most of Epworth crowds around to see what this man is all about. He seems completely at ease and happy to meet us, while his followers look uneasy. He pulls out an ancient chillum from a well-worn travel pouch and hands it to the man beside him who loads it with charas. Then, with a grand gesture, he wraps the mouth of the chillum in a dirty cloth, holds it up in offering to the heavens, and yells (just like Ganesh Baba in Darjeeling), "Om Shiva Shankara, Bom Bom Bolay!" Taking an enormous pull from the chillum, he explodes in violent coughing, and then laughs as he passes the chillum around, along with handfuls of peanuts and betel leaves. Now, arms and hands gesticulating, he expounds about the fresh air, the sun, and the clouds in Hindi, as a chela translates in halting English. His openness has the effect of relaxing everyone, and soon we're all laughing and jabbering away; all that is, except James who sits quietly against a tire of his van. This is so unlike him that I'm concerned, until I realize that this is Sunday, and James has taken his "one or two tabs of acid."

Baba returns every Sunday for the next several weeks. We move his show into the large porch off our bedroom, the one we call the "puja room" because of the many posters we've hung on the wall of Hindu deities. Each visit is pretty much the same, and all, even his chelas by now, are happy and relaxed.

During a full moon eclipse, Shanti the dog gives birth to five puppies in our kitchen. Sammy and Ninny, beside themselves in excitement and joy, immediately claim a puppy each. Bhole Baba is delighted when we present him with a puppy, saying through his translator that he now has a true companion on the road. Herat Singh assures us that he will be able to find homes for the other two puppies, although I'm not so confident that they won't end up like their emaciated mother, Shanti, when she first appeared at our door.

The monsoon rains are over. The days are filled with sunshine, with white puffs of clouds floating by on gentle fall breezes. Our time at Epworth is coming to an end. We have less than a month left on our temporary visas, and we still want to see the Taj Mahal and visit Jaipur before leaving the country. James and family have already left, bound for Delhi where we plan to meet up with them. Chris has hitched a ride with them to Delhi on his way to Ganeshpuri, outside of Bombay, returning to the ashram of his guru, Swami Muktananda (the same teacher of John from Manali), where he'd been for two months prior to Almora.

On the Sunday before Jean and I are scheduled to leave Almora, I walk with Baba after his visit down the road past Chota Bazaar. We part at a crossroads with a hug, knowing we'll never see each other again. I give him a brass hair clip I've used ever since leaving New York to tie back my hair. He reaches into his pouch and pulls out a red-hued rock and, saying a mantra over it, indicates through his large gestures that this will give me strength. We come from two vastly different worlds and don't speak each other's language, but I feel as though I'm saying goodbye to a dear brother, and I know he feels the same way.

We keep putting off the inevitable task of saying goodbye to Epworth and our friends. "One more day, one more day" becomes our mantra. Finally, the day arrives. A taxi pulls up on our front lawn. Mary, Rogan and Jim, Wynn, Sally and the children, Jennifer, Herat Singh, and even Jack, the dog who has been with us since Christian Hill, crowd us with hugs and promises to see each other again.

We vow to return one day to Almora and beautiful Epworth. (As it turns out, we do return two years later. Mary is still there, as delightful as ever, and Jennifer as well, who has changed her name to Janobai, is now twenty years old and married to an older Englishman named Neil.)

A four-hour bus ride, avoiding potholes from the monsoon rains, down to the base city of Kathgodam, and an overnight train through Bareilly, brings us back to Delhi. This time, at James's recommendation, we book a big, comfortable room in the Hotel Continental Annex, just behind Connaught Place's Regal Cinema. James and family are in a room down the hall. It's only ten o'clock in the morning, but James is smoking his chillum already. The family doesn't seem happy. Matteo doesn't look any healthier, and now we're told their van has developed engine trouble. They also don't know where they'll go next. One plan is to return to Ibiza, where they lived for two years before coming to the East. We can see that there is tension between James and Shelley. James mopes, while Shelley seems more wired than ever. We leave them to go to a favorite restaurant nearby, only to return to hear them yelling at each other down the hall.

I say to Jean, "I wonder how the children are coping with this?"

"Probably nothing they haven't heard before," she responds.

The next morning, James tells us that they are leaving the center of the city to a campground on the outskirts. "We need the space to figure out our next move."

We wave goodbye as they drive away, the van sounding strangely wheezy. We hope that little Matteo will survive his illness. We never do see them again.

Dear Mom, Pop and Nancy,

Well, here we are in Delhi, after nearly five months of quiet Almora life. It's certainly a change! Congratulations Dad on being promoted to V.P., making you an official V.I.P. (Does this include a salary raise as well? How much do we get? None. Huh.)

We'll be in Delhi until tomorrow when we train to Agra (we think) to view the Taj Mahal, and then on to Jaipur, below Delhi, in Rajasthan, a state we've heard a great deal about. Jaipur, in the midst of the Rajasthan desert, is known as the "Pink City" because of its stone coloration. We've heard that Jaipur is unsurpassed in quality and originality of cloth materials, so we go to buy a little. Then to Delhi again (in about 2-3 weeks) and overland, via Afghanistan of course. As you understand by now, these are only tentative plans. We'll just have to see.

With all the new travelers in India this fall, we look upon ourselves as "old-timers." Over a period of nearly a year, we've traveled quite extensively in this country and can speak pretty good "pigeon" or "market" Hindi. So we delight in serving as information banks for newcomers here. We're both now healthy and happy. Say hello to Uncla, Grandma and Tanta, to the Cranes, and the Fiedels. Love, Brus & Jean

We run into Chris as we cross a street in opposite directions. He's staying at Sony's, yet another guesthouse on Jan Path Lane. He was about to leave Delhi on his way back to the ashram in Ganeshpuri when he found out that his guru, Swami Muktananda, was in Delhi. He invites us to join him for Swami's darshan so, later in the day, we three take a taxi to a large house in the New Delhi suburbs. Chris tells us during the short drive that Swamiji stresses the keys to a spiritual life are devotion to the guru and karma yoga, or selfless work for the benefit of others. The sounds of chanting and music upon arriving inform us that the darshan has already begun. We're directed to the back lawn of the house where an enormous tent has been erected. Inside, hundreds of people are crowded up to a platform where Swami Muktananda is seated on a throne. Chris and I stand at the rear of the men's section, while Jean finds a seat in the back of the women's area. We watch as person after person prostrates to Swami, leaving offerings of money, gifts, and flowers on a long table next to his throne. Several people sing songs and recite poetry. Muktananda, perhaps in his forties, looks every bit the bored monarch, rarely acknowledging all the attention. After an hour or so, Jean and I nod across the tent to each other. I tell Chris we're leaving but that we'll come and find him at Sony's the next morning. Just then, a remarkable thing happens. Chris and I watch as Jean rises to leave, placing her hands in *anjali,* or prayer gesture, to Swami and says namaste. Swami Muktananda looks directly at her over the crowd, smiles, and waves! Uncertain if his gesture is meant for her, she repeats her action, and he waves to her again! All heads in front of her turn to see just who it is that Swamiji is waving to. Somewhat embarrassed, Jean bows and backs out of the tent to escape the attention.

Chris is astounded! He tells me, "During all the darshans I've been to, Swamiji has almost never given this much attention to one person. He must see something special in Jean."

This comes as no surprise to me.

We find Chris the next morning strumming his guitar in the gardens of his guesthouse. After a breakfast together nearby, he asks us if we want to go with him to see a man named Baba Bidi.

"Who is he?" I ask.

Chris replies, "I was told by a guy here that he's a psychic guru and that a lot of travelers see him to find out where to go next. I thought I'd just go to see what he's all about."

Chris has been given directions, so we soon pull up in a taxi to one in a row of small houses on the outskirts of Old Delhi. A blonde, heavyset Western woman answers our knock and escorts us into a small room with cushions placed around a low round table. Baba Bidi is enormously fat. He doesn't rise but greets us cordially as we settle on the cushions. Before him on the table are platters of rice, *subji*, dal, fruit, and sweets, continuously refreshed by the Western woman during the time we're there. We request that Baba gives us a reading. He smiles widely, displaying just two *pan*-stained teeth, then nods to the Western woman, who collects our offerings of rupees. Once we've paid, Baba lights a cigarette with an expensive-looking lighter and, beginning with Chris, then Jean and me, launches into an uninterrupted stream of consciousness for an hour. His cigarette bobs up and down in his mouth as he speaks, ash dropping on his belly. When each cigarette is done, he lights a new one, so we're enveloped in a cloud of smoke. Although we're all listening intently, we're soon confused by his long, run-on sentences, often seeming to contradict what he's just said before. Attempts by us to clarify statements are ignored, perhaps considered interruptions to his flow of words. At the end of his monologue, he gives us a big, satisfied smile, indicating that our time with him is over. On the way back to Connaught Circus, I ask Chris if he understood what Baba Bidi was saying to him.

"At first, I thought I did. Then I didn't," he responds.

Jean and I can only agree. We're left to ponder whether we just weren't capable of understanding his lofty insights, or if we were taken in by a "snake oil salesman."

We spend the next day with Chris, taking him to Raisika (the restaurant young Eric had introduced us to nearly a year before) for their famous "Russian Rolls." We also visit Kumar Galleries, learning from Kumar that our friend, Roslyn, was still in Europe traveling with her guru. We bid goodbye to Chris at day's end. He's bound to Ganeshpuri in the morning, and we're leaving that evening directly to Jaipur, having decided that a visit to Agra and the Taj Mahal can wait.

The next afternoon, we run into Cindy at the American Express. She and her husband, Bob, were at Ananda Ashram for the first weeks of our arrival there, leaving with others disgruntled by Swamiji's "attitude." She tells us over lunch that she's waiting for Bob to return from Germany, where he's selling Indian clothing.

Then she says, "After Bob returns, we plan to go on a ten-day meditation retreat."

"Oh?" Jean asks. "Where?"

"It's in a hill station called Dalhousie. That's in Himachal Pradesh."

"Where did you hear about it?"

"Some friends took the same course before. They were psyched up about it, said it was the best thing they'd ever done."

Cindy goes on to say, "It's a Buddhist retreat with a man named Goenka. He's a Burmese Indian who goes all over the place giving these retreats. Seems to have a lot of Western followers."

I ask, "Can anyone go?"

"Yeah, they told me you just show up on the first day. You don't have to be a Buddhist or anything. They say the teachings are free, that you just have to pay for your accommodations."

We learn from Cindy that the retreat begins on October 5. We think this may be a good way to calm and strengthen ourselves for the long, tiring journey back west. Also, revisiting the Himalayas again before leaving India is enticing. We thank her, saying we may see her and Bob at the retreat after we return from Jaipur.

Our initial plans to spend a week or two in Jaipur change after hearing about the meditation course in Dalhousie. Now our priority is to quickly shop for clothes to sell back in the States. The overnight train deposits us at the Jaipur station in the morning. Seasoned travelers by now, we quickly find a rickshaw driver to take us to a government tourist bungalow we've heard about, just outside city center. On our way, we notice many buildings are pink hued.

I ask the rickshaw driver about this, and he replies, "Oh yes, this is why we are known as the Pink City. The older buildings like the City Palace, Amer Fort, and Albert Hall Museum are built of red and pink sandstone. But these more modern ones are simply painted this color."

He proudly adds, "Many tourists come to our famous city. If you would like, I can take you to the best places. It is true that I am named after Amer Fort. My name is Amer."

I say to Amer, "What interests us is shopping. Do you know good bazaars where we can buy cloth and other things?"

"Oh yes. I will take you to the markets if you like. There are many to choose from."

We arrange for Amer to meet us at the tourist bungalow later in the day.

With Amer's help, we spend the next two days rummaging through bazaars. We've given ourselves a budget of 1,500 rupees, and so are picky about the items, choosing only those that we feel we can sell in New York. The best shop we find is the Rajasthan State Emporium, which has many choices of colorful dresses, many with the hallmark Rajasthan mirrors sewn into the fabric. For just 700 rupees, we leave the emporium with two sizable bundles of cloth.

Our one respite from shopping comes when Amer drives us to the city zoo. Both of us love to see wild animals, albeit captive, but this zoo is disappointing. Not as bad as the Darjeeling zoo, many of the animals still have too little room to roam and exercise. The birds, tigers, monkeys, and even the snakes, look bored and worn out.

Our work in Jaipur done, Amer drives us to the railway station in time for the overnight train back to Delhi. We give him a large baksheesh, and he happily assures us he will be at our disposal whenever we return to Jaipur. Though we have comfortable enough berths, sleep is impossible due to the loud music and laughter of a boisterous group of teenagers sharing our compartment. They're determined to stay up all night. We gather from their conversations that they're on vacation from school and returning to their families in Delhi. Any attempt on my part to tell them this is an overnight sleeping compartment is met with more laughter. I think to myself, whatever happened to the authority of the white British Raj? Certainly lost on today's Indian youth, and even with all this disturbance, it's a healthy change.

We've now overextended the two-month temporary visas we received in Almora due to my hepatitis. The responsible thing would be to go to the Foreign Registration Office and plead for another extension. But we're so determined to go to the meditation course we decide to follow the old adage, "It's better to beg forgiveness than ask permission," rationalizing that, as we're already late, two extra weeks won't make much difference. We stay in Delhi this time just long enough to mail parcels of Rajasthan cloth and purchase train tickets to Dalhousie.

ELIXIR

Oct. 2 Delhi

Hi,

 Well here we are in Delhi again, after two days only in Jaipur. We bought goods there and have shipped them to N.Y. Tonight we are taking the train to Dalhousie, which is north of Delhi & in the Himalayas again. We are going for a 10-day course in Burmese Buddhist meditation, that runs from Oct. 5-15th, then we return again to Delhi for our overland trip home. We should leave India around Oct. 20th if everything works well. I have not received any mail from you since Almora—I know my friends have forwarded your last letter, but there have been continuous holidays all over India, and everything inc. Am. Express has been closed. So I'll pick up all my mail here when we return from Dalhousie, and find out all the info from you then. Do you have any idea where you'll be for Christmas? I'm sure your letters are filled w/ questions and news for me, and I don't know any of it. I hope all is well w/ everyone there. We are both well, Brus' hepatitis seems to be all gone but we still watch his diet. His energy is hard to keep up with, I was never one to be extremely bouncy!

 Delhi is quite hot! We are sitting in an outdoor café having our morning coffee and a persimmon. In a month we should be enjoying pomegranits (sp.?) and melons in Afghanistan, and then <u>quickly</u> across Iran to Turkey, and then by boat to Greece from Istanbul. Also we hope to fly to N.Y. from Greece, we heard it should cost $125 chartered flight. We shall see …

Give my love to all around, ask Carole if her friends are still in Iran, she never ans. my letter, and I would like to visit them for a stay in Tehran. Hope all is well and the weather is nice—Write soonLove, Jean and Brus

A blessedly quiet overnight train to the base city of Pathankot, and a three-hour bus ride through the Himalayan foothills, bring us to Dalhousie, a former British hill station at about 6,500 feet. We check into a room at a large resort hotel named the Grand View, where the course is to be held. We're a couple of days early, with only a few travelers, the hotel owner and chowkidar family around, so we spend our first day exploring the town. Like Darjeeling, the town has stately Victorian-style houses overlooking a splendid range of snowcapped peaks. The crisp mountain air feels so invigorating after the hot plains of Jaipur and Delhi! We find a small Tibetan market where we enjoy a delicious lunch of *momos* and *thukpa*.

We return to the Grand View at dusk to find that several more people have arrived for the meditation course. We have dinner with another American couple, Robert and Beth, who have just come overland to India. They tell us they've had a difficult time on the Great Hippie Trail, and think they may just fly back to the States after the course. A couple of hours of sharing our adventures over the past year seems to convince them to explore India a bit further.

Francis, the course manager, arrives the next day. He's a quiet, thoughtful man who has been taking these ten-day courses with Goenka, whom he calls Goenkaji, for the past two years. This is the first time he has actually managed a course and admits that he's a bit nervous to have to coordinate accommodations and food for the hundred expected participants. He wonders if he'll even have time to meditate with all the work he envisions. He's excited, though, that his younger brother, James, whom he hasn't seen in over a year, will be coming to his first meditation course. Sure enough, a couple of hours later, James arrives, and he's none other than our friend James from Darjeeling! We're all delighted to see each other again and have a lot of stories to share since we waved goodbye at the "toy train" station.

Now James asks, "But whatever happened to Bagus, the puppy I left with you at the Sham Rock? Did you bring him back to the marketplace?"

"No," Jean replies, "we took her with us. We changed her name to Tashi Deleg, Tashi for short."

We then recount our months with Tashi and her sad passing at Ananda Ashram. James has been living in Nepal since we parted, running a successful export business of Tibetan clothing and relics. It strikes us just how different the effusive James is from his quiet older brother.

We also spot George and Lynn, the couple we spent time with on the beaches of Puri. They left us to go to Calcutta and on to Nepal, but decided instead to explore Southeast Asia, visiting Thailand and Malaysia. This is their first course as well, and Lynn is nervous, not sure if she can spend all that time meditating.

The rest of the participants, mainly Westerners of all ages, arrive the next day. Francis is busy collecting the 100-rupee room fee per person and assigning rooms: five people in each room, as the hotel only has twenty rooms. Mats cover the floor of each room, with blankets and pillows supplied. Sexes are separated, even married couples, with men in one wing, and women in the other. Francis tells us that this is ordered by Goenka, so that each participant has the optimal opportunity to work on their own and not be distracted with relationships.

Later in the day, Goenka arrives with a short, stout woman and a contingent of Indian and Burmese students. Francis tells us that this is his wife, who has just arrived from Burma and is taking her first course as well. A portly man with short graying hair, Goenka wears Western clothes. After our time with the robed and bearded Swamiji, he looks very ordinary, like anyone you'd pass on a Delhi street.

The course begins right after a buffet dinner. The hotel's large dining room has been converted to a meditation hall, accommodating over a hundred mats and cushions facing a central platform, with a chair for Goenka, who now enters with his wife and close Indian followers. He takes his seat while his wife and the others take their seats on the reserved cushions in the first row. Francis welcomes everyone, emphasizing that from now until the end of the ten days, we are all expected to maintain silence, writing notes only to the teacher or Francis regarding any needs or difficulties. We're encouraged to refrain from reading and writing during the course to concentrate solely on the meditation techniques. We're also expected to remain on the hotel grounds unless there is special permission to leave. He then introduces S. N. Goenka, who has been closely surveying his new students during Francis's instructions. Smiling, Goenka gives us our first introduction to vipassana meditation. He tells us that one must first develop strong concentration before actually practicing the technique of *vipassana*, or "insight," meditation. To develop our concentration, we must focus our attention on our breath as it passes the outer part of the nostrils. It is unnecessary to follow the in and out breath beyond this point of the "nose door," but to just remain there. When we lose our attention, simply return to the breath at this point of the nostrils. I'm struck by the deep, mellow timbre of Goenka's voice, so relaxed, almost hypnotic, reminding me of Bela Lugosi's character, Dracula. We then practice the concentration exercise for an hour. For many, this is their first foray into meditation, and there's a lot of shifting and coughing.

The session ends at 9:00 p.m. with Goenka, in his deepest Dracula voice, saying, "Now take rest, take rest." We retire to our rooms to sleep with strangers. I know I'm not the only one who has difficulty sleeping this first night.

Our daily schedule remains more or less the same over the next ten days: 4:00 a.m. wakeup; 4:30 to 6:30, individual meditation in our rooms, where we have the option of sitting with Goenka at 5:45 in the main meditation hall as he sings devotional songs in Pali and Hindi; 6:30 to 8:00, breakfast (usually porridge, fruit, and tea) and relaxation (for many a walk on hotel grounds); 8:00 to 9:00, group meditation; 9:00 to 11:30, individual meditation in our rooms; 11:30

to 1:00 p.m., lunch (usually rice, dal, and *subje*) and relaxation; 1:00 to 2:00, group meditation; 2:00 to 5:00, individual meditation; 5:00 to 6:00, tea and fruit; 6:00 to 9:00, teacher discourse and group meditation; by 10:00 p.m., lights out. With such an intensive schedule, by the end of the first day, most of us feel as though we've been sitting on our butts for a year!

Goenka's discourse each evening focuses on the *sutras*, or teachings of the Buddha. Each of these teachings seems to speak exactly to my day's meditation experience. I feel at first as though he's reading my mind but, as the days pass, I realize that he is well aware of the progress on the path of meditation and unfolds the *sutras* accordingly.

I'm exhausted at first, trying so hard to stop thoughts and focus on the breath at the "nose door." I'm not alone. Most everyone is wandering around during relaxation periods with gloomy faces. After just the second day, several people, including Robert and Beth, leave the program. I wonder if they'll now go back home or explore India further. Concerned about how Jean is doing, I "illegally" slip her a note on the third day. Her secret message back reads that she's tired too, but rests whenever her body tells her to. A wise perspective. I, of course, in my bullheaded drive and enthusiasm, am determined to follow the schedule to the letter.

During his discourse on the evening of the third day, Goenka introduces the vipassana technique. He directs us to now move the attention from the door of the nose to the top of the head. With the concentrated mind, we then "sweep" the body from head to toe and back again, simply noticing sensations without judgment, such as hot, cold, pleasant, and painful; in other words, just observe the rise and fall of all phenomena within the body through the "mind's eye" of an impartial observer. If one becomes flooded with thought, or overcome with emotion, simply return to the breath at the door of the nose to restabilize one's concentration before returning again to the "sweeping" technique. The vipassana technique, Goenka tells us, serves to purify the mind by ridding oneself of mental blocks and controlling emotions. Such work will initially intensify emotions, presenting themselves fully so as to better see them clearly. In the days immediately following this initial instruction on the technique, our meditation hall is filled with expressions of intense emotion—coughing, sighing, laughing, crying, complaining, even people falling asleep and off their cushions—as we each work to explore our sensations by sweeping our bodies. Goenka continues to encourage us, often saying, "Work, work," pronounced "vurk," "for the benefit of all beings."

As days pass and our practice deepens, Goenka's evening discourses reveal further aspects of the dharma, or teachings of the Buddha. The purpose of our work, he says, is to develop insight, or wisdom. He tells us that the Buddha is also called the tathagata, or the one who sees the world exactly as it is, without conceptual blinders. We learn of the "three gems:" *anicca, dukkha,* and *anhata. Anicca* translates as "impermanence." Everything is constantly changing: seasons, weather, hopes, fears, feelings, sense of self. The living die and are reborn, nothing remaining the same, nothing seen as permanent.

Dukkha means "suffering," which can be expressed as the Four Noble Truths. First there is suffering; all beings suffer the experience of sickness, old age, and death. Even the discomfort of a nagging bug bite is an expression of suffering. Second, the cause of suffering is attachment to the "three poisons": passion for what is desired, aggression or avoidance of what is not desired, and ignorance of one's essential nature. Third, there is an end to suffering, or *Nirvana;* beyond the clouds of the conceptual mind, this is the clear sky of reality. The fourth Noble Truth describes the way out of suffering through the "Eight-Fold Noble Path," which includes Right View, Intention, Speech, Action, Livelihood, Effort, Mindfulness, and Concentration (all of which we are trying to emulate during this course).

The third gem, *anhata,* is the truth of selflessness. The sense of "I" or "me" is not solid, but a construct of mental objects and nothing more. The more one investigates this sense of "me," the more one realizes that "me" is everywhere and nowhere. What size or shape is this "me"? What color? Is it inside or outside the body? It can't be found. To illustrate, Goenka cites a Buddhist expression: "There is Nirvana, but no one to enter." He also tells us that the three gems are inseparable from each other; to understand one completely is to understand all. At the end of each evening, after his discourse and an hour of practice, Goenka says, in his deep Dracula voice, "Take rest, take rest, for the benefit of all beings, take rest."

Days into the course, as I'm sitting in the meditation hall in the early morning listening to Goenka singing songs in Pali, I experience my whole body relax into an upwelling of love for him. His singing, which I initially considered strange, is now more beautiful than any music I've ever heard! Something releases within me, a surrender to an openheartedness that brings me to tears. I sit in this blissful state for a long while. Could this be the "elixir" that Joseph Campbell describes as the ultimate discovery of the hero's journey? I don't know, but a doorway or portal has opened, and a certainty arises that I am on the right path in my own hero's journey. From this moment on, I approach vipassana meditation with greater confidence, the practice itself becoming more inspired and less of a struggle, and now, like Francis, I call our teacher Goenkaji.

In the afternoon of the eighth day, a violent thunderstorm breaks, interrupting everyone's meditation. Many leave the meditation hall to dance and run around in the rain. The storm is a welcome respite from the intensity of the course. It helps many students approach the last two days with renewed energy. For others, however, it marks the end of their practice. They spend most of the last days lounging and chatting on the grounds outside.

Goenkaji presides over an optional refuge ceremony on the last day of the course. For those of us who participate in this short ceremony, we take refuge with him in the Three Jewels: the *Buddha* as teacher, the *dharma* as the Buddha's teachings, and the *sangha* as those who follow the Buddha's teachings. The refuge vow is a precious gift from Goenkaji, essentially introducing us to our basic natures. From this moment on, Jean and I consider ourselves Buddhists.

The course ends with a general question and answer session with Goenkaji. When asked how we should proceed in our practice from here, he counsels that it would be good for each of us to find the time and place to meditate for one or two hours a day. He adds that this is not a meditation for those who want to live in caves, but to live well-concentrated and balanced lives among fellow beings. And so I begin to practice vipassana meditation for at least an hour each day, whatever and wherever our traveling or living circumstances might be. Jean sometimes joins me.

S. N. Goenka and his party leave the morning after the course ends. We decide to stay on for a few more days to socialize with friends. James leaves back to Nepal and his business the following morning, and George and Lynn say goodbye in the afternoon, bound again for South India. Many students are headed to Goenkaji's next vipassana course in Bikaner, a city in northwest Rajasthan. Finally, Francis and we are the only ones left. He's also going to Bikaner, this time just as a participant with no other responsibilities. He tells us that his concerns about not being able to take part in this course's daily meditations were realized, as he ran around day and night, responding to the many requests of the participants.

"For a course with no talking, the people I dealt with were yelling loud enough through their written messages!"

We say goodbye to Francis as we leave by bus and train back to Delhi. We hope to see each other again, a distinct possibility as Jean and I certainly intend to go to future vipassana courses.

10-25-71

Dear Dad, Mom and Nancy,

Happy Halloween! This is the last aerogramme from India; soon we'll be able to talk with our mouths rather than pens. We leave for the border tonight, will (hopefully) "fly" across Pakistan and be in Kabul again in two days. Perhaps we'll spend two weeks in Afghanistan and "dash" across Persia to Istanbul, and then down to Greece. Depending on air fare, we may even fly from Athens to N.Y. So that's the move and we hope it takes us to you in time for Christmas. Jean discovered in a recent letter from her folks that they won't be in New York for Christmas (not until the end of January) so, with your permission she'll join us in a Westby-Olsen Christmas. We're greatly looking forward to it.

Yesterday, Jean and I went to Agra to see the Taj Mahal. What more can I say. Yet another beautiful experience. Love Love, Brus and Jean.

We stay at Jain's Guest House on Jan Path Road this time. We plan to stay only a couple of days in Delhi, with time enough for a day trip to Agra to finally see the Taj Mahal before taking a train to Firozpur on the border of Pakistan. We're more than a month over our extended visas now so, as all visitors to India must obtain exit visas to leave, we have no choice but to return to the Foreign Registration Office and "face the music." After a long wait, the same officer we saw six months before ushers us into his office. His large desk, piled with papers, looks exactly the same as it did then, lending the impression that he's been sitting there the whole time waiting for our return.

When he sees our expired visas, he states accusingly, "Do you know we have been looking for you two for the past month?"

I lie, "We're very sorry but, just as I was recovering from hepatitis, I had a relapse. I only now feel strong enough to travel."

He's now on a roll, puffed up with self-importance, throwing our visas down on a pile of papers. "I was out of the office," (so, he does leave his office!), "when my negligent assistant granted you this medical extension by telephone. I would never have done that! Now you have laid this mess at my door!"

He seems conflicted between indignation and a way to relieve himself of this predicament, until Jean says quietly, "We have already bought tickets to leave in two days for Firozpur."

The dark clouds in his mind give way to bright blue sky. She has offered him a solution!

"I will contact Pondicherry, and they will send your exit visas directly to Firozpur. Just see that you are on that train."

His demeanor transforms to reasonable, even cheery, as he wishes us a safe journey. We go directly from his office to the train station, where we buy tickets for two days hence to Firozpur.

We take the next morning's train three hours to Agra, the ancient capital of India. The train platform is crowded, and as we're about to board, a fat Indian man grabs Jean's butt. All of our equanimity from the vipassana course is gone in an instant! I kick, then punch at the man, both blows missing; but Jean doesn't miss, and the man hurries away down the platform rubbing the scratch marks on his face. We find our seats in an open car and soon calm down, somewhat satisfied that the man literally feels the pain of his action.

We pass a long train of armed Indian soldiers and tanks on the way. A passenger in the seat in front tells us that the train is headed for the India-Pakistan border. He adds that war is imminent between the two countries over an Indian independence movement in the Muslim country of East Pakistan. We'd heard rumors back in Almora that there was trouble brewing between the two countries. We understand little of the causes for this conflict but are now struck with the urgency to get through the India-Pakistan border as soon as possible.

We arrive in Agra at noon and take a rickshaw to the Taj Mahal. We've seen pictures of the Taj before (and I even sent a postcard to my parents), a great domed white building bordered by towering minarets at each corner, but nothing prepares us for our first view. A long, rectangular fountain opens to this magnificent structure that, set against blue sky and white billowy clouds, seems to be floating in the air, unbound to the earth. A number of Indian and Western tourists, along with hopeful tour guides, professional photographers, and vendors selling postcards of the Taj and various deities are milling around the fountain. We decide to join a small tour group, giving the guide a couple of rupees each.

Our guide is an older man with a wide smile. He has probably been giving tours for many years. When everyone has paid, he leads us along the fountain toward the building, speaking in a surprisingly loud voice, "The Taj Mahal is actually a mausoleum. It was commissioned by the Moghul emperor, Shah Jahan, in 1632 to honor his favorite wife, Mumtaz Mahal, who had recently died giving birth to their fourteenth son." This is the same Shah Jahan who built the Shalimar Gardens we visited in Lahore. "It is made entirely of ivory and marble. Most of the materials, as well as the twenty thousand artisans who built it, came from Persia, and it took twenty years to complete."

As we approach the high, arched entrance, our guide continues, "Shah Jahan planned on building a second structure, a Black Taj, on the other side of the Yamuna River behind us. The two structures were then to be connected by a marble bridge. However, twenty years of taxing his subjects to build this Taj had caused great unrest, and so his son finally overthrew him. Sadly, the second Taj was never built."

Upon entering, the guide's voice echoes throughout the great domed chamber. "In the center of this room, you can see two large marble caskets surrounded by a marble screen. These are for Shah Jahan and Mumtaz Mahal. And yet, this is but a display. Two smaller caskets in a chamber directly below this one actually contain their bones. Also, all of these surrounding walls were encrusted with precious gems. Sadly, over the years, thieves have stolen every last one of them." The tour ends with our guide gratefully accepting everyone's baksheesh.

Jean and I now rickshaw to the nearby Agra Fort, the original residence of Moghul rulers, including Shah Jahan, before he shifted his capital to Delhi during the building of the Taj. This red brick structure has great arched gates in the four directions, the western "Delhi Gate" being the largest and most impressive with its white marble inlay. We roam around the fort for a time but, after visiting the Taj Mahal, not much here holds our interest. We hop on another rickshaw to catch the late-afternoon train back to Delhi.

That evening and the next day in Delhi, we run into a number of participants from the vipassana retreat, most bound for the next course in Bikaner. We make plans to have a final meditation at Jain's Guest House in the afternoon before Jean and I catch the night train to Firozpur. We're enjoying Russian Rolls at Raisika, when Ronn walks into the restaurant! We haven't seen him since Ananda Ashram. He tells us that, after Pondicherry, he went to Assam to study and practice at an all-Indian ashram.

"I was the only Westerner there. Many had never even seen a Westerner. I was treated like a king!"

Ronn is pale as a ghost. He is so skinny and weak that I ask him if he's okay.

"Well, you remember that I have anemia. Now I'm afraid it's getting worse. I'm going to relatives in Israel, where I hope to get healthy working on a kibbutz."

"So, we'll be heading in the same direction for a while," Jean says. "Why don't we travel together?"

"We can certainly meet up in Afghanistan, but I'm too weak to go overland again. I'm taking a plane directly to Kabul in a couple of days. We can meet up there. Then I'll try to find the cheapest ticket to Istanbul."

We make plans before leaving him to connect with each other through the American Express in Kabul.

Fifteen of us meditate for an hour in the gardens of Jain's Guest House. I wonder what Mr. Jain and the other guests think of all these people sitting in absolute silence. At the end, we bid each other farewell, expressing hopes that we'll be together again at future vipassana retreats.

I look out the window of the cab ride to Old Delhi Station, taking in all the sights and smells on the way, and thinking to myself how much change this city has seen in us: from "green" overland explorers wondering where to go next, to seasoned travelers, more confident and self-directed with each passage we've made through this city.

We arrive at Firozpur Station the next morning after a restful night's sleep in third class berths (no partying teenagers!). We look for Arjun, the rickshaw driver who first introduced us to India over a year before, but he is nowhere to be seen. Another rickshaw takes us to the border, just a few miles away. As we feared, a large convoy of tanks rumble past us on the way, and the fields along the road are covered with soldiers' tents. We're met by a Sikh official at the border.

Taking our passports and visa papers, he says with some amusement, "So you are leaving? What is the matter, don't you like India?"

"Oh yes," I respond. "We'd really like to stay longer but we must return to our families."

He takes some minutes examining our papers. Seeing that we have overextended our stay, he declares, "It looks as though your wish to stay in our country has been granted. These papers are not in order. You have no permission to leave."

I counter as calmly as I can, "We were told by the officer in Delhi that he would contact Pondicherry, where we first extended our visas, and they would send on the permissions to exit."

"But I have received no papers from them," he replies. "No, you must go directly to Pondicherry now to receive proper permissions."

The enormity of his reply hits us like a brick! Trains from here to Pondicherry and back will take us days, if not weeks! The border will probably then be closed because of the war!

Jean now pleads with him, "Oh please let us go. We don't want to be caught in a war!" Then she begins to cry.

As always, Jean's magic tears take their effect. The hard countenance of the Sikh officer melts.

Nothing is said for a long moment, but then he offers, "There, madam, please don't cry. Perhaps your exit papers are in another pile of papers."

He yells a command in Hindi back to a subordinate, who returns minutes later with two slips of paper.

"Ah, just as I thought. Your exit papers were covered up."

We can't express enough gratitude to him, knowing that he has succumbed to a woman's tears and found a way to help us leave. He personally escorts us to the border guard, wishing us a safe journey.

Crossing the border, we look back at Mother India who has taught us so much during our time there. We make a vow never to forget her lessons and that we will return one day. We have since been fortunate to be able to fulfill our vow, but that's another story.

RETURN

Oct. 28—Kabul

HAPPY HALLOWEEN!

Well, we made it to Afghanistan—got here Weds. night. Fortunately, Pakistan is a small country to cross & it was done w/ very little problem & very little sleep, so today was very quiet. This country is just as nice as it was last year—only even more Westerners passing through. It has such a strong Russian influence in look and sound of the lang. The things to buy are very exciting and although we will try to conserve ourselves carefully, we have questions as to whether we'll have enough money when we get to Athens to fly to N.Y. So ... before you leave N.Y. you could send the rest of my balance (round figures) to Athens, Greece, First National City Bank, so we would not have to worry when we get there! Tell them to hold for us as we expect to be there mid-Nov. & stay for approx. 3 wks. & try to find a charter flight to N.Y. for $125 each. (We've heard it's possible) & if not we will go into Europe & find a cheap flight. Even if we don't use the money it's better than being stuck when we get there!

The weather is getting colder now, but we've been given warm enough clothes for now. We may go through North Afghanistan, to Bamiyan (sp.?) where there is a 150 ft. Buddha they've excavated. This is such a nice country & friendly people—although they're mostly Muslim, they're not like the Pakistanis and Iranis.

We are both feeling well & are excited (at least now that we've made the big move of leaving India) about going back—it won't be

long now—hope all stay well 'til we get to Turkey for new news. Be
happy—Love and kisses, Jean and Brus

The Indo-Pakistani War, a thirteen-day conflict resulting in the creation of the new Indian state of Bangladesh, breaks out days after we leave. By then we're safely in Kabul, having crossed Pakistan in record time. We meet up with Ronn shortly after arriving. He's now sporting seven stitches on his chin, having fallen down one of the many infamous potholes plaguing the streets of the city. The stitches, along with his preternatural paleness, make him resemble one of the walking dead!

We're having a final lunch in our hotel's downstairs restaurant with Ronn before he catches another "puddle jumper" to Herat, when a bearded man comes up to our table and says to me, "I know you!"

I look at him for a long time before it dawns on me. "Jimmy!" I yell as we hug each other.

I haven't seen Jimmy since high school. We were mere acquaintances then, but now, thousands of miles from home, we somehow recognize each other through our shaggy beards. We soon become as close as old friends, spending the rest of our time in Kabul together. He's headed to India for the first time, having come from Maui, Hawaii, where he's lived for several years. He has many questions about the places and people we experienced in India, says he's going to check out Ananda Ashram, and maybe take a vipassana course as well. As a parting gift, he gives me a bamboo flute he made in Maui, which I still carry with me wherever I go.

Jean and I are among the few returning west, like salmon swimming against an eastward current of travelers on the Great Hippie Trail to India. The streets of Kabul, Kandahar, and Herat are packed with travelers. We pass through these cities quickly as, to our travel-weary minds, they seem less interesting than we remember. Many of our conversations with people we meet now are question and answer sessions about where to go and what to do in India.

We admit to each other that we feel a certain pride in our roles as "senior advisers."

We again connect with Ronn in Herat. His stitches have been removed and he looks better than he did in Kabul. He introduces us to an Englishman he just met named Peter, who's had severe dysentery during his two months in India and is returning to England to recuperate. Peter is soft-spoken, speaking just above a whisper, and is so gaunt and pale he makes Ronn look healthy by comparison. In fact, Ronn is feeling well enough now to try traveling overland, and, with Peter joining us, we take a bus through the Iran border to Mashhad. As on our way to India over a year earlier, I feel as though we are not doing justice to this city by only allowing one day to tour its mosques and markets before moving on to Tehran, but we're all invested in traveling through Iran as quickly as possible.

We stay again at the Amir Kabir in Tehran, its lobby familiarly crowded with travelers. We wander through the marketplaces of the city, this time not intimidated at all by stares and occasional cat-calls. We also visit the international Tehran Community School. At first, the teachers didn't know what to make of us, Jean in a Tibetan chuba, and me in loose Afghan clothes, complete with embroidered vest and traditional skull cap. When Jean tells them she is Carole's sister, they immediately warm up to us, asking many questions about India. We spend the next two evenings having dinner with the teachers in their apartments. It's eye-opening to see washing machines, electric ranges, televisions, valuable Irani lamps, carpets, and tapestries in each apartment, benefits for these teachers living on Western salaries in a country with a low cost of living.

The four of us purchase first class train tickets for a several days-long ride to Istanbul, covering thousands of kilometers, for Irani rials amounting to just $16 per person! We have a spacious compartment to ourselves and plenty of provisions that we've bought in Tehran. We're left to ourselves during the day, with porters folding down our berths and providing clean sheets at night. The train climbs through low, treeless dark hills to the border of Turkey, where we must disembark and take a four-hour ferry over the emerald waters of Lake Van. The "first class" compartment on the train awaiting us on the other side is seedy, with ripped upholstery, torn window curtains, and filthy windows, but at least we again have the compartment to ourselves.

Peter has been withdrawn and complaining about body pains since we left Tehran. Now, as the train descends into eastern Turkey, his skin and eyes begin to turn yellow. I know the signs immediately: hepatitis! Soon, he's too weak to sit up, so we help him climb up into a berth. We worry that Peter has infected us and try to review with him any time we may have shared the same food and drink. In the end, we just have to hope for the best. Peter planned to proceed by train to Spain, but now he knows he must either recuperate in Istanbul or fly home to England. Peter sleeps through much of the remainder of the two-day trip, only asking for water occasionally.

Arriving at the Istanbul station, we walk Peter onto the ferry crossing the Bosporus to the European side of the city. We again check into the Gungor Hotel in Santa Sophia. Manuel, the owner who helped us so many months before, is delighted to see us.

"You are both so skinny now!"

"You're right, Manuel," I reply. "We've lost a lot of weight. Our plan is to fatten up in Greece before we return to the States ..."

Jean adds, "... and my mom dies of shock when she sees how skinny I've become!"

Manuel says, "Well, you're definitely in better shape than most returning travelers." Now eyeing Peter and Ronn, he adds, "But your friends don't look so good."

We explain to Manuel that Ronn is anemic, and Peter has hepatitis. He immediately provides each of them with a separate room. He then helps Peter to call his parents, who are apparently wealthy enough to immediately arrange a charter flight for him directly to London. Our last image of Peter is of him weakly waving from the back of a taxi as he heads to the airport.

Ronn has also bought a ticket to Tel Aviv and leaves the following day. We'll miss him as we've come to enjoy his quiet, friendly presence since we first met at Ananda Ashram. We promise to keep in touch and do correspond regularly for a while. (Our last letter from Ronn says that, after spending some months on a kibbutz where he has regained his health, he is going to a desert retreat to undertake intensive studies in the kabbalah. After so much time in Hindu ashrams, he now seems to have made a connection between yoga and esoteric Judaism.)

We say goodbye to Manuel soon after this and fly to Athens. One look at this city, with its modern high-rises amid ancient Greek temples and theaters, is a comfort to know that we are back in Europe and that much closer to home. We stay in a guesthouse near the main plaza and spend a week sightseeing and eating souvlaki, moussaka, and spanakopita. We find several letters from both of our families awaiting us at the American Express office where, just outside the building, dozens of travelers carry signs offering vans and airline tickets for sale and seeking rides to other countries in Europe and North Africa.

Fri. Nov. 26th
Dear Everybody,
HAPPY (late) THANKGIVING!
Here we are in Athens and loving it! We got our money yesterday with no problem—thanks for sending as much as you did. We needed it! Today we bought our plane ticket home—$166. Each— total $332. There were no cheaper flights for this time of year. So, on Dec. 20, we fly to London, on the 22nd to Amsterdam and connect with a KLM flight to N.Y. on that day!
Tomorrow we take a boat to Crete. There is a small fishing village on the south side called Agia Galini. (Friends have been there & loved it!) We had several ouzos on the square, toasted to you. We find the people warm & friendly & helpful—I think you should find an apartment here & forget about N.Y. The weather has been somewhat rainy, then sun & warmth.
So many changes since we've been away! Brus's brother Randy expects his 3rd child any day now. How are you doing Barb? Can't

*believe I'm going to be an aunt! Soon we'll be talking on the phone
and I can tell you more about our travels then—can I call collect?
We are both well and Happy—hope it's the same for everyone there.
Love and Kisses, Jean and Brus*

Although we've enjoyed touring the ancient sites, especially the
Acropolis and Parthenon, we soon tire of the crowds, noise, and
car exhaust of Athens. Through word-of-mouth, the communica-
tion that has served us well throughout Asia, we learn of a quiet
village in southern Crete called Agia Galini. Thinking this sounds
like a good place to spend some time fattening up on rich Greek
food before returning to the States, we book evening tickets on the
overnight ferry from the nearby port city of Piraeus to the northern
Cretan city of Iraklion.

The crowded ferry features a bar, and soon many people are
drunk on ouzo and retsina and dancing to music so loud that sleep
is impossible. We get into a conversation with three other travelers: Bill, his girlfriend, Colleen, and Bart. They've just arrived from
the cold weather in Germany and are seeking warm Mediterranean
sunshine. It's their first time in Crete as well, so they decide to join
us in checking out Agia Galini. A two-hour bus ride from Iraklion
through the verdant hills of central Crete brings us to the southern coast and the fishing village of Agia Galini. We stay only long
enough to have lunch—and the best goat's milk yogurt with honey
that I've ever eaten!—and buy provisions before we set up a makeshift camp in an olive grove just outside the village. Our three new
friends have good sleeping bags and tarps, while Jean and I have
long since exchanged our sleeping bags for thin bedrolls, but the
earth floor in the grove is soft, and we are soon lulled to sleep by
the chirruping of crickets and warm Mediterranean breezes.

The next day, we all venture farther down the beach, perhaps a
kilometer from Agia Galini, where we set up a more "permanent"
camp by a shallow ravine winding down from the hills behind us
to the sea. Most of the day is spent building walls from the ravine's
large, rounded rocks and covering them with a roof of tarps. At

day's end, we proudly assess our new abode, large enough to sleep the five of us.

We settle into a "family" routine over the next two weeks. Men carry water from a well near the village and comb the hillside for firewood, while women shop for supplies. Everyone takes turns cooking and cleaning. With plenty of time, and nobody but us on this far stretch of beach, we sunbathe naked. Jean and I meditate every morning, and I practice playing the flute Jimmy gave to me in Kabul. Bill and Bart try fishing (in vain) from the shore with lines and hooks they bought in the village. We all get along well, enjoying these lazy, sunny days to the fullest.

Then one afternoon, we see great dark clouds building over the sea, coming ever closer to land. The wind picks up, growing colder with each minute. The first drops of rain send us inside our house and, almost instantly, we're besieged by a violent thunderstorm tearing at the tarped roof! We huddle together throughout the night, nobody sleeping through the thunder, howling winds, and torrential rains. The storm has not let up one bit by morning. We're soaked, along with everything we own, and shivering with cold.

There's nothing to do but huddle, until Jean comes up with an idea. "We have to do a sun dance. We have to supplicate the Sun Gods to drive away the storm!"

We all look puzzled as she rises and starts dancing in the wet sand, singing "Om Namo Shivaya" over and over. We're all soon dancing, laughing, and singing our own songs, especially the Beatles tune, "Here Comes the Sun." If nothing else, I think, at least we're not as afraid anymore. Just a half hour after our sun dance begins, the sun pokes through the clouds, and the rain and winds abate until only a slight drizzle remains.

Bill yells, "We did it! We drove the storm away!"

Yelling our gratitude to the Sun Gods, we quickly gather our wet belongings and hustle down the beach to the village, where we book two rooms at a small hotel. Minutes after we check in, the eye of the storm passes by, and the storm rages throughout the rest of the day and night.

I awaken to bright sunshine streaming through our window. After a tasty breakfast of eggs, rolls, and coffee, we all make our way down the beach, now etched with rivulets cluttered with rocks and debris. We find an abandoned walking cane on our walk and wonder if its owner was washed out to sea. Arriving at our site, we're amazed that all that's left of our house are rocks and shreds of tarps at the bottom of a now deeper and wider ravine. Without comment, we know that we're lucky to be alive.

Our friends leave the next day, Bill and Colleen bound for Morocco and Bart back to his home in Princeton via Switzerland. (We'll see Bill and Colleen again, staying for a month in their apartment in Berkeley.) We stay on for another week before returning to Athens, enjoying a relaxed village life and good food, particularly the fried fish, yogurt, and ouzo.

The airline tickets we'd previously purchased in Athens to New York via London were much more expensive than we'd planned. Now we find ourselves arriving at London's Heathrow Airport with almost no money and a full day before the connecting flight to New York! Our only option is to try to sell some of the items we've bought on the road back from India. Late evening finds us at the entrance to the Piccadilly tube station. I'm standing with a hopeful smile, trying to flog an ornate Afghan necklace, while an exhausted Jean sits in tears atop our backpacks. We've been here for hours, with people hurrying by, not one person showing the faintest interest in us or the necklace. Suddenly, a thin man carrying an umbrella who must have passed us, rushes back up the tube and hands me a pound saying, "Here, take this. I don't want your damned necklace," before disappearing back down the tube.

This pound, comparable to five dollars, is enough to buy us cots for the night in a commons room of a local hostel. Jean remembers upon waking the next morning that she has been carrying a "lucky" two-dollar bill in her wallet the whole time. We cash it at a nearby bank, giving us enough for mashed potatoes and candy bars until the evening flight.

The plane from London stops in Amsterdam for more passengers, where we have to disembark and recheck our carry-on bags. Jean and I are the only passengers frisked by airport security, most likely due to our long hair and Eastern clothing.

My mother and sister meet us at the gate in New York's Kennedy Airport. We're overjoyed to reunite again, but I can see by their glances at us two skinny people—me in *pyjamas* and an Afghan vest, and Jean in a Tibetan *chuba*—that they wonder just who it is that's returning to them.

Then my mother smiles and says, "Welcome home. Just in time for Christmas!"

POSTSCRIPT

Jean and I are married the following summer on a hot and humid day in Oyster Bay, New York. We have a potluck wedding, with family and friends bringing food trays, salads, and a giant wedding cake. The only expense for the day is a keg of beer bought by Jean's father. Friends have hung remarkable mobiles from the surrounding trees, while others dress as minstrels, playing celebratory music throughout the day. The ceremony itself is held in the middle of a loving circle in front of a stained-glass church window propped against an oak tree. David, an old friend dressed as the Wizard of Oz, serves as the officiant as Jean and I, both in Indian dress, exchange vows. For wedding gifts, we receive new backpacks, sleeping bags, and car tires for our upcoming journey through the States, my mother whispering to me, "I remember when we used to get silverware and china."

We fulfill our vow to return to Mother India a year later, this time flying directly to Delhi. Over the next two years, we stay in Almora again for several months, do vipassana retreats in Bodhgaya and Burma, trek in Nepal, tour Southeast Asia, live in Bali, and work in Tokyo. As with our first journey, the valuable lessons we receive from friends and their stories propel us forward, and, of course, the stalwart "kite string" of letters to and from home continue to provide us the unconditional support for our ongoing quest of discovery on the hero's journey.

ACKNOWLEDGMENTS

I have many people to thank for their gifts of support in helping me to write this memoir. First and foremost, Jean, my wife and traveling companion, continually inspires me by her gifts of love and wisdom.

I thank my daughter, Kirsten, whose own wonderful memoir has inspired me to write mine. She is an enthusiastic cheerleader, helping me with her technological skills and instilling in me a "can do" attitude. Her gift is encouragement.

For her excellent help in editing the many drafts of this memoir, I thank my sister-in-law, Carole Wilson. She focused on structure and grammar, challenging me to review how I might describe a person or experience more clearly. Hers is the gift of precision.

Thank you to friends Deb and Ed Shapiro, and Mary and Andy Dinsmoor. In combing through the manuscript and giving suggestions for improvement, they offered me further clarity.

Thank you to Josh Freel, Senior Publishing Associate of Waterside Productions, and Ken Fraser, Graphic Designer of Impact Book Designs, for their tireless help in converting a rough draft into a most presentable book. Theirs are the gifts of skill and patience.

Finally, I thank all those whom Jean and I met on the Great Hippie Trail. Their friendship and stories taught us so much. Through them we came to understand that whatever our differences in background and language, we can communicate clearly through the heart. Our many encounters reminded us that, in truth, we're each not that different, and this world is not so big after all.

Made in the USA
Las Vegas, NV
25 September 2022

55944804R00148